Euclid and Terex
EARTH-MOVING MACHINES

Eric C. Orlemann

Motorbooks International
Publishers & Wholesalers

First published in 1997 by Motorbooks International Publishers & Wholesalers, 729 Prospect Avenue, PO Box 1, Osceola, WI 54020-0001 USA

Library of Congress Cataloging-in-Publication Data

Orlemann, Eric C.
      Euclid & Terex earth-moving machines / Eric C. Orlemann.
          p.   cm.
      Includes index.
      ISBN 0-7603-0293-6 (paperback : alk. paper)
      1. Earhmoving machinery. 2. Euclid Road Machinery Company.
      3. General Motors Corporation. Euclid Division. 4. General Motors Corporation.
Terex Division. I. Title.
      TA725.066   1997
      629.225--dc21   97-15493

On the front cover: The first of the redesigned Euclid R-X haulers, model 10LLD. A single GM Diesel 12V-149T, turbocharged engine rated at 1,000 gross horsepower powered this model.

On the frontispiece: C-6-1 crawler dozers roll off the line in 1960.

On the title page: Euclid released the production version of the Tandem TS-14 scraper in July 1964. Shown at work in August 1964 are some of the first units delivered into service.

On the back cover: Top: Euclid new equipment introduction at the GM Milford Proving Ground, September 1954. The TC-12 crawler tractor is shown pulling a Euclid BV Loader. GM Corporation **Bottom:** The models on the 350-ton-capacity Terex 33-19 Titan hauler show just how big this beast actually was. The 33-19 measured 25 feet, 7 inches wide and 66 feet in length. GM Diesel Division Archives

Edited by Micheal Dapper
Designed by Katie Finney

Printed in Hong Kong through World Print, Ltd.

Contents

Preface

The author would like to express his sincerest thanks and appreciation to all of the individuals who gladly shared their stories and time in my pursuit of information on the "green iron." I would also like to especially thank all of the GM, Euclid, and Terex personnel, both current and retired, for sharing so much of their time, whether by phone or in person, and for providing any requested information.

I would like to personally thank the following individuals for their extra effort in making sure this project would succeed. They are John G. Addams, Ralph J. Bernotas, Chuck Krouse, Louis R. Best, Madonna Duaso, George Kenyon, Dan Hopkins, Joe Pleichner, Anthony J. Craig, Charles C. Gray, Warren Brisson, Don Blackmore, Paul L. Cooper, Floyd C. Joliet, Martha Glasgow, Bob Fleming, Rudy Sudrla, Bruce Kurschenska, Ian Hamilton, and Roger Hull.

Special thanks is also needed for the assistance provided by Stephen Grimes of Grimes Photography, Inc., and to Don Frantz and J. Keith Haddock of the Historical Construction Equipment Association (H.C.E.A.) for access to their archives.

> *"But how are we going to feel if we don't try?"*
> Raymond Q. Armington
> January 12, 1907–
> April 19, 1993

Two individuals stand out for going the extra mile in providing assistance and generally guiding my way through the background and history of the companies and machines that make up this book. They are Alvin E. Nus and William A. Borthwick. Without their help, this project would never have gotten past the planning stage.

I would also like to pay tribute to the many photographers, both staff and subcontracted, who in some cases spent their entire careers recording Euclid and Terex machines at the factory or in the field. Quite often, their contribution went unnoticed in the year-to-year business of producing machines, but their work lives on as a testament to the fantastic creations of the GM years. Some of these contributors include Ron Nelson and Jack Grimes, who performed most of the work at Diesel Division in Canada, and Jim Makuh, Otto Sieber, and, especially, Brad Kish. Brad alone was responsible for about 70 percent of all images taken of GM Euclid and Terex equipment between 1953 and 1981. An incredible legacy of work.

Eric Orlemann

Introduction

"A taste for the green iron." This is what was usually said of contractors or individuals who purchased Euclid or Terex equipment instead of the more common yellow variety. My earliest recollections of the "green iron" are from the late 1960s, when I was eight or nine, riding in the back of the family station wagon. On the way to the Tri-County Shopping Center, just north of Cincinnati, we would pass the W.W. Williams Company, an equipment dealer whose machines were all painted green. Not just any green, mind you, but a bright, almost lime-like shade. I would beg my mother to slow down as we passed the dealership so I could get a better look at the dozers, loaders, and haulers. Lined up in the dealer's lot, right next to the road, were the haulers, with their dump box bodies raised, as if to salute the passing motorists. I would press my face up against the glass in the back of the car as the lot faded from sight. This scene would be repeated as we came home from shopping, usually at night. As we passed the dealership again, the equipment was bathed in the warm glow of spotlights, especially the units closest to the road. It was a scene I would see many times over the years, and it always was the highlight of shopping excursions to that part of town. To this day, I can close my eyes and see those machines lit up at night in the dealer's lot, as if I had just seen them yesterday.

One day, while approaching the dealer, in my usual seat in the back of the station wagon, I noticed something was amiss. The green equipment was gone, replaced by blue-colored BFI garbage trucks. I wondered what had happened to all the green trucks. The old W.W. Williams signs were gone, as were all the green machines. When I passed the lot months later, I always hoped the green equipment would return, as if it somehow were just parked in the back, out of sight for some reason. But it never did. I always wondered what had happened, but school and the pressures of being a sixth grader were bearing down on me, and I gradually forgot about the old dealership, especially when the new expressway was finished, which no longer took us by that dealership.

I purchased a book in 1983 titled *Mammoth Vehicles of the Land, Air & Sea*, written by John H. Bradner. While paging through it at the bookstore, I came across two images of the Terex 33-19 Titan hauler. I remembered seeing photos of the truck back when I was in junior high school, though at the time, I didn't know exactly what I was looking at. Bradner's book, and especially the image of the Titan, with its dump body raised, rekindled memories of that old dealership. The hunt was now on for the green iron.

At first, my research was typical of most when seeking information on an unknown subject: find a dealership. Not finding one in Cincinnati at the time, I was off to the library and to more dead ends. Now mind you, I wasn't doing this every day, just whenever I had a little extra time. There were periods when a few years would go by before I would get the inclination again to search out more information. In 1986, I was given the book *GM...The First 75 Years of Transportation Products*, produced by the editors of *Automobile Quarterly* magazine. In it, I found an image of a haul truck referred to as a Titan 33-15C. It struck me as unusual that the early history of Euclid Division, and the more recent history of Terex Division, was not even mentioned, let alone covered. If GM didn't even care about its earth-moving engineering achievements, why should I? Thank goodness, I didn't keep that attitude long.

For the next few years, this fascination with the green iron was mainly spent following up leads in my spare time, of which I unfortunately had little. Slowly but methodically I started to put together a small library concerning these past GM divisions. Numerous long distance phone calls were made in the process of gathering this historical information, making that AT&T phone bill each month always an unwelcome sight in the mailbox.

I could never understand why it seemed that every other major division or product line of GM had been written about in some way. The automobile creations were well covered, as were most of the trucks, including many of the military variations. The railroad hobby magazines and books covered just about every EMD locomotive that ever came out of the La Grange and Diesel Division plants, so why not the earth-moving machines? I started to feel that this history must be recorded in book form, to help preserve a very important piece of GM history. Of course, this was easier said than done, and it was made all the more difficult by a lack of printed research material on the subject. It looked like this project was going to have to be done from scratch.

Many times, I wished I had never started on the project in the first place. The knowledge that so-and-so had just thrown out their photo files on Euclid or Terex the month before was, at times, almost too much to bear. There were instances when I missed important finds by as little as two weeks before they were thrown away, or "turfed," as a Canadian dealer put it. These files had existed for years, sometimes decades, being left alone in one piece. How come, just at the time I was trying to put this information together, everyone seemed to be having an attack of spring-cleaning fever? For me, it was a case of being two steps to the left, instead of two to the right. If I was going to pull this off, I was going to have to make sure that I was in the right place, at the right time, to keep this material from being destroyed. Part of this was achieved through numerous contacts built up over the years with individuals in the industry. It also helped that many of the clients I worked for were in the surface mining industry. I always justified my troubles with this project by telling myself that if it were easy to find this information in the first place, someone else would have already produced a book, making mine irrelevant.

Needless to say, the images were found, the interviews done, and the copy was written. Most of this was accomplished between my advertising photo assignments at various surface mines throughout the United States and my other book projects, mainly between 1992 and 1996. I think that this whole experience can be summed up in one simple statement: Time sure flies when you're having fun.

The focus of this book on Euclid and Terex equipment involves the GM years of production. It also covers the earlier Euclid Road Machinery Company, and the activities of both companies as they exist today, just not in the same depth or detail as the GM period.

Model Nomenclature

With the number of model variations produced by Euclid and Terex, the model identification coding can be very confusing, especially during the Euclid Road Machinery and GM Euclid Division years. During the early years, machine variations were referred to by their engineering model designations. Starting in the mid-1950s, GM also used a sales model designation in conjunction with the engineering identification. In many areas of the book, the sales model identification is listed first, followed by its engineering designation, such as a Euclid R-50 (12LD).

Standard sales model designation type unit codes are as follows:

R: Rear Dump
B: Bottom Dump
CH: Coal Hauler
S: Scraper
TS: Twin-powered Scraper
SS: Tractor Scraper
C: Crawler
TC: Twin-powered Crawler
L: Loader
BV: Belt Conveyor Loader

In sale model designations for haulers and bottom dumps, the first letter stands for the type of unit, and the second set of numbers is for the tonnage. For example, R-50 stands for rear dump hauler rated at 50 tons. In the case of a crawler dozer, such as TC-12, the second set of numbers stands for the total number of engine cylinders. In scrapers, such as a TS-24, the last digits referred to the struck cubic yard capacity of the unit. For loaders, such as the L-30, the number stands for the average cubic yard class the model falls into, which in this case is 3.0 cubic yards. An L-7 unit would have a capacity range of 0.7 cubic yards.

Engineering model designations are made more complicated by the sheer number of model variations.

Engineering model types for rubber-tired equipment were divided into four major categories: Rear Dumps, Tractors, Trailing Units, and Prime Movers. BV belt loaders and the crawler dozers were not part of this four-category system, because of the limited model types produced.

Following are some examples of standard engineering designation codes.

A 12LD Rear Dump, for example, breaks down as follows:
12 is the model design sequence number
L is the vehicle axle size class
D is the primary power source

Drive axle class designations break down this way:
Q: Under 10 tons
U: 10–15 tons
F: 5–25 tons
T: 22–40 tons
L: 30 tons and over
FF: 34–45 tons
LL: 50–105 tons

Power designations break down this way:
D: Diesel
B: Butane
G: Gasoline
E: Electric
T: Turbine
O: Over-hung tractor; no power designation

Tractors, such as a 49LDT, break down as follows:
49:    Model design sequence number
L: Vehicle axle size class
D: Primary power source
T: Denotes that tractor is used in combination with a trailing unit

Trailing Units are divided into the following three types:
SH: Scraper
W: Dirt, Rock, or Coal Wagon
CH: Coal Hauler
For example, in the model 33SH, the first numbers refer to the model design sequence, and the second set of digits stands for the type of trailing unit, in this case, a scraper.

Prime Movers are divided into the following four categories:
QPM
UPM
FPM
TPM
For example, in the model designation 3UPM, the Prime Mover designation's first number refers to the model design sequence; the first letter refers to the axle type, as indicated for the Rear Dumps; and PM stands for a prime mover, usually of the four-wheel-drive variety. Models included under this designation include front-end loaders, wheel dozers, and tow tractors.

Starting in the late 1960s, many of the engineering model designations were being dropped. The old system was finally phased out of use by 1977, during the GM Terex years.

Note that this sales and engineering model designation system was retained by Euclid, Inc., when the hauler product line became part of White Motor Company. Today, Euclid-Hitachi Heavy Equipment still uses this designation system, with slight modifications due to the expanding product line.

The
Pioneering Spirit

By the turn of the twentieth century, the old ways were giving way to the new. From the late 1800s to the early 1900s, the process of working the earth was becoming ever more mechanized. The horse and mule teams were stubbornly giving way to steam-, gas-, and diesel-powered machines. More productive methods of farming were needed for a growing populace, better roads were needed for the growing number of automobiles the public had fallen in love with, and an increase in the production of energy by such means as dams and powerplants was necessary. All would need the talents of energetic engineers to design the earth-moving machines that could make these things possible.

One of these engineers was George A. Armington. It can be said that George Armington and his sons were to Euclid Road Machinery, as Daniel Best and Benjamin Holt were to Caterpillar.

George Armington was born on August 3, 1865, in Milford, Massachusetts. After graduating from M.I.T. in 1887, he became head of the Mechanical Engineering Department of Case School of Applied Science. In 1889, he left his teaching position and joined the Otis Steel Company in Cleveland as a structural engineer. In 1895, George moved on to become superintendent of the Phoenix Iron Works, of which he was made director the following year. But working for someone else's company was not how George wanted to spend the rest of his life.

In January 1897, George Armington set out to start his own company, and formed G. A. Armington & Company.

The first Model 1Z truck in January 1934. It was the first rear dump hauler to be built by Euclid. The 1Z model was powered by a 100-horsepower Waukesha gasoline engine, and was equipped with a dump body rated at 7 cubic yards. This truck is considered the first true off-highway rear dump designed from the ground up solely for that purpose. Before this, off-road haulers were modified trucks based on standard road-going units. In 1935, these trucks picked up the trade name "Trac-Truk," based partly on the extra-traction tire lugs that were standard on the early models. Later, these tracks were replaced by larger tires, but the Euclid Trac-Truk name remained unchanged.

This new venture specialized in engineering and manufacturing hoisting equipment, such as hand, steam, belt, and electric cranes. Things were not what George expected. It was a case of biting off more than he could chew. A false start, maybe, but the lessons learned would come in handy in the not-too-distant future. In 1898, he joined the management group of the Cleveland Crane and Car Company. But George did not hold controlling interest in the company. Again, he found himself wanting.

George Armington moved his family to a farm in Wickliffe, Ohio, in 1902. He started another new company, the Armington Electric Hoist Company, in 1907, in a building on his Ridge Road property in Wickliffe. All of what George had learned over the years would now be brought to bear. This venture would mark the beginning of what would eventually become the Euclid Division of General Motors. But we still have a few more decades to go before that will come to pass.

By May 1909, it was already time to find larger manufacturing space for the new company, and the plant was moved to a new location on Chardon Road in Euclid, Ohio, just northeast of Cleveland. It was at this time the business name was changed to the Euclid Crane and Hoist Company. The farm in Wickliffe was retained and would become the major testing area for many of the earth-moving machines that were yet to come.

George A. Armington had five sons—Arthur, Stuart, Everett, George Jr., and Raymond—all of whom would play important roles in molding the company into a true contender in the earth-moving business. These men would become the first true pioneers of the "green iron."

The eldest of the five sons, Arthur P. Armington, joined his father's company in 1915 as an engineer after graduating from Case Institute. Next to join the family business was Stuart F. Armington, the second-eldest son, in 1926. He came to the company as an engineer, but soon assumed some of the responsibility of product engineering and field contacts. In 1929, George E. Armington Jr., joined the company, also as an engineer. In 1931, Raymond Q. Armington followed his brothers into the business and took over some of the company's management

The first Euclid wheeled scraper, a 1/2-yard unit built in 1924, is being pulled by a Fordson tractor down Euclid Avenue, at Chardon, in Cleveland, Ohio. For extra traction, the tractor is equipped with Euclid Fordson Traction Lugs attached to the outside of the rear wheel rims.

duties. Shortly after Raymond started with Euclid, Everett F. Armington, the last of the five brothers to join the company, took the position of sales manager.

Arthur Armington is probably the person most responsible for starting to steer the company's future interests toward the earth-moving side of the business. Arthur, with the aid of his father, designed and built a small crawler tractor. Even though this crawler was never released commercially, it proved to be an important test bed on the Armington farm in the evolution of many of their inventions.

The Euclid company was starting to become very well known for its industrial lifting devices. As the business started to expand and prosper, so did Arthur's experiments in designing earth-moving equipment. In a corner

This experimental Euclid Model ZW Bottom Dump was the first tractor and 8-yard bottom dump trailer combination built entirely by Euclid. The picture is dated December 14, 1933; at the time, the unit was still in its early design phase. Before Euclid built this tractor, the company had tried using a modified Chevrolet truck chassis with a prototype 5-yard bottom dump trailer.

of the shop set aside especially for his use, he would build and test his concepts' viability as marketable products. A few wheel tractors were built and tested, but none was found suitable for production. At about this time, Arthur's interest in tracked and wheeled tractors shifted to scrapers. This is where he thought a weakness existed in the marketplace, and he envisioned Euclid as the company that could exploit it. He was right.

In 1924, Euclid introduced its first two models of scrapers. The first to be released was a rotary scraper. The Euclid Automatic Rotary Scraper was drum-like in appearance and could be pulled by any number of tractors on the market at the time. Capacities started at 18 cubic feet and would eventually reach 56 cubic feet. As this type of unit scraped the surface of the ground, a different type of unit was needed if the earth was to be plowed or loosened because of being too hard. Shortly after release of the rotary model, Euclid introduced its wheel scraper. The Euclid Wheeler, as it was sometimes called, was of 1/2-yard capacity. With its narrower digging blade and cutting teeth, it was ideal for hard, compacted ground. These units would find great acceptance with various earth-moving contractors. Many of these types of Euclid Wheelers were teamed up in trains of three to five, pulled by a single crawler tractor of 60 to 75 horsepower. One of the most popular of these units was the Euclid Contractor's Special, a heavy-duty 1 1/4-yard wheeler scraper designed for continuous use in hard ground. These units weighed about 4,350 pounds.

With the acceptance of these early scrapers in the marketplace, it was decided that a new division within Euclid should be set up to address this new customer base. So in 1926, the Road Machinery Division of the Euclid Crane and Hoist Company was created.

In 1927 and 1928, large public works programs across the country required moving massive amounts of earth. These projects included roads, flood control systems, earth-fill dams, and various other large construction jobs. If these projects were to be completed, more efficient methods of earth-moving would soon have to be invented. Because of this demand, the production of scrapers was increased, with many improvements made to increase their reliability and ease of operation.

In 1928, Euclid added its next product line, in the form of crawler wagons. These cart-type wagons operated on steel tracks or crawlers. They were pulled by crawler tractors and were able to dump from the rear, or from either side, depending on the model. These models of heavy rock and dirt hauling wagons would eventually be known as Euclid Tu-Way haulers. Additional versions included log and pipe crawler wagons that were produced at the same time as the earth-moving units.

In 1929, when George E. Armington Jr. joined the company, one of his first projects was the development of the wheel wagon. This early hauler had steel wheels and was to be pulled by a crawler tractor. It was hoped

The first true production Euclid Model 1ZW bottom dump was released in early 1934, not long after the 1Z rear dump was introduced. This unit featured a redesigned bottom dump trailer that was stronger and better engineered than the experimental ZW prototype's version. The quickest way to tell the two tractors apart is by the front bumper. The prototype ZW's front bumper is a steel bar, while the production 1ZW has a larger steel one, like the one used on the 1Z rear dump.

that this model would improve working times as opposed to the units with crawlers. This was an important first step in a development that was yet to come— Euclid's bottom dump hauler.

Experiments by George Jr., who had a keen interest in hydraulics, would soon lead to the development of hydraulically operated crawler and wheel wagons and bulldozer attachments. Many of the models of crawler tractors built by Caterpillar, Allis-Chalmers, and Case could use the Euclid bulldozer. They were very popular and put Euclid into greater competition with R.G. LeTourneau, a manufacturer whose similar products depended, at the time, on other companies' machines, especially Caterpillar crawlers.

The incredibly rapid expansion of the Road Machinery Division made it necessary to separate the earth-moving part of the business from the crane and hoist part of the company. On July 11, 1931, the Euclid Road Machinery Company was incorporated. This company would remain a subsidiary of the Euclid Armington Corporation until January 1, 1933, when there was a complete separation of the two companies. From January 1933 on, greater emphasis would always be placed on

the earth-moving part of the business. Products in the early 1930s consisted of wheel and crawler wagons, special log pipe wagons, bulldozer blade attachments and related hydraulic controls, and sheepsfoot tamping rollers. The smaller rotary and wheel scrapers were slowly phased out of production.

The need for faster, more productive, off-road earth-moving equipment was very evident to the management of Euclid, and in early 1933, steps were taken to address the situation. Contractors needed vehicles with crawler tractor toughness and the speed of the rubber-tired trucks then in use. The first unit built by Euclid to combine some of these traits was a hybrid of sorts. It combined a Euclid-designed five-yard bottom dump trailer with a specially modified Chevrolet truck chassis, which had a shortened wheelbase and a specially designed drive axle. It was also equipped with 13.50x24 tires, the largest then available. Three of these units were built and put through a series of rigorous earth-moving tests, with mixed results. The modified tractors were inadequate for the heavy-duty work for which they were intended, and the bottom dump trailers were not large enough. The tires also suffered from poor traction and floatation in

The Euclid Model 1SH tractor-pulled scraper was the first self-propelled model designed and built by Euclid. The first and only unit produced, shown here working on October 17, 1938, was rated at 12 cubic yards for its tilting scraper bowl. The tractor was a Euclid 4FDT model, powered by an HB Cummins diesel engine.

less-than-ideal conditions. Clearly, if Euclid was going to produce a heavy-duty hauler, it was going to have to build the tractor itself, from the ground up.

In late 1933, Euclid started testing its newly developed rubber-tired tractor. It featured a 100-horsepower Waukesha gasoline engine and a special Euclid-designed rear axle for severe duty use. The tire industry had just released a new, larger 17.5x24 tire, which was used on the tractor. In conjunction with the development of the tractor unit, a new 8-yard-capacity trailer was also built. This experimental semi-bottom dump would become known as the Euclid Model Z (sometimes referred to as the ZW). Considerable sales resistance was experienced by Euclid in getting the industry to accept the Z hauler. Also, many design and mechanical features still had to be worked out, but gradually, the hauler proved itself on road and earth-fill dam projects throughout the country. The unit soon became so popular that Euclid was building one unit per day.

During the building of the bottom dump, Euclid realized that a rear dump unit would also be needed to handle hauling duties on large construction job sites. Until this time, off-road haulers were nothing more than beefed-up standard road units built by various manufacturers. The need for a rear dump, off-road hauler, built from the ground up, was real. In January 1934, Euclid unveiled the new truck, the 7-cubic-yard capacity Model 1Z "Trac-Truk." The Euclid Trac-Truk was the industry's first hauler designed strictly for off-road service. Even though Mack Trucks had introduced a 14-yard heavy-duty hauler, the Model AP Super-Duty Truck, in 1931,

for use on the Boulder Dam project, it was still based largely on existing road-going versions of Mack's famous AC Bulldog models.

The success of the Euclid Model Z haulers would point the way for the future of the company, and to a certain extent, the rest of the industry. Improved versions of the original concepts were continuously released. In September 1935, the first of three experimental Model 1Z bottom dump coal haulers were produced for Truax-Traer Coal Company, in Fiatt, Illinois. New models of rear dumps were also introduced, such as the 5-yard Model B and 7-yard Model D haulers. In 1936, the first of the Euclid "F" series (later known as "FD") haulers was introduced, and it had some of the features for which Euclid trucks were to become known. Diesel-powered engines replaced the early gasoline units, and planetary final drive axles were incorporated. Also, the new "Pioneer" trademark was added to all products. In the years to come, the pioneer character in the logo would be referred to as "Pioneer Pete." This nickname was not official company policy, but the name stuck anyway, as these things often do.

Two side endeavors to the earth-moving part of the business emerged during the mid-1930s. Around 1934 and 1935, Arthur Armington's interest in railroads prompted a brief venture into the production of diesel-electric switch engines. Locomotives in two sizes, 35 and 55 tons, were produced. The Railway Transportation Division was formed at the Chardon Road Plant and appropriate staff was hired. But due to limited sales outlets and poor financial conditions, the project was abandoned in 1936. The second diversion involved the idea of "piggy-back" transporting of highway trailers on railroad flat cars. At least two Euclid trailers were designed and built with removable wheels and solid rubber suspension systems. Again, the lack of capital forced the abandonment of these projects in 1937.

Arthur Armington was the main catalyst and guiding force of the development of the Euclid earth-moving equipment, but in March 1937, he died after several long months of ill health. This was a tremendous blow to the company. Arthur had been responsible for steering the young company through many difficult times while establishing new Euclid product lines.

In mid-1937, the company experienced a period of financial strain caused by its rapid expansion and lack of operating capital. For the next several years, a more conservative approach to operations was undertaken. Main objectives were to reduce inventories, collect on customer debts, and improve cash flow. During this period, refinements in product design and operation were stressed, and a strong sales force was established in the field. These efforts paid off, with Euclid ending the decade stronger than ever.

In October 1938, Euclid began testing a newly designed scraper, the 1SH. Pulled by a 4FDT tractor, this 12-cubic-yard unit marked Euclid's return to the scraper business after the discontinuation of the rotary and wheel scrapers of the 1920s. Other early developmental scraper models built around this time included the 12-cubic-yard Model 2SH in 1939, and the Model 3SH, incorporating a twin bowl ejector-type design, also in 1939. In 1940, Euclid introduced its first experimental over-hung tractor-powered scraper, the 10-cubic-yard

In 1940, Euclid released its first self-propelled, over-hung front-engine scraper, the Model 1MGT-5SH. The first unit (pictured) was a 10-cubic-yard scraper that steered with its rear wheels. Later, more advanced Euclid types were steered by hydraulic cylinders between the tractor front and the scraper rear.

Model 1MGT-5SH. Next to follow was the Model 2MDT-7SH scraper, also introduced in 1940. Though these last two models looked very modern, they relied on rear-wheel steering, which allowed the scraper rear end to wander from side to side, as the steering wheels would get caught in existing tire ruts in the working area. Another problem arose when the scraper worked close to edges. As the scraper turned away from the cut, the rear end would sweep out over the embankment, and hang up the unit.

By the end of 1940, total sales to date of the new types of earth-moving equipment introduced in the 1930s included 331 rear dumps, 843 bottom dumps, and 23 Model FT-2SH scrapers. Of this total, 295 of these units were sold in 1940 alone. But development of new models, such as the scrapers and the BV conveyor belt loaders, would have to wait. There was a war in Europe and in the Pacific that would determine what would be produced, not just by Euclid, but by all manufacturers.

Early in 1942, it appeared to Euclid that it was going to have to convert its manufacturing facilities to the production of military items. Up until this time, the War Production Board felt the current supply of off-road hauling equipment was adequate for the war needs. But when the earlier production quotas for coal, iron, and other raw materials could not be met with the equipment then available, Euclid was authorized to continue production of its standard equipment. Since the company produced the only true heavy-duty off-road haulers then available, these were in the most demand. The "Eucs," as they were becoming known, needed little modification before being purchased by various government agencies. In fact, just about the only things they needed were a dimmer switch for the lights and a flat coat of OD green paint.

During the war years, Euclid introduced two new rear dump models. In 1942, the first 1LD hauler was released, and in 1944, the first 1TD hauler. These were very robust trucks, whose looks would be evident in models for years to come.

When the war ended, Euclid found itself in a very enviable situation. During the war, new equipment was not made available to contractors unless they were performing essential war work. This meant that most of the machines in the construction industry were worn out. The equipment used in mining, quarries, and other industrial complexes was in no better shape. With no factory conversions to contend with, since none had been needed for war production, Euclid went right to work filling the new equipment orders that were flooding into the office. Something would soon have to be done to keep pace with the demand for more equipment—not only in quantity, but also in productivity.

Customers were asking for bigger loads, faster cycle times, and most important of all, more power. And more power is just what they were going to get.

Two Is Better
Than One

Up until 1946, Euclid Road Machinery had been using the same manufacturing facilities that had given birth to the company on Chardon Road, just east of Cleveland, Ohio. Factory space had been expanded only slightly, in 1937 and 1942, and an aggressive expansion program was needed if production was to meet the tidal wave of orders pouring into the offices. Euclid took the first step to meet these needs in 1945, when the company purchased 37 acres at St. Clair and 222nd Street in Euclid. At this location, the first section of St. Clair Plant No. 1 was completed in 1946. This structure consisted of 66,500 square feet of manufacturing and office space, making it almost three times larger than the Chardon Road facilities. One of the outstanding features of this new plant was the assembly line production of heavy-duty off-highway equipment, one of the first such assembly lines in the industry.

With work on larger production facilities under way, the Euclid company made a more concentrated effort in the development of its Model BV Loader. Preliminary work had started on the 1BV Loader concept in 1940, but because of World War II, further work had to be delayed for a few years. This prewar unit was dismantled and improved upon. The BV Loader did not hit its stride until the release of the Model 3BV Loader in 1946. In total, 23 of the Model 3BV units were built, with great acceptance now being shown by contractors who were looking for high-speed earth-moving capabilities. The BV loaders used a conveyer belt-type of design to load the high-speed, rubber-tired, bottom-dumps of the day—Euclid's own to be precise—by means of a crawler tractor that could pull the unit. Any of the larger units built by the various crawler manufacturers could be used to pull the BV through various materials, such as sand, hard clay, and

The 1LLD model line was not officially released by Euclid until 1953, and even then, it was considered a special-order unit. In 1953, this 1LLD was painted in the new green color that was introduced just after GM purchased Euclid Road Machinery. It would still be about another year before the lighter, "Hi-Lite" green color would be introduced.

shale. The tractor operator controlled all functions of the BV by means of three levers mounted within easy reach on the back of the crawler. The wide cutting blade and moldboard plow would send a steady flow of material to the conveyer belt and into a bottom-dump hauler that was traveling next to the loader. This way, a fleet of haulers could be matched to one BV Loader so there would always be one by its side, ready to be filled. With the unit working in the right material, there was no cheaper way to move earth. Different models of the BV Loader were built until the last unit, an 18BV model, was shipped on December 12, 1956, to India.

The next problem that Euclid would have to address was the lack of more powerful engines and suitable tires. Development had not kept up in these two areas, and demand increased from customers eager to tackle the larger construction contracts that soon would be awarded for dams and highways. Adding an engine to double the horsepower output was the logical solution. But unless a suitable heavy-duty transmission could be found, one that was also reliable, the attempt would fail, as a few of Euclid's competitors would learn the hard way.

At General Motors Corporation's Allison Division, work was under way on a transmission that would eventually address the problems that Euclid was experiencing with the quest for more power for heavy-duty earth-moving applications. During World War II, an Allison transmission had been developed for military vehicles and tanks with engine output ratings of over 500 horsepower. In many instances, they were coupled in multiple-engine configurations, especially in tanks that needed large amounts of power in the most demanding conditions imaginable. Since conventional shift transmissions had already reached a fairly stable degree of reliability, major improvements throughout the industry were not really needed. What was needed was an automatic drive system that would reduce operator fatigue, lessen driver errors in shifting, increase ease of operation, and of course, provide a better means of transmitting power from the engine to the drive wheels. The system that would address these problems was the Allison Torqmatic Drive.

The Euclid 50FDT-102W "Twin-Power" bottom dump was the first Euclid model designed to utilize two separate drivetrains, one in the front tractor, and the other in the rear 18-cubic-yard capacity bottom dump trailer. Both engines were GM Diesel 6-71 units, each with its own Allison Torqmatic transmission. Total rated output for both engines was 380 gross horsepower. Pictured here on November 22, 1948, is the first unit built, shortly after its final assembly at the St. Clair plant.

The first self-propelled scraper model built to utilize the twin-power concept was the Euclid 51FDT-13SH, introduced in February 1949. This model shared the same engine and transmission combinations as were first installed in the 50FDT-102W bottom dump. Pictured is the first 16-cubic-yard unit undergoing early engineering field trial testing in February 1949.

The Euclid 1FFD rear dump was the first hauler built by Euclid with twin-power, side-by-side-mounted GM Diesel 6-71 engines, each with its own Allison Torqmatic transmission. Total power output was 380 gross horsepower. The truck's capacity was rated at 34 tons. Pictured is the first 1FFD on February 18, 1949, fresh off the assembly line at Euclid's St. Clair plant.

The commercial development of this Allison transmission commenced immediately after the war. Euclid started to experiment with the Torqmatic Drive in 1946 and 1947. Even though mechanical and field application developments would need to be addressed, it was apparent the semiautomatic type of transmission with full power shift capability was the way for the company to go. It was decided to fund a vigorous engineering effort to adapt the Allison unit for heavy earth-moving duties.

The Allison Torqmatic Drive consisted of a combination of a torque converter, which would automatically adjust for any minor variations in load and road conditions, and a full power shift transmission. The Allison transmission was of the planetary type, with engagement accomplished through hydraulically actuated clutch plates. This allowed for the unit to be shifted instantaneously under full power and with a full load. This system was the only one available that could have made possible Euclid's "Twin-Power" concept. The use of torque converters and semiautomatic transmissions eliminated the engine synchronization problem, and permitted

two transmissions to be shifted simultaneously by the operator. Only one lever needed to be shifted into any of the system's forward speeds for engagement.

The first Euclid model to be produced incorporating the Twin-Power concept was the Euclid 50FDT-102W Bottom Dump. The first unit rolled out of the factory in November 1948. This unit was powered by two GM Diesel 6-71 engines, rated at 190 horsepower each, coupled to Allison TG602 transmissions. One engine, transmission, and torque converter was in the front tractor, and a duplicate set was in the rear of the trailer, driving the rear wheels. The load capacity of the bottom dump was 18 cubic yards of earth, or about 57,000 pounds. This hauler performed extremely well in adverse conditions, such as on steep grades, soft fills, or deep sand, due largely to its four-wheel-drive capability.

With the success of the early testing program of the twin-engine bottom dump, Euclid's attention now turned toward adapting the system to its tractor scrapers. In June 1948, Euclid had re-entered the scraper market with the single-engined 47FDT-11SH. This was the company's best

When the 50-ton-capacity 1LLD was introduced by Euclid Road Machinery in May 1951, it was the largest rear dump hauler then produced in the industry. The 1LLD was powered by two six-cylinder, Cummins NHRS-600 engines rated at 600 gross horsepower total. Each engine was connected to its own Allison Torqmatic transmission and torque converter. This 1LLD belonged to Western Contracting Corporation of Sioux City, Iowa, and is shown working in 1952 at the Fort Randall Dam Project in Pickstown, South Dakota. Western was the contractor that originally asked Euclid to build its 50-ton-capacity hauler. This 1LLD was not the first unit built, but it was one of the trucks delivered in the first factory order.

scraper to date, featuring hydraulic cable operation of the scraper functions and a 14-cubic-yard capacity. The next step in the evolution of the scraper was adding power to the scraper portion of the unit. The first prototype Euclid Twin-Power scraper model produced, in February 1949, was the 51FDT-13SH. This model was equipped with the same Allison Torqmatic Drive and GM Diesel engines found in the twin-engine bottom dump, with the same power ratings. The scraper featured hydraulic cable controls and a 16-cubic-yard capacity. With dual power, this unit had the ability to work in areas that single-engined units were not well suited for. The twin-powered scrapers could dig, haul, and spread their loads in most conditions without the assistance of push tractors. Of course, push dozers were used with the scrapers in many instances because contractors would send these machines into the worst operating conditions imaginable to maximize the units' operating potential. Production versions of the early twin-power scrapers Euclid released in 1950 included the GM Diesel-engined 68FDT-17SH, and the Cummins-powered 66FDT-16SH.

While the twin-engine concept was being implemented in the scraper line, the hauler engineers at Euclid were also working on their version of Twin-Power for rear dump applications called the 1FFD. The big 34-ton capacity, tandem-drive truck was unveiled in February 1949. While the goal for twin engines in the bottom dump and scraper models was better mobility and greater capacity, the goal in a rear dump application was—plain and simple—power. At the time, there was not a single engine with suitable power-generating capacity to meet Euclid's needs. Any engine that could generate the power was so large and heavy that it actually reduced payload capacity. It was a classic case of one step forward and two steps back. To address this problem, the engineers installed two currently available engines, side by side, in the front of the truck. Each engine would be mated to its own semiautomatic transmission and torque converter, and would drive one of the rear tandem-axles. In this case, the left engine drove the front drive axle and the right engine drove the rear one. Both engines were GM Diesel 6-71 units, rated at 190 horsepower apiece, with a 380-horsepower total output. The transmissions were Allison TG-607RM units. Payload capacity was 34 tons, or 68,000 pounds, with an empty truck weight of 64,000 pounds. A twin-powered Cummins version of the hauler, the 4FFD, with two NHB diesels rated at 200 horsepower each (400 horsepower total), was released in 1951. More-powerful GM Diesel engines, rated at 436 total horsepower when used in a pair, and Cummins units, rated at 400 total horsepower for two engines, were installed in both models by 1956.

The Euclid FFD proved to be a very tough and popular truck with mining operations across the country, especially in the Mesabi Iron Range area of Minnesota. With its 34-ton capacity, it was the largest rear-dump hauler Euclid had to offer in 1949 and 1950. But the quest for a larger truck to carry greater payloads is never-ending

for manufacturers of such machines. The next record-breaker was just around the corner.

Around 1950, officials from the Western Contracting Corporation, located in Sioux City, Iowa, approached Ray Q. Armington, then president of Euclid Road Machinery, about the possibility of Euclid developing a larger rear-dump hauler. With the bigger road-building and dam projects coming up for bids, Western realized that only the largest possible hauler would meet its requirements. Ray Armington agreed to meet Western's challenge, and after some discussions, it was decided that Euclid would design and build a 50-ton capacity hauler, making it the largest ever produced for its time. So confident was Western of Euclid's engineering abilities, the company placed an initial order for 10 trucks, even before they received final design specifications and long before the first prototype was to be ready. Before one of these first 10 trucks could be delivered, Western placed an additional order for 10 more units; right after the first truck was delivered, Western ordered yet another 10.

In May 1951, the first mighty Euclid 1LLD hauler rolled off the production line. It was similar in layout to the FFD truck, only larger. The LLD design incorporated the twin-power concept, this time in the form of two six-cylinder Cummins NHRS-600, four-cycle diesel engines mounted side by side under the hood. Combined power output from these engines was 600 horsepower at 2,100 rpm. These units supplied power to the rear tandem-drive axles through Allison transmissions (Model TG-607RM), and torque converters (Model TCG-604), one unit each to an engine. The truck weighed in at 104,000 pounds empty, and 204,000 pounds with a full load.

Euclid built three pilot LLD haulers that underwent a little over a year and a half of preliminary field testing. One LLD was shipped for testing in the Mesabi Iron Range, working in deep pit operations. Another truck went to work in the anthracite coal fields of Pennsylvania, and the first unit went to Western Contracting Corporation. By November 1952, Western had received 19 of the 50-ton haulers from its original orders, with all of the trucks, including the first pilot model, assigned to the Fort Randall Dam Project in Pickstown, South Dakota. The early LLD haulers were classified as special order trucks and did not become standard production models until 1953. In 1957, the R-50 designation was assigned to the 50-ton capacity LLD model line.

Euclid's FFD and LLD haulers have always been some of the company's most memorable trucks, with new models being added well into the early 1960s. (These models are covered in a later chapter.) These haulers were instantly recognized as "Eucs." The company might have made larger-volume sellers, and would eventually build bigger-capacity models, but I doubt they will ever be remembered like these twin-engined, tandem-drive haulers. "Pioneer Pete" never looked as good as he did on the sides of these trucks.

The General and the Super-Dozer

The Euclid Road Machinery Company was experiencing continued growth and sales through the late 1940s and early 1950s. In 1945, Euclid had about 400 employees. By 1950, this number had risen to 1,200. Additional properties consisting of about 60,000 square feet were purchased on another corner of St. Clair and 222nd Street. This plant and office space would be known as St. Clair Plant No. 2. Also, expansion at St. Clair Plant No. 1 in 1948 and 1951 more than tripled the size of the complex. The company may not have had the size of some of its competitors, but when it came to off-road haulers, it led the industry.

This expansion of Euclid's manufacturing capabilities was necessary to keep up with the worldwide demand for its products. To help further solidify its international sales network, a new plant was established at Newhouse, near Motherwell, Scotland. This move would also help the company keep its share of the sterling markets, because of a dollar shortage and the devaluation of the British pound. Also of great benefit was the excellent skilled labor force and access to ports capable of handling large machinery for export. Euclid Great Britain, Ltd. shipped its first truck, an R-15 (B5FD) rear dump, in January 1951. Early on, only a few models of haulers were manufactured abroad, but within a few years, a larger variety of scrapers and crawler dozers would roll off the assembly lines in Scotland. In the future, this plant would become a very important asset to the company, in more ways than one.

In January 1966, the designation for the TC-12 model was officially changed to the 82-80 series. One of the first of these new units to carry the new designation was this 82-80 (BA) unit, being demonstrated in Boca Raton, Florida, on December 22, 1965, a few days before the name change announcement. This model's major specifications were unchanged from the TC-12-2 version, but the weight had gone up a bit, and was listed at 71,250 pounds. Note the modified Euclid trademark triangle logo on the side of the dozer. In late 1964 the new logo was introduced without "Pioneer Pete" in the triangle. By the end of the first quarter of 1965, the pioneer trademark had been removed from all buildings and new machines.

In the early 1950s, the sales environment in the earth-moving field started to change for Euclid. Even though sales were up and product acceptance from customers was extremely high, the company's reliance on a limited product line caused management great concern. Euclid's competitors were starting to take a closer look at the market niche that the company had created for off-road haulers. These manufacturers were starting to feel that this market was now large enough to justify the sizable investment required for the design and engineering of these products. Up until this time, Euclid was the industry leader by far in the off-road hauler business. Euclid realized that the playing field was going to get a lot more crowded in the not-too-distant future.

The other concern for management came from a growing awareness that, more and more, customers were looking for dealers and manufacturers that could supply a full product line. Customers didn't want to have to buy a hauler from Euclid, a dozer from Caterpillar, and a scraper from LeTourneau. The company that could offer the most complete line of earth-moving equipment was going to be in a better position to give customers what they wanted. As the need for better roads and bridges increased, so did the need for more and more heavy-duty equipment to get the jobs done. The demand for more power created by generating plants and dams, and construction of the superhighway system, would mean orders for earth-moving machines in unprecedented numbers. Other manufacturers also realized this. They recognized that the best way of quickly broadening one's product line was to form an alliance with another company that offered equipment that complemented their own. So consolidations of competitive firms started to take place, resulting in more-cohesive dealer networks, offering full product lines from a single source. Euclid did not have the necessary capital reserves to develop a full product line in time to meet the growing demand. The company just wasn't large enough. If Euclid was going to flourish in this new competitive environment, the Armingtons were going to have to find an ally quickly. And that is just what they did.

Where Euclid Road Machinery saw competition, General Motors Corporation saw opportunity. With the growing demand for heavy-duty off-road equipment, the need for large diesel engines would be on the increase.

On September 15, 1954, at the GM Milford Proving Grounds, Euclid introduced its new-and-improved equipment lineup to Euclid dealers and trade reporters. At the show were the first four prototype TC-12 crawler tractors, equipped in various configurations to demonstrate the crawler's overall performance in earth-moving applications. The TC-12 shown pulling a Euclid BV Loader has the second-generation sheet metal body panels, which were more rounded than the first test units, but still functioned only as a temporary design until the final forms were approved. *GM Corporation*

Even though GM supplied Detroit Diesel engines to some of the earth-moving equipment manufacturers, including Euclid, the engines of choice were the Cummins diesel units. Other companies, such as Caterpillar, Allis-Chalmers, and International Harvester, made their own lines of engines to go into the majority of the machines they produced. The only way to ensure that Detroit Diesel engines would play a large part in the burgeoning off-road industry was for GM to become a participant. By 1952, GM was well on its way to establishing its own earth-moving equipment line, which was to be handled by the GM Truck and Coach Division. To do

this, individuals whose knowledge and experience could expedite development of the new product lines, from companies such as Caterpillar and Cummins, were brought on board. The first areas that GM would focus on were haul trucks and crawler dozers.

The two individuals brought over from Caterpillar, Russ C. Williams and John Carroll, were to head up crawler development, with their first assignment the development of a "super-dozer." Williams was the man leading the super-dozer program. Before joining GM in 1952, Williams had been with Caterpillar for a long time. He was laboratory engineer with Caterpillar for nine years before being appointed project engineer in the research department. From 1944 to 1947, he was staff engineer, working on tractor and earth-moving research projects, which led to his promotion to assistant director of research, in charge of research on all tractor and earth-moving equipment projects.

Needless to say, Caterpillar was not very happy with the departure of key employees to a company such as General Motors, a company that loomed as a great threat. Here was a company that had the engineering capabilities, factory output, and dealer network that would give it immediate access to the industry. It also produced its own engines, transmissions, and accessories, much to the dismay of Cummins. And there was also the company's deep cash reserves—provided by its automotive products—that could sustain the research needed to make reliable and productive equipment. Preliminary research had just gotten under way on the super-dozer, now called the TC-12, when a knocking was heard at General Motors' door. It was the Armingtons from Euclid, and boy, did they have a proposition for GM.

Both parties quickly realized that this was a match made in heaven, a win-win situation for all. Here was a company that produced the best off-road haulers in the world, saving GM millions in developing a new truck line from scratch. To Euclid's benefit, GM had the finances and resources needed for serious growth, and it was well under way to developing a significant product it lacked, a crawler tractor. So on September 30, 1953, General Motors Corporation acquired the Euclid Road Machinery Company. Euclid was officially made a division of GM on January 1, 1954, with Raymond Q. Armington appointed as general manager.

Even though the ownership of Euclid, as a company, passed from the Armington family, their legacy would continue. The founder of the original business, George A. Armington Sr., had passed away in 1954 at the age of 89. But he was able to see the company that he and his sons built become a part of General Motors. Stuart and Everett Armington retired in 1953, with George E. Armington Jr. joining them in 1958. This left Ray as the last of the sons to be associated with Euclid Division until his retirement, after seven years as general manager, on June 1, 1960. In these years, Ray Armington guided the new division through a period in which Euclid's engineers flexed their creative muscle and showed the industry exactly what they were capable of.

After the purchase of Euclid Road Machinery, General Motors went right to the task of reorganizing its engineering resources to meet the new challenge of developing a full line of earth-moving equipment. Since Euclid had one of the best hauler product lines in the industry, GM halted development of its own hauler program, which had barely been started, to give full attention to the crawler tractor program. Russ C. Williams and John Carroll were transferred from GM Truck and Coach Division to Euclid in 1953 to supervise the new crawler development. Even though Williams would have his

Shown here at the GM Proving Grounds in July 1954 is Euclid's first experimental test version of the twin-powered TC-12 crawler dozer. At this stage in the model's development, it was covered in crude metal body panels while the design department finalized the look the production version would take.

hand in many projects, the twin-engined Euclid TC-12 "super-dozer" was his baby, while Carroll would watch over the development of the single-engined dozer project, to be called the C-6.

These new dozer programs called for a rapid expansion of plant and manufacturing facilities. The St. Clair factories were already at capacity and were not well-suited for the heavy tooling and specialized facilities the crawler tractors would require. As a stop-gap measure, 426,000 square feet of the Electro-motive Division of Cleveland Diesel, on Clinton Road, was acquired in 1954, to build crawler tractors and over-hung scrapers. The plant was not really being utilized by GM, since most of the work that was being done there had already been transferred to LaGrange, Illinois.

In the meantime, plans were made for a new plant, specially suited to building crawler tractors, in Hudson, Ohio, not far from the St. Clair facilities. One of the reasons the new plant was not built next to any of the existing ones was the U.S. government's insistence on "decentralization" of large industrial manufacturing facilities during the Cold War. Ground was broken for the new plant on March 28, 1957, it was completed in 1958, and assembly line production started in 1959. With a 668,897-square foot manufacturing area, it was probably the industry's most modern and best-equipped factory producing earth-moving equipment. In 1961, GM added another 347,574-square foot building. It opened in May 1961, to help consolidate Euclid's varied business activities in a more central location. Some of the administrative offices from St. Clair were moved to Hudson, which helped open up space for greater engineering and experimental working areas. In 1962, the remaining activities at the Clinton Road facility were finally moved to the Hudson plant.

From its conception, the TC-12 dozer was designed to be the most powerful, maneuverable, and productive crawler tractor in the world. It was to be unlike any other

Pictured in January 1955 is the first preproduction version of the TC-12, covered in the preliminary fiberglass body panels. These were made to test the fit and overall look of the crawler, and were an aid in the construction of the final sheet metal forms. At this point in the TC-12's life, it was powered by two six-cylinder, GM Diesel 6-71 engines rated at 388 gross horsepower and 365 fhp at 1,800 rpm total. Each engine was attached to its own Allison CRT-5530 Torqmatic transmission. Operating weight of the crawler tractor was 58,100 pounds, with no attachments.

The TC-12 carried both of its radiators in the rear section of the crawler, just behind the operator. Air was drawn in through the top vents and expelled out of the two large rear radiator sections. The unit shown in early 1956 shows the nicely rounded metal body panels that gave the dozer its unique look.

big crawler the industry had ever seen. The TC-12 was powered by two GM Diesel engines, each mounted in a separate chassis. The chassis were hinge-mounted by a large cross-shaft at approximately the center of gravity of both chassis. This allowed the two halves of the tractor to oscillate over uneven terrain. Each chassis half consisted of a mainframe, gearbox, transmission, and final drive gearing for driving the sprocket on the roller frame and track system. Each GM Diesel engine was directly connected by a driveshaft into the torque converter mounted on the Allison transmission. The Allison Torqmatic Drive controlled the volume of power that was transmitted to the drive sprocket with Euclid planetary reduction gearing.

With independently powered tracks, incredibly tight pivot steering could be achieved by counter-rotation of one of the crawlers. In practice, by manipulating the forward and reverse direction selector controls for each track, the operator could pivot the tractor around its own center a full 360 degrees. No other production crawler had this ability. Before this, the only way to control forward motion in dozers was by throttle and brake. Because of its full power shift capabilities, a smooth flow of power was always available on demand to match speeds to scrapers for push loading, pulling large equipment for steady production, and higher working speeds, no matter how big the load. There was no master clutch or tedious shift pattern, resulting in less operator fatigue and greater productivity. Another unique feature of the crawler was its rear-mounted radiators. Front-mounted radiators were more prone to damage because of the severe working environment encountered by the front end of a dozer. By moving them to the rear, there was less chance of them

being punctured during dozing operations. Also, the fan blasts from the radiators helped to keep the dust stirred up by the crawler away from the operator.

The first TC-12 prototype started its engineering evaluations in July 1954, at the General Motors Proving Grounds. At this point, the crawler was not much to look at. Covered with crude sheet metal forms, it was the test bed of the powertrain and other mechanical aspects of the unit. The sheet metal styling would fall into the hands of Charles M. Jordan, the newly appointed chief designer of the Euclid Electro-motive Studio, in 1954. Jordan had joined GM Styling in 1949, and for the next four years, he served as assistant chief designer in the Chevrolet Truck Studio. Jordan's team studied the prototype in the field and made numerous sketches of the unit. These then were taken to the Euclid Engineering Department in Cleveland, where the layouts of the crawler and the requirements of the tractor, in reference to the sheet metal shapes, were discussed. Back in Detroit, a set of goals was established by the team as to the major points the sheet metal designs would address. The designs would: increase the function of the tractor; provide superior comfort and visibility for the operator; improve access to mechanical components that were covered; maintain maximum compactness of the shape of the unit; and provide a design shape that suggested the appearance of "leaning into the load," as if it were pulling something.

After all the preliminary design layouts were gathered together, an accurate one-tenth-scale layout was made of the final proposal. From this, a one-tenth-scale clay model was fashioned, and later, a plaster mold was made. A one-tenth-scale model was built from plaster, wood, and aluminum, and the model was painted and decals were applied.

This 1956-vintage TC-12 dozer was one of the first equipped with the Gar Wood Model 151-E front-mounted cable control unit. It would soon become evident under hard working conditions that this setup, and the entire front end in general, needed to be redesigned and strengthened considerably.

In September 1954, the scale model and layouts were presented to the Euclid management and engineering staffs. After approval for continued research, a full-size, two-dimensional scale layout of the TC-12 was produced. After approval by Euclid, the full-size clay-and-wood mock-up could be produced. During this period of the design process, close contact was maintained between GM Styling and Euclid Engineering. Other than repositioning the radiator core 3 1/2 inches forward and remounting the instrument cluster, most changes were small. Once the full-size clay mock-up was completed, a wooden track segment was produced and set alongside the model. Wooden models of the

headlight assemblies and rear radiator intake and exhaust grilles were also fixed into place, and the completed model was painted. Once this stage was approved by Euclid, the styling was complete. Now it was time to take the scale model and turn it into reality. A set of templates was made from the clay model to aid draftsmen in preparing detailed surface drawings to be used by anyone concerned with the body shapes. In addition to this, plaster molds were made of the body shapes, and male plaster casts were sent to Euclid to aid in the manufacturing process of the TC-12.

To get an accurate overview of the new crawler, it was decided that a prototype would be built using fiberglass

Groundbreaking ceremonies were held on March 28, 1957, for Euclid's new Hudson, Ohio, assembly plant. Power ratings for this version of the Euclid TC-12 were 436 gross horsepower and 413 fhp at 2,100 rpm. Operating weight for the crawler tractor was now up to 62,500 pounds.

body panels produced from the GM Styling female molds. In January 1955, the preproduction prototype rolled out of the Clinton Road plant. The design had some hints of automotive themes, but on the whole, it was unique. One might love it or hate it, but there wasn't another tractor that looked quite like the Euclid TC-12.

But even before the first preproduction version had been produced, Euclid Division showed off its new-and-improved equipment lineup to dealers at a special preview at GM's Milford Proving Grounds on September 15, 1954. Four of the engineering prototype TC-12 tractors in different pushing and dozing applications were on display. These were the first of about 20 units scheduled for engineering evaluation testing. These models had more-rounded lines than the first engineering unit, but were never intended for production. The field study units were made to test different operating configurations and components while the final sheet metal designs were being approved.

The first Euclid TC-12 dozers were powered by two GM Diesel 6-71, two-cycle, six-cylinder engines, with a

These early TC-12 units, pictured push-loading a Euclid TSS-40 scraper in 1963, were equipped with the Gar Wood hydraulic blade control cylinders. Most of the crawlers that had this option belonged to Western Contracting Corporation. These dozers were part of Western's original orders for these units back in 1955 and 1956.

combined power output of 388 gross horsepower and 365 fhp at 1,800 rpm. Each of these diesels was connected to its own three-speed Allison CRT-5530 Torqmatic transmission. These early TC-12 crawler tractors could be distinguished from later versions by the use of only seven track rollers per side, in conjunction with the older final drive designs. There were also no rear wraparound air intakes just below the two main vents, on top of the main radiator shrouds. This TC-12 model has generally been considered a preproduction model, since the final mechanical designs were still in a state of flux. About 84 of these units were built between 1954 and early 1956, including the pilot models.

The big Euclid twin-powered dozer started to hit its stride with the improved TC-12-1, introduced in October 1956. On the outside, the crawler tractor did not look much different from the previous version, but closer inspection of the undercarriage shows this model had eight track rollers per side instead of seven. Still more significant improvements could be found under the hood. The power output of the TC-12-1 was increased significantly to 436

This view of the TC-12-2 from October 1963, shows off the crawler's strong lines that made the unit so recognizable in the marketplace. The newer front end may not have had the automotive styling of the early units, but it was certainly a lot stronger, and provided an improved area for the mounting of a front cable control unit.

In February 1958, the updated TC-12-2 model of the twin-engined dozer was released with an increased power output of 454 gross horsepower and 425 fhp. Extra radiator air intake vents were installed just below the main rear ones, and a newly redesigned front end took care of the blade control mounting problem. This TC-12-2, shown working in 1959, is equipped with the Gar Wood ECF-12 front-mounted cable control unit, with a Gar Wood Full "U" Dozer blade. The weight of the new model was now up to 69,000 pounds, without attachments.

Shown here in June 1964 are the redesigned radiator housings and rear fenders on the prototype TC-12-3 (SN#34496) crawler dozer. Also new were the front end and the operator control area. These design changes were in keeping with Euclid's other dozer programs at the time, but it was decided that the costs involved were too much for such a limited-market machine, so the project was canceled.

The first of the more-powerful 82-80 (DA) models was this unit, pictured in the back lot of the Hudson plant on December 21, 1967. The "DA" version was equipped with improved GM Diesel 6-71N engines, now rated at 476 gross horsepower and 440 fhp, total. The operating weight of the tractor was 73,000 pounds, and with all of the attachments shown, the dozer tips the scales at 105,260 pounds complete.

gross horsepower and 413 fhp at 2,100 rpm. The two transmissions were also upgraded to Allison CRT-5531 units. Only about 149 units of the TC-12-1 were ever built.

In February 1958, the first Euclid TC-12-2 version was readied with further improvements, which included an entirely new front end assembly. The old version, with the rounded sheet metal and twin headlights, was now gone. The new design, with heavy-duty nose guards, was better suited to the task of mounting twin blade control cable mounts. The older front was just too flimsy to properly support large bulldozing blades in tough working conditions over long periods. The new front end may not have had the distinctiveness of the old one, but it was definitely more functional.

Other changes were found in the back of the crawler, where there were redesigned planetary final drives. Also, the rear radiator shrouds behind the operator now sported additional air inlet vents on either side of the main top grids to allow more air to be drawn into the cooling system. Also, a new Donaldson dry-type air cleaner system was now standard. Engine and transmissions were the same units as before, but the dozer had lost a little power in the transition, with lower ratings of 431 gross horsepower and 402 fhp at 2,100 rpm. In 1959, the engine power figures were revised upward again to a more respectable 454 gross horsepower and 425 fhp at 2,100 rpm. The TC-12-2 was by far the most popular version of the big super-dozer, and about 512 units were produced between 1958 and 1965.

The GM Powerama, the World's Fair of Power

During the 1950s, and ending in 1961, General Motors had a traveling automotive show called the "Motorama" that showcased different GM products in various show-stopping ways. The show was open to the general public, and Motoramas were truly a fair, a circus, a museum, and a car show, all rolled into one incredibly expensive traveling event. It was staged in several large cities every year, with various themes relating to GM's many technological achievements. The stars of these shows were typically the futuristic concept or "dream" cars, built to draw audiences into the shows, but also to highlight GM's technological and design achievements. Each division also had its latest production models on display, so the connection between the concept cars and the vehicle you could actually go to a dealership and buy was not lost on the attendees. One of these traveling extravaganzas stood out as different from all of the others. If the Motoramas catered to the automobile side of the GM empire, why not an additional show that highlighted some of the more interesting industrial concerns of the company? Thus was born the GM "Powerama." The Powerama, billed as the "World's Fair of Power," was held in Chicago at Soldier Field, from August 31 to September 25, 1955. The Powerama was a one-stop affair, unlike the Motoramas, which traveled to several large cities. The Powerama was divided into areas featuring key division displays, including Allison, GMC Truck and Coach, Electromotive, Detroit Diesel, and Frigidaire. But the show is best remembered for the Euclid displays and the use of the earth-moving equipment in the live stage shows, with Lake Michigan in the background.

The live stage shows, referred to as the World's First Technological Circus, and titled "More Power to You," consisted of the following acts, choreographed by Richard Barstow: Mechanical Mastodons, Farm Tractor Hoe-down, Salute to America's Railroads, The Crawler Mambo, The Truck Fashion Parade, and Diesel Dopey the Clown. Other programs included aerial performances from the end of a truck crane boom, a live elephant comedy act, a 10-girl rough-rider troupe, and dazzling dancing beauties. Did I mention that Diesel Dopey the Clown was also there? Well, he was.

The stage shows featuring Euclid equipment were very different from what one might expect of shows featuring green earth-moving machines. The most entertaining programs featured the TC-12 dozers demonstrating their outstanding maneuverability. In one act, two TC-12 crawler tractors were pitted against five elephants in a series of demonstrations, choreographed to the music of "I Can Do Anything Better Than You." In the end, the dozers would always win the competition, much to the disdain of the audience, which was usually rooting for the elephants. In another act, TC-12 dozers showed off their moves while "dancing the mambo," with a stage full of mambo dancers. With the dozers' ability to counter-rotate its crawler tracks, they could hold their own in the dance number. Along with the demonstrations featuring TC-12 dozers, the Euclid scrapers also had a chance to get into the act. The scrapers performed the usual dirt-moving exercises, with TC-12 and C-6 push dozers, but they were also involved in a rough-riding act. With cowgirls saddled up on the goosenecks of the scrapers doing rope tricks, it was certainly a sight to see. These, along with the other shows, ran four times every day.

The outside Euclid Division display consisted of Euclid S-7, S-18, and TS-18 scrapers; TC-12 and prototype C-6 crawler dozers; and FFD and LLD rear dump haulers. But the absolute star of the outside exhibit was the LLD, 50-ton-capacity hauler, which had been converted into a swimming pool, complete with bathing beauties and a diving board. The hauler, christened the S.S. *Euclid*, was a one-of-a-kind 2LLD, specially built for the show, utilizing GM Diesel 6-110 engines, with Allison TG607 Torqmatic transmissions. The original Euclid 1LLD was equipped with Cummins engines, something that would be unacceptable at an event that sang the virtues of GM diesel power. So a special version was built using a standard 1LLD with the Cummins engines being replaced by two GM Detroit Diesel units. Another departure from production versions was the installation of a new-style operator's cab, one that was just being introduced to other Euclid hauler model lines. The 2LLD's cab and engine combination would not make it into a production-version truck until mid-1957, when the GM-powered 3LLD was introduced. Along with the bathing beauties floating around in big inner tubes, there were also some very impressive springboard diving exercises into the back of the 50-ton-capacity truck. Even when filled with water, the dump box wasn't all that deep and would constantly leave the audience gasping when the divers would go off the spring board. The haulers' sides were extended by plexiglass clear side boards to keep the crowds that were close to the demonstration from getting soaked.

Did I mention that Diesel Dopey the Clown also performed diving comedy acts into the back of the 2LLD S.S. *Euclid*? Well, he did.

The hauler-as-a-swimming pool demonstration was so popular that it appeared again at the GM Motorama "Key to the Future" show, held in Miami, Florida, in February 1956. The same 2LLD rear dump was called back into service, along with the trucks' divers, bathing beauties, and clown act, that included, yes that's right, Diesel Dopey the Clown. Entertainment just didn't come any better than this.

Even though the Powerama was an incredible triumph as far as attendance, publicity, and positive press reports were concerned, the cost to GM to stage and put on the show was a real budget-buster. All Motorama shows were expensive projects, but the Powerama was more costly than others, and was not to be repeated again.

At the 1955 GM Powerama, this Euclid 2LLD, 50-ton-capacity hauler, christened the S.S. *Euclid*, was converted into a swimming pool to demonstrate the size of the dump body, which was considered quite large for its day. *John G. Addams*

The Euclid LLD served as one of the main attractions at the Powerama, especially when the diving demonstrations were held in the back of the water-filled dump body. *John G. Addams*

This Euclid TC-12 crawler tractor, equipped with a scraper push-guard, could certainly hold its own when it came to "dancing the mambo" with a troupe of mambo dancers. With the ability to counter-rotate its crawler tracks, the TC-12 was one of the most maneuverable dozers ever created. *John G. Addams*

Throughout 1959, the Euclid TC-12-2 was one of the major stars of Euclid Division's "Big Three Demonstration" equipment showcase that was traveling around the country, giving customers hands-on experience operating the big dozer. The shows also included the S-18 and TS-24 scrapers, demonstrating to potential buyers the productivity and profit advantages that these machines, in various combinations, could provide.

Euclid started developing an upgraded version of the TC-12-2, identified as the TC-12-3, in 1963. This model incorporated many of the newer design elements that had recently found their way onto the latest C-6 dozer. Among numerous detail changes, three areas received major redesigns. The front end had a new beefed-up design, with an improved cable wind for the blade control. The rear side quarters and radiator shrouds now looked more squared-off, like the C-6-3 crawler but with an extra cooling unit. The operator controls were also completely changed from previous versions. The experimental prototype was finished in June 1964, but for whatever reason, the update program was canceled. Costs, more than anything, probably influenced the decision to end the project, since other dozer model lines being developed needed large amounts of funding to get them off the ground. Only one TC-12-3 unit was ever built.

The TC-12-2 remained in production relatively unchanged, except for the addition of an extra 56-gallon fuel tank on the right side and redesigned side radiator air intake vents in late 1960. In January 1966, the nomenclature for all of the Euclid crawler tractors was changed to the "82-series," with the TC-12 now being referred to as the Euclid 82-80 (BA). Despite the names, both dozers were mechanically identical. The "BA" model was in production from 1966 to mid-1967, with only 30 machines being listed as being produced.

The first batch of 15 units of the new Euclid 82-80 (DA) dozers started rolling out of the Hudson plant in December 1967. The DA model 82-80 dozer featured the most significant changes to the twin-powered crawler to date, and was by far the most powerful version ever built. Its two GM Diesel 6-71N, six-cylinder engines combined to produce 476 gross horsepower and 440 fhp at 2,100 rpm. Also new were the three-speed Allison CRT-5533 Torqmatic, full power shift transmissions, with Allison 550-3E torque converters. Changes made to the undercarriage included going back to seven track rollers per side, instead of eight. This version was the last to be designed and built as a Euclid Division model, before the antitrust settlement went into effect (more on this later). But that was not the end of the 82-80 dozer. A few more years of life were still ahead for the big twin-powered crawler, but in the future, it would be carrying the Terex name instead.

Shown at the Hudson plant in December 1967 is a Euclid 82-80 (DA) twin-engined crawler, secured in place and under load, undergoing a full systems and component testing session. This was done to make sure the tractor was fully operational and up to specification before delivery. While in motion, the tracks were covered with a water-based coolant and lubrication fluid, to help minimize any needless wear and tear on the undercarriage during the testing procedures.

A Taste for
the Green Iron

General Motors had ambitious plans for its new Euclid Division. Resources were allocated to all areas of the earth-moving division. Along with the crawler tractor program, new designs of self-powered scrapers were to be introduced early on and preliminary design work started on wheeled tractor loaders. Even the color of the equipment was to be changed. For years, Euclid machines were painted a dark green, much like a military olive drab, but glossy instead of a matte finish. During the war manufacturing years and immediately afterward, most of the equipment was painted army surplus O.D. green. Because of material shortages during the war, this was all that was available. From about 1946 to 1953, the dark green paint color was used. But after the acquisition, GM felt the old color was out of step with the times. It was felt a new color was needed that reflected the dynamic changes taking place with the new product line. Some early color suggestions were silver, white, and a pastel powder blue. One can only imagine fleets of light powder puff blue Eucs working all over the country. Thankfully, more rational minds prevailed and an evolution of the green color was used instead. In late 1953 and throughout most of 1954, a brighter green, sometimes referred to as a Sherwood Forest green, was used.

Though this new green was not as dark as the older color, GM management still felt it was not making a bold-enough statement. Management wanted Euclid machines to be clearly identifiable from a distance, and not be confused with the competition's offerings, especially the bright yellow equipment from Caterpillar and LeTourneau-Westinghouse. The new color would be more of a willow green, bright like yellow, but with a touch of green. This new color would eventually become known as Hi-Lite Green. Euclid would go through numerous shade variations in 1955 and 1956, trying to

find the right color combination that was fade-resistant from the sun and durable enough to take the wear and tear of earth-moving life. Overflows of diesel fuel, grease, and abrasive materials would be the norm. Early examples of paint shades "chalked" or faded in the sun. But eventually a compromise was reached that had the brightness of the yellow-green management was looking for, plus the desired durability. Over the next decade, the color would become more of a dirty lime green, but all of these variations were still considered Euclid Hi-Lite Green.

Euclid Over-Hung-Engined Scrapers

Even though GM had put considerable resources to work in the development of its crawler tractor, other areas were also being given the means to match, and even surpass in many instances, the competition's offerings. Most notable was the new over-hung-engined, self-propelled scrapers introduced to the Euclid dealers, and the press, on September 15, 1954, at the Milford Proving Grounds. (This was the same show at which the prototype TC-12 tractors were introduced.) The new Euclid scrapers, the S-7, S-18, and TS-18, featured all-new designs. Euclid had experimented with this type of scraper concept before with the model 5SH, 6SH, and 7SH scrapers (see chapter 1). The downfall of these designs was their use of rear-wheel steering. In 1946, Euclid built one experimental engineering prototype scraper, the 28FDT-9SH. This unit was powered by a single Cummins HBIS600 diesel engine rated at 275 horsepower. The rear 9SH scraper had an 18-cubic-yard capacity. What made this unit unique was its use of hydraulic jacks, connected to the gooseneck, to steer the scraper, since the tractor did not steer relative to the scraper bowl. This gave the scraper the ability to make 90-degree turns. Also, all scraper functions were controlled hydraulically, rather than by cables.

But at the time, funds were too short for an engineering project of this complexity. Resources were instead being concentrated on development of a line of scrapers to be used with existing Euclid four-wheeled rubber-tired tractors. These became the Euclid Model FDT 12-yard and the TDT 15.5-yard scrapers. In 1952,

Released at the same time as the L-20 series was the larger L-30 front end loader. The first of these released was the 9UPM, rated at 3 cubic yards. The loader was powered by a GM Diesel 4-71 engine rated at 152 gross horsepower and 144 fhp. This L-30 is shown in July 1962 working at a cement plant in Montana, and it's equipped with the optional larger tire and wheel combination.

The S-7 (3UOT-26SH) was the smallest single-engined, over-hung scraper produced by Euclid. The S-7 was powered by a GM Diesel 4-71 engine rated at 138 gross horsepower when introduced in 1954. Output was increased to 143 gross horsepower by the end of 1955. The S-7's capacity was rated at 7 cubic yards struck and 9 cubic yards heaped. The unit is shown in its original dark Euclid green in late 1954.

Euclid engineers experimented with a four-wheel-drive scraper unit called the Model 19SH. This was a single-rear-engined design that ran its driveshafts around the outside of the scraper bowl to the front axle. The operator sat just forward and on top of the scraper itself. But due to the mechanical complexity of the drive system, the project was abandoned. With the release of the new scraper model lines, the problems encountered by the earlier experimental 5SH and 9SH models were corrected by the new Euclid S-7 and S-18 units. The quest for a four-wheel-drive model, started by the 19SH, was found in the twin-engined TS-18. All three scrapers featured GM Diesel engines, "No-Spin" limited-slip differential, hydraulic controls, and advanced ease-of-maintenance designs. These models were the start of an incredible line of great earth-moving machines that would establish Euclid over the next 13 years as one of the industry's premier scraper manufacturers.

The smallest scraper in Euclid's over-hung engine model line was the S-7, introduced in 1954, and officially released for sale in 1955. Engineering model numbers for the first type of S-7 specified a 3UOT-26SH tractor front

The S-7 was offered with a Hancock Model 12E2 (4UOT-12E2) elevating scraper in 1964. Even though this unit had two engines, the rear unit was for driving the elevator on the scraper and not the rear wheels. The front engine was a GM Diesel 4-71 rated at 148 gross horsepower and 135 fhp. The rear-mounted elevator engine was a GM Diesel 2-71 rated at 65 gross horsepower and 61 fhp. The total payload was 12 cubic yards heaped.

and scraper back combination. The S-7 was powered by a single GM Diesel series 4-71, two-cycle, four-cylinder engine rated at 143 gross horsepower. Power was transmitted through a Fuller 5CB-650 five-speed transmission to the Euclid heavy-duty drive axle, with planetary final drive and No-Spin differential. Capacity of the 26SH scraper was 7 cubic yards struck and 9 cubic yards heaped. With its 90-degree turning ability, the S-7 could make a continuous turn in 28 feet. This was a very important feature for this size class of scraper, since many of its work assignments were in tight, restricted areas, such as between buildings and houses. In 1957, an upgraded 4UOT-26SH model of the S-7 was released featuring the Allison Torqmatic Transmission, Model CT-3340, instead of the earlier Fuller unit. A bit more power was also available, with engine power now rated at 148 gross horsepower and 135 fhp. In early 1964, the S-7 received its first significant sheet metal change to the front end. Gone were the trademark bug-eyed headlights; they were replaced by a more traditional lighting system. Also introduced in 1964 was the S-7 Hancock, model 4UOT-12E2. This unit consisted of a standard 4UOT tractor front, with a 12-cubic-yard capacity Hancock 12E2 Elevating Scraper for the rear section. The supplier of the rear scraper, Hancock Manufacturing Company, located in Lubbock, Texas, furnished Euclid with the completed rear units, which were then connected to the front drive tractors. The scraper loading elevator was powered by a single GM Diesel 2-71 engine, rated at 65 gross horsepower and 61 fhp, mounted in the rear. This engine did not power the rear axle and it is not considered a true twin-power scraper, since only the front wheels were driven. The front tractor portion of the S-7 Hancock was virtually unchanged from earlier models. This version of the S-7 was best suited to working in loose material, such as sand, gravel, loam, and clay mixtures. Hard, sun-baked, or highly plastic clays were not recommended for this type of scraper.

Euclid Division introduced its fourth new model of an over-hung-type scraper, the S-12, in mid-1955. The S-12, model 78FOT-29SH, was the next size up from the S-7 in Euclid's product line, with a 12-cubic-yard struck and 16-cubic-yard heaped capacity. The 78FOT tractor was powered by a GM Diesel 6-71, two-cycle, six-cylinder engine, rated at 218 gross horsepower. Transmission for the early S-12 was a Fuller 5F-1220, five-speed unit. The S-12 was considered a medium-sized unit, built for jobs where the S-7 was too small, and the S-18 too large and costly. The S-12 also shared the same basic design benefits that other Euclid scrapers offered at the time. The S-12 sold well, but was discontinued in 1962 because of a shift to larger machines in the marketplace. In 1965, an 18-cubic-yard capacity Hancock Model 218 Elevating Scraper was offered as an option to be added to used S-12, 78FOT tractors. These were intended for current owners of the S-12 or dealers who had taken them in on trade.

The first S-32 (47LOT-79SH) scraper is shown in September 1966 at the Hudson plant. The S-32 replaced the S-28 in Euclid's scraper line, and was the largest single-engined over-hung type built by the company. Only the tractor-pulled models were larger, as far as capacity. The S-32 was powered by a GM Diesel 12V-71T engine rated at 520 gross horsepower and 498 fhp. Payload capacity ratings were 32 cubic yards struck and 43 cubic yards heaped.

The Euclid S-18, model 27LOT-28SH, single-engined scraper was introduced in 1954. Along with the key features that all early Euclid scrapers shared, the S-18 was equipped with an Allison CRT-5630 Torqmatic transmission for smooth power delivery in all working conditions. The S-18 was powered by a GM Diesel 6-110, two-cycle, six-cylinder engine, rated at 300 gross horsepower. Capacity of the 28SH scraper was 18 cubic yards struck and 25 cubic yards heaped. All controls of the scraper were hydraulic. In 1957, an improved version of the S-18, model 30LOT-28SH, was released. This version had an improved Allison CLT-5640 Torqmatic transmission, replacing the previous unit. Except for a tire and wheel upgrade on both axles, all other major specifications remained the same, including the engine. In the following year, 1958, the S-18 scraper portion was upgraded to the 31SH unit. The scraper featured a redesigned bowl that increased the load capacity to 21 cubic yards struck and 30 cubic yards heaped. The power output of the 30LOT tractor was also increased to 325 gross horsepower to cope with the extra weight. Except for new gear ratios, the transmission and engine combination remained the same.

NEXT PAGE: The S-18 (30LOT-31SH) scraper was one of the original three over-hung-engined models introduced by Euclid in 1954. The two S-18 scrapers pictured working in 1960, alongside a Euclid TS-14 unit, were the last versions of the scraper to be released before the model was upgraded into the S-24 version in 1961. These S-18 models were powered by a GM Diesel 6-110 engine rated at 325 gross horsepower in 1958, and 336 gross horsepower in 1959. They carried payload capacities of 21 cubic yards struck and 30 cubic yards heaped.

In 1958, the S-12 (78FOT/TS-1622) was offered with the 22-ton-capacity Easton TS-1622 rear dump trailer, which was rated at 14 cubic yards struck and 16 cubic yards heaped.

Euclid offered a bottom dump trailer in 1957 to be used with the S-12 over-hung tractor. Pictured is the first prototype S-12 bottom dump (78FOT-130W) unit built, rated at 13 cubic yards struck and 19 cubic yards heaped, with a maximum 20-ton payload.

In early 1961, Euclid replaced the S-18 with the new S-24 scraper, model 39LOT-46SH. The S-24 featured a new front-end design with repositioned headlights, and grilles and nose piece alterations. The new 39LOT tractor was powered by a GM Diesel 12V-71, two-cycle, 12-cylinder engine rated at 432 gross horsepower and 392 fhp. The transmission was a five-speed Allison Torqmatic CLT5840. In 1962, this transmission was replaced by an improved version of the Torqmatic, a six-speed Model CLT-5860. Capacity of the 46SH scraper was 24 cubic yards struck and 32 cubic yards heaped. In late 1962, an improved version of the S-24, model 39LOT-55SH, was released. Changes to the tractor were minimal. A bit more power was available from the GM 12V-71 engine with a 398 fhp rating. The gross rating remained the same, 432 horsepower. The big news was in the new 55SH scraper, which featured the "Full-Load" Power Apron-Bowl Control System. Unlike the previous system that relied on a hydraulic jack pulling a short cable attached to the apron to open it and gravity to close it, the new apron was now operated by hydraulic cylinders on either side of the scraper body. The apron-bowl control system automatically closed the apron and picked up the bowl with one motion of the control lever by the operator. The bowl design of the scraper was now longer, with a larger throat opening. This permitted dirt to flow easier and faster into the scraper bowl, with better distribution. The next version of the S-24, model 39LOT-76SH, was introduced in 1966. Again, the tractor remained the same, but the new 76SH scraper rear unit replaced the previous 55SH version. Capacity ratings remained unchanged.

Euclid introduced the S-28, model 38LOT-50SH, in 1963. Though larger than the S-24, it was not a replacement for that unit. It was an entirely new model in the product line, as opposed to the S-24, which was a replacement for the S-18. The S-28 was powered by a

GM Diesel 12V-71N, two-cycle, 12-cylinder engine rated at 475 gross horsepower and 441 fhp, connected to an Allison CLT-5960 Torqmatic, six-speed, full power shift transmission. Scraper capacity was 28 cubic yards struck and 38 cubic yards heaped. Features included "Dirt-Flo" action, a Euclid term referring to the way dirt would flow into the newly designed clean-sweep low bowl of the scraper. Another aspect of Dirt-Flo improvements was a single-lever control for the operator for all three bowl functions of the scraper.

The Euclid S-28's replacement, the larger and more powerful S-32, model 47LOT-79SH, was introduced in 1966. The S-32 was powered by a GM Diesel 12V-71T, two-cycle, 12-cylinder engine rated at 520 gross horsepower and 498 fhp, mated to a six-speed Allison CLBT-5965 Torqmatic transmission. Capacity of the scraper was 32 cubic yards struck and 43 cubic yards heaped. The S-32 utilized all of the scraper features found on the S-28, but the term "Dirt-Flo" was no longer being used to describe them, since almost all of Euclid's scrapers now contained these design innovations.

In the 1950s and early 1960s, special rear dump trailers, often referred to as "rockers," were available for the single-axle front tractor of some Euclid's scrapers. These trailers were of an extremely rugged design, specially suited to the task of hauling rock. Some were of Euclid design, while others were supplied by outside manufacturers. The Euclid S-7 rear dump, model 3UOT-129W, introduced in 1956, was one of the earliest units made available as a rocker. The 129W trailer had a capacity rating of 8 cubic yards struck and 11 cubic yards heaped, with a maximum 12-ton load weight. The unit dumped by means of a single three-stage hydraulic cylinder. This same rear dump was also available for the 4UOT tractor front. Both tractor specifications were the same as their scraper counterparts. In 1966, outside supplier Athey, offered a 15-ton rocker, model E915R, for use with the

The smallest two-engined, four-wheel-drive, over-hung scraper built by Euclid was the TS-14 (6UOT-38SH), introduced in July 1959. The early TS-14 models were powered by a pair of GM Diesel 4-71 engines rated at 148 gross horsepower and 134.5 fhp each, for a total of 296 gross horsepower and 269 fhp. This TS-14 pictured working in 1960 is equipped with a scraper bowl whose capacity is 14 cubic yards struck and 20 cubic yards heaped.

Euclid 4UOT tractor. In 1957, the Euclid S-12 was offered in a bottom dump configuration, and in a rocker version in 1958. The S-12 Bottom Dump, model 78FOT-130W, had a capacity of 13 cubic yards struck and 19 cubic yards heaped, with a 20-ton payload weight. The S-12 Rear Dump, model 78FOT-TS-1622, utilized an Easton TS-1622, variable-wheelbase, rear dump trailer. Capacity for this unit was 14 cubic yards struck and 16 cubic yards heaped, with a 22-ton load rating. Many parts of the trailer were interchangeable with the 78FOT tractor, such as the tires, wheels, spindles, and brake parts. The Euclid S-18 was also offered in a rear dump form, model 30LOT-131W, in 1956. Utilizing a Euclid-built rear dump trailer, the rocker had a 23 cubic yard struck and 32 cubic yard heaped capacity, rated at 35 tons. Easton also produced a rocker in 1959 for the S-18 (30LOT) tractor, the model TS-2635. Similar in design to the unit it built for the S-12, the Easton was rated at 23 cubic yards struck and 26 cubic yards heaped. Payload capacity remained unchanged from the Euclid version at 35 tons.

Euclid's twin-powered scraper model line shared many of the same features as its single-engined counterparts. The biggest difference was an additional engine, installed at the end of the scraper, driving the rear axle and giving the unit all-wheel-drive capability. And of course, with an extra engine, power output was almost doubled in some applications. The smallest of Euclid's two-engined scrapers was the TS-14, introduced in 1959. The first model, a 6UOT-38SH, was powered by GM Diesel 4-71, two-cycle, four-cylinder engines, rated at 148 gross horsepower and 134.5 fhp each, mated to full power shifting Allison CLT-3340 Torqmatic transmissions. Power ratings and transmissions were the same in the rear scraper, as they were in the tractor unit. Capacity for the scraper was 14 cubic yards struck and 20 cubic yards heaped. The TS-14 turned out to be a very popular model for Euclid. Tough and scrappy, it was an excellent choice for contractors with small-to-medium-sized jobs where a larger scraper model would be too big or expensive. In 1961, the TS-14 received a cosmetic face-lift. The original bug-eyed headlights were replaced with more-common units and the grille shroud was cleaned up. No other major mechanical changes were made at this time. The first significant

43

Shown in February 1964 is the first 7UOT-61SH model of the Euclid TS-14, which featured many improvements over the previous version, most notably the GM Allison, full power shifting transmissions. The front sheet metal had been revised in the 1961 model of the scraper, but the rear body panels of this newer unit were now squared off, as opposed to the rounded versions from 1961.

In July 1964, Euclid officially released the production version of the Tandem TS-14 (7UOT-63SH-62SH) scraper, also referred to as the TTS-14. Shown at work in August 1964 are some of the first units delivered into service. These models were powered by three GM Diesel 4-71 engines, rated at 444 gross horsepower and 403 fhp.

mechanical upgrade for the TS-14 occurred in 1964, with the release of the 7UOT-61SH model. Engine specifications remained the same as the previous TS-14, but new 4-speed Allison CLT-3341 transmissions were introduced to replace the older models. Minor modifications were made to the scraper bowl assembly, along with a redesigned, squared-off rear radiator shroud replacing the round-cornered version. The next version of the TS-14, model 13UOT-81SH, introduced in late 1966, would receive substantial changes to its drivetrain, compared to its predecessors. The 13UOT tractor was powered by two identical GM Diesel 4-71N, two-cycle, four-cylin-

Euclid produced its first Tandem TS-14 (6UOT-60SH-38SH) model in September 1963, undergoing field trial testing at the GM Milford Proving Grounds in May 1964. The tandem version had payload capacity ratings of 28 cubic yards struck and 40 cubic yards heaped.

45

The Tandem TS-14 (7UOT-63SH-62SH), shown working in June 1965, is equipped with the optional comfort cab. The scraper would fill the front bowl first, and then the second. It did not load both scraper bowls simultaneously.

The TS-18 (29LOT-27SH) was the first production twin-powered, over-hung scraper model built by Euclid. The front and rear engines were GM Diesel 6-71 units with a total rated output of 436 gross horsepower. The payload capacity was 18 cubic yards struck and 24 cubic yards heaped. This TS-18 pictured at the St. Clair plant around August 1954 was the first unit built. It was officially introduced at a special dealer preview at the GM Milford Proving Grounds in September 1954.

der engines, rated at 320 gross horsepower (160 horsepower apiece) and 288 fhp (144 fhp each). Both transmissions were six-speed Allison CLT-3461 Torqmatics.

To add to the versatility of the TS-14, Euclid introduced tandem scraper bowl configurations to the model line to increase payload capacity. Several large contractors had built their own versions of this model by combining two TS-14 scraper units over a year before Euclid released its factory-built units. The prototype Euclid Tandem TS-14 (also referred to as the TTS-14), model 6UOT-60SH-38SH, started its testing program in September

1963. This early unit was basically a standard TS-14 unit, modified to accept the additional 60SH scraper installed between the original tractor and scraper combination. After months of testing at the GM Milford Proving Grounds, a production version, model 7UOT-63SH-62SH, was released in July 1964. The Tandem TS-14 was powered by three GM Diesel 4-71, two-cycle, four-cylinder engines, one in the tractor and one in each of the rear scraper units. Each of these engines produced 148 gross horsepower and 134 fhp (the rear 62SH engine produced 135 fhp), for a total output of 444 gross horsepower and 403 fhp. The two throttle-control pedals could be used separately or together, one controlling the tractor engine, the other controlling the two rear engines simultaneously or individually by means of a switch. Both the 7UOT tractor and the rear 62SH scraper unit used their own four-speed Allison CLT-3341 Torqmatic transmission. The center 63SH scraper utilized a different transmission model, an Allison CLT-4440 unit. These Allisons, with their integral torque converters, required only one control valve for simultaneous shifting of all transmissions by the operator. Total combined capacity for both scraper bowls was 28 cubic yards struck and 40 cubic yards heaped, with a 94,000-pound maximum payload rating. In late 1966, the upgraded version, model 13UOT-82SH-83SH, was released, and was being referred to as the Euclid Tandem-14. The new engines were improved GM Diesel 4-71N engines, each now rated at 160 gross horsepower and 144 fhp (the rear 83SH engine rated at 145 fhp), for a total power output of 480 gross horsepower and 433 fhp. Transmissions for the tractor and rear scraper bowl were six-speed Allison CLT-3461 units. The middle 82SH scraper engine was mated to an Allison CLT-4460 transmission. Capacity and load ratings remained the same as in the previous model. Only 23 units of this last model of Tandem-14 scraper were built, 20 in late 1966 and three in early 1968. Euclid also offered a 84SH scraper bowl field conversion kit for owners of existing standard TS-14, model 13UOT-81SH, scrapers. This way, any single-bowled scraper unit could now be "tandemized" to suit a contractor's varying job requirements.

The first twin-powered over-hung scraper produced by Euclid was its TS-18. The TS-18, model 29LOT-27SH, was introduced in September 1954, and went into full production in 1955. The TS-18 was essentially an S-18 with an extra engine attached to the rear scraper bowl, giving it all-wheel drive. All of the key features found in the S-18 were also present in the TS-18. The major differences were mainly in the drivetrains. The TS-18 was powered by GM Diesel 6-71, two-cycle, six-cylinder engines rated at 218 gross horsepower each, for a maximum power output of 436 gross horsepower. These units were connected to full power shifting, three-speed Allison TG-600 Torqmatic transmissions. The engine, torque converter, transmission, drive axle, brakes, and tires found in the 27SH scraper had the same basic specifications as the corresponding components found in the 29LOT tractor front. Capacity for the scraper unit was 18 cubic yards struck and 24 cubic yards heaped. In early 1956, a more powerful model option was offered for this scraper called the TS-18 Special. Differences were in the 29LOT tractor drivetrain. A more powerful GM Diesel 6-110, two-cycle, six-cylinder engine and three-speed Allison CRT-5000 transmission now resided under the hood up front. Power ratings were now up to 300 gross horsepower for the tractor, for a combined total of 518 gross horsepower. The rear engine ratings in the scraper remained unchanged.

In January 1957, the TS-18 was upgraded into the new TS-24 (31LOT-33SH), which would become one of the greatest scrapers Euclid ever produced. The TS-24's front tractor was powered by a GM Diesel 6-110 engine and the rear unit was a GM Diesel 6-71. Combined power ratings for these engines was 518 gross horsepower. Pictured in 1959 during one of the special "Big Three Demonstration" events held throughout the United States is a TS-24 (now rated at 563 gross horsepower and 524 fhp), being push-loaded by a TC-12 crawler dozer equipped with an additional operator training seat.

In 1957, the Euclid TS-18 was upgraded into a new model, now called the TS-24. The TS-24, model 31LOT-33SH, was a natural evolution of the previous TS-18 Special that was offered in 1956. Engines in the TS-24 were a GM Diesel 6-110, two-cycle, six-cylinder unit in the 31LOT tractor, rated at 300 gross horsepower, and a GM 6-71, two-cycle, six-cylinder unit in the rear 33SH scraper, rated at 218 gross horsepower. Total power output of the scraper was 518 gross horsepower, the same as the TS-18 Special. Transmission for the front engine was a three-speed Allison CRT-5630 Torqmatic, and the rear engine was connected to an Allison TG-600 unit. Payload capacity of the scraper was 24 cubic yards struck and 32 cubic yards heaped. This new capacity of the 33SH rear unit was achieved mainly by the lengthening of the previous TS-18 scraper bowl. The width of the bowl remained the same.

In 1959, the power output of the TS-24 standard engines was increased to 336 gross horsepower and 317 fhp for the 31LOT tractor, and 227 gross horsepower and 207 fhp for the rear 33SH scraper, totaling 563 gross horsepower and 524 fhp. Engine and transmission models were the same type used in the original TS-24, and the payload capacity remained unchanged.

Early 1963 brought more significant changes to the TS-24 scraper line. The new model, 31LOT-56SH, shared many of the features found on the 55SH scraper bowl of the S-24, introduced just a few weeks earlier. The TS-24 now featured the "Full-Load" apron-bowl control system described earlier on the S-24. Drivetrains, power ratings, and the payload capacity remained the same as for the previous model. The biggest change to the

47

This model of the Euclid TS-24 (39LOT-56SH) from December 1965 was powered by a GM Diesel 12V-71 engine in the front tractor and a GM Diesel 6-71 unit in the rear. Total power output was rated at 659 gross horsepower and 605 fhp. Payload capacity was the same as previous TS-24 models, at 24 cubic yards struck and 32 cubic yards heaped. In August 1966, this version was replaced by the model 43LOT-78SH of the TS-24 scraper.

31LOT tractor was a redesigned front end. In mid-1965, the tractor of the TS-24 was upgraded to a new version, initially referred to as the TS-24 Special, model 39LOT-56SH. The 39LOT tractor of the TS-24 was very similar to the version used with the S-24 scraper. The front engine was a GM Diesel 12V-71, two-cycle, 12-cylinder unit, rated at 432 gross horsepower and 398 fhp, connected to an Allison CLT-5840, four-speed Torqmatic transmission. The rear scraper portion was powered by a GM Diesel 6-71, six-cylinder engine, rated at 227 gross horsepower and 207 fhp. The rear transmission was an Allison TG-604, 3-speed unit. The total power output from the engines was 659 gross horsepower and 605 fhp. The next version of the TS-24 was the 43LOT-78SH, introduced in 1966. This version was more of a refinement of the previous 39LOT-56SH model. All major specifications remained the same. In April 1967, a prototype TS-24, model 44LOT-67SH, was built as a replacement for the 43LOT-78SH. But for whatever reasons, this model never made it into full production.

The largest standard-production, twin-powered, over-hung type scraper built by Euclid was its big TS-32, model 47LOT-80SH, officially released in 1966. The

The largest regular production, twin-powered, over-hung scraper built by Euclid was the TS-32 (47LOT-80SH), shown here in September 1966 at the Hudson plant. This model was originally the prototype TS-28, back in October 1963. The TS-32's tractor was powered by a GM Diesel 12V-71T, and the rear scraper used a GM Diesel 8V-71T engine. Total power output from both engines was 865 gross horsepower and 818 fhp. Capacity of the scraper was 32 cubic yards struck and 43 cubic yards heaped.

TS-32 shared the same 47LOT tractor front that was also used with the single-engined S-32. Power was supplied by a GM Diesel 12V-71T, two-cycle, 12-cylinder engine up front (rated at 520 gross horsepower and 498 fhp), and a GM Diesel 8V-71T, two-cycle, eight-cylinder unit at the rear (rated at 345 gross horsepower and 320 fhp). Total power output was 865 gross horsepower and 818 fhp. The front engine used an Allison Torqmatic CLBT-5965, six-speed, full power shift transmission and the rear engine was connected to an Allison CLBT-5865, six-speed unit. Payload capacity for the 80SH scraper bowl was 32 cubic yards struck and 43 cubic yards heaped. The TS-32 featured all of the key features found on other large Euclid scrapers, including a Dirt-Flo-designed bowl, large throat opening, three-stage snap-out ejection system for quickly moving the load out of the scraper, and full hydraulic controls. The TS-32 was a contractor's dream come true for even the largest earth-moving projects.

All of Euclid's twin-powered scrapers could be factory or dealer-modified for coal stockpiling applications. The TS-18, TS-24, and TS-32 were the scrapers most commonly converted to coal duty, but the TS-14 found its small niche with a few operations that involved feeding furnaces at steel and coke plants, with as many as five different coal types at a single location. Modifications usually included side-boarding of the scraper bowl to increase payload volume for the lighter coal material, enclosed cabs for the operators, and an improved air filtering system for the engines. Though each application of a coal scraper was custom built to the owner's particular requirements, specifications could be based on the more popular units in the field. A TS-14 with 54-inch sideboards could haul 20 tons of coal per trip. Early TS-24 units with 36-inch sideboards increased their capacity to 36 cubic yards struck, with the later 43LOT-78SH models (with special stretched bowls) achieving capacities of 45 cubic yards struck, using 40-inch sideboards. The big TS-32, when equipped with 40-inch sideboards, could handle 47 cubic yards struck and 55 cubic yards heaped.

Euclid Tractor-Pulled Scrapers

Euclid had established its line of two-axle, tractor-pulled scrapers, often referred to as six-wheel scrapers, well before GM entered the picture. The six-wheel scraper model was well-suited to job locations where the haul roads were longer than a half-mile and were well-maintained, to maximize the scraper's higher top speeds, compared to the over-hung type. The two-axle tractor also offered better riding ability and superior steering control at high speeds. The over-hung models tended to ride harder and to sometimes get into a "loping" cycle, requiring the scraper to be slowed down. If the traveling distances were short or in very uneven terrain, then the over-hung scrapers were the machines of choice. Euclid offered three tractor types, matched to specific scraper units. The smallest, the FDT series, pulled scrapers with capacities in the 12-cubic-yard range. The TDT series

The 15.5-yard tractor scrapers were introduced into the Euclid product line just before GM purchased the company. The model shown here, the 23TDT-21SH, equipped with the Allison Torqmatic transmission, was introduced in 1955, and would eventually replace the previous 22TDT-21SH model from 1954, which was equipped with a manual Fuller gearbox. The 23TDT-21SH was powered by a single GM Diesel 6-110 engine rated at 300 gross horsepower. Capacity ratings for the 21SH scraper bowl were 15.5 cubic yards struck and 21 cubic yards heaped. The first Euclid 15.5-yard machines introduced were the models 7TDT-14SH in 1950, and the 8TDT-14SH in 1951.

handled scrapers with capacities ranging from 15.5 to 18 cubic yards. The LDT series pulled all of the large-capacity units, ranging from 24 to 40 cubic yards. These combinations were fairly consistent, with only one or two exceptions.

The smallest of the six-wheel scrapers released by the Euclid Division were the 76FDT-18SH with a Cummins engine and the 77FDT-18SH with a GM Diesel unit, both in 1955. Both of these scrapers replaced previous models 70FDT-18SH and 71FDT-18SH, which were introduced in 1951. All of these units had rated capacities of 12 cubic yards struck and 16 cubic yards heaped, and were known as Euclid 12 Yard Scrapers. In 1958, an improved model was released called the Euclid SS-12, model 77FDT-40SH, with GM Diesel power. The SS-12 nomenclature had been introduced in 1957, but this unit was the first to carry that designation from the very beginning. The 40SH scraper was the same as the 29SH unit used with the over-hung-engined S-12, except with a different pull yoke. Euclid also offered the 13-cubic-yard capacity 89W bottom dump dirt trailer for use on all of the previous FDT tractors mentioned. The SS-12 continued in production until about 1960, when the model line was discontinued.

In the next class up in size, using TDT tractors, were the Euclid 15.5-yard scrapers. Just before being acquired by GM, Euclid had just released the 12TDT-21SH and 14TDT-21SH scrapers in 1953. Both of these machines were rated at 15.5 cubic yards struck and 21 cubic yards heaped. GM introduced updated versions of these models

The SS-33 (34LDT-42SH) was first released by Euclid in November 1959. The SS-33 was powered by a GM Diesel 12V-71 engine rated at 432 gross horsepower. The payload capacity of the scraper was 33 cubic yards struck and 43 cubic yards heaped.

In 1961, Euclid released an upgraded version of the SS-33 called the SS-40. Shown here in August 1962 is a special version of the SS-40 (43LDT-51SH) built for Western Contracting Corporation. This unit was powered by a GM Diesel 16V-71 engine rated at 530 gross horsepower. Regular versions of the SS-40 (49LDT-52SH) were powered by a GM Diesel 12V-71N rated at 475 gross horsepower and 441 fhp. Load capacity for all SS-40 models was 40 cubic yards struck and 52 cubic yards heaped.

The 16TDT-23SH, introduced in 1954, was the first GM twin-powered six-wheeled scraper model to be introduced by GM Euclid division. This version replaced the previous 68FDT-17SH model from 1950. The 16TDT-23SH was powered by two GM Diesel 6-71 engines rated at 380 gross horsepower total. The 23SH scraper capacity was rated at 18 cubic yards struck and 24 cubic yards heaped.

with the 22TDT-21SH (GM Diesel), in 1954, and the 28TDT-21SH (Cummins), in 1956. The 22TDT was upgraded to the 23TDT-21SH, in 1955. All of the tractors used with the 15.5-cubic-yard scrapers could also be ordered with the 17-cubic-yard, Euclid-built 122W bottom dump dirt trailer.

In late 1956, Euclid introduced the new SS-18, which replaced the 15.5-yard model. First of the SS-18 units to be released was the 23TDT-36SH (GM Diesel), followed by the 14TDT-36SH (Cummins) in 1958. Both of these units were rated at 18 cubic yards struck and 25 cubic yards heaped. Like the 15.5-yard tractors, all of the SS-18 units could also be ordered with the 122W bottom dump trailer.

Euclid introduced the new SS-24 scraper in 1957, not as a replacement for the SS-18, but as an additional model to broaden its product line. The first SS-24 models to be released were the 33LDT-32SH (Cummins) and 28LDT-32SH (GM Diesel) scrapers. The SS-24 proved to be a very popular machine with contractors, and during its life it received many model upgrades. These include the 37LDT-32SH (GM Diesel) in 1959, the 34LDT-32SH (GM Diesel) in 1962, the 49LDT-59SH (GM Diesel) in 1965, and the 36LDT-77SH (Cummins) in 1966. All SS-24 models were rated at 24 cubic yards struck and 32 cubic yards heaped.

Another model produced by Euclid using LDT tractors was the SS-28, introduced in mid-1963. The first of these released was the 49LDT-53SH (GM Diesel), followed by the 36LDT-53SH (Cummins), in 1964. Capacity ratings were 28 cubic yards struck and 38 cubic yards heaped. The 53SH shared all of the major features found in the Euclid S-28 scrapers rear 50SH unit and both machines were in production at the same time until being phased out in 1966.

November 1959 saw the introduction of the big Euclid SS-33 scraper. The SS-33, model 34LDT-42SH, was powered by a single GM Diesel 12V-71, two-cycle, 12-cylinder engine, rated at 432 gross horsepower. Scraper capacity was 33 cubic yards struck and 43 cubic yards heaped. The SS-33 was a big-volume, high-speed producer that Euclid engineers quickly found had greater potential for even larger load capacities. In 1961, Euclid introduced the SS-40, model 34LDT-47SH (GM Diesel), scraper. This early SS-40 was basically an SS-33 with a modified scraper bowl with sideboards. This increased payload capacity to 40 cubic yards struck and 52 cubic yards heaped. The 34LDT tractor remained unchanged. The next step in the evolution of the SS-40, model 43LDT-51SH, was introduced in August 1962. This SS-40 was powered by a GM Diesel 16V-71, 16-cylinder engine, rated at 530 gross horsepower. Even though the 51SH scraper unit was a new design, the payload capacity remained the same as previous models. This SS-40 model was a special-order unit and not carried in the standard product line, with the majority of them being purchased by Western Contracting Corporation.

The regular-production SS-40 scrapers were updated in 1963, with the 49LDT-52SH (GM Diesel) and the 36LDT-52SH (Cummins) model units. The 49LDT tractor was powered by a GM Diesel 12V-71N, two-cycle, 12-cylinder engine, rated at 475 gross horsepower and 441 fhp, connected to a six-speed Allison CLBT-5960 Torqmatic transmission. The 36LDT utilized a Cummins NVH, four-cycle, 12-cylinder engine, rated at 450 gross horsepower and 421 fhp. The transmission was a six-speed Allison CLBT-5860 unit. The Cummins engine was a good performer, but most of the SS-40 scrapers delivered were equipped with the more-powerful GM Diesel. These became the last of the SS-40 models produced. By mid-1968, all of Euclid's six-wheel scraper models were discontinued.

Most of the six-wheeled scrapers built by GM Euclid Division were single-engined types. But a few special order models were produced for some of the company's largest customers featuring twin-engined power. These scrapers were truly the direct descendants of Euclid's first twin-power scraper concept from 1949.

The first two-engined models introduced by the Euclid Division were the 15TDT-22SH (replacing the 66FDT-16SH) and the 16TDT-23SH (replacing the 68FDT-17SH), in 1954. Both of these units had rated payload capacities of 18 cubic yards struck and 24 cubic yards heaped. In 1958, Euclid offered two larger twin-engined models, the 28LDT-37SH (GM Diesel) and the 33LDT-37SH (Cummins), with the latter also referred to as the TSS-24. The tractors were the same models that were used on the SS-24 scrapers, and the 37SH scraper unit was essentially the 33SH rear scraper bowl from the TS-24, but with a different hitch. Rated capacities for both models were 24 cubic yards struck and 32 cubic yards heaped, with a total power output of 543 gross horsepower. A special version of the TSS-24 was produced in late 1958 (model 37LDT-37SH) for one of Euclid's largest customers. The 37LDT tractor was powered by a GM Diesel 6-110T, two-cycle, six-cylinder engine, rated at 360 gross horsepower. The 37SH scraper was powered by a GM Diesel 6-71, two-cycle, six-cylinder, rated at 218 gross horsepower, for a combined total of 578 gross horsepower. Capacity ratings remained the same as previous TSS-24 models.

The pinnacle of Euclid's design and engineering efforts in tractor-pulled scrapers were two specialty models produced for Western Contracting Corporation. This was the same contractor that had purchased the first large fleets of Euclid 1LLD rear dump haulers and TC-12 super-dozers. Western had confidence in Euclid's ability to produce, and the company would not disappoint them. The first unit built was the TSS-40, model 43LDT-54SH, in March 1963. The 43LDT tractor was powered by a GM Diesel 16V-71, two-cycle, 16-cylinder engine rated at 530 gross horsepower, connected to a six-speed Allison CLBT-6060 Torqmatic transmission. The rear 54SH scraper bowl was powered by a GM Diesel 8V-71,

In late 1958, Euclid produced a special fleet of TSS-24 (37LDT-37SH) scrapers for Morrison-Knudsen, Kaiser and F&S, for use on the Navajo Dam Project. The front 37LDT tractor was powered by a GM Diesel 6-110T turbocharged engine, and the rear 37SH scraper utilized a GM Diesel 6-71 unit. Together, the engines were rated at 578 gross horsepower. Payload capacity for the TSS-24 was 24 cubic yards struck and 32 cubic yards heaped.

The TSS-40 (43LDT-54SH) was a special-order model built for Western Contracting Corporation in March 1963. The TSS-40 was powered by a GM Diesel 16V-71 engine in the tractor, and a GM Diesel 8V-71 in the rear scraper unit, with a power output totaling 810 gross horsepower. The scraper was rated at 40 cubic yards struck and 52 cubic yards heaped. Factory records indicate that four TSS-40 units were built for Western.

The Tandem TSS-40 (53LDT-65SH-66SH), also referred to as the TTSS-40, was the largest production scraper model ever built by Euclid. Five of these giants were produced for Western Contracting, with the first unit rolling out of the factory in August 1964. The TTSS-40 was powered by three GM Diesel 16V-71N engines, rated at 1,740 gross horsepower and 1,690 fhp.

two-cycle, eight-cylinder engine rated at 280 gross horsepower, mated to a six-speed Allison CLBT-4460 unit. Total power output was 810 gross horsepower. This enabled the TSS-40 to obtain a top speed of 37 miles per hour on level ground. Payload ratings were the same as the SS-40, at 40 cubic yards struck and 52 cubic yards heaped. Western ordered a total of four TSS-40 scrapers.

The next scraper model to be produced for Western was the three-engined Euclid Tandem TSS-40, model 53LDT-65SH-66SH, better known as the TTSS-40. These monsters were the largest scraper models ever to be factory built by Euclid. The specially prepared 53LDT tractor, 65SH, and 66SH scraper units all used the same engine and transmission packages: the GM Diesel 16V-71N, two-cycle, 16-cylinder engine with the six-speed Allison CBLT-6061 Torqmatic transmission. The combined power ratings for all three engines was 1,740 gross horsepower and 1,690 fhp. The rear axle of the tractor and both rear ends of the scrapers were powered. The front axle of the tractor and the dolly between the two scrapers were not driven. At each end of each axle were large, dual wheels, except the front steering axle of the tractor (which had a single wheel at each end), giving the unit a total of 18 tires. Payload capacity of the TTSS-40 was 80 cubic yards struck and 104 cubic yards heaped, or a maximum of 250,000 pounds (125 tons), with a loading time of about two minutes. Total gross vehicle weight was 526,000 pounds (263 tons). The first TTSS-40 was unveiled at the Euclid factory in

August 1964. By the end of September 1964, the first unit was already at work for Western on the San Luis Canal aqueduct project in Modesto, California. A total of five TTSS-40 scrapers were built for Western.

Euclid Bottom Dump Haulers

The FDT, TDT, and LDT tractors were also the power behind Euclid's bottom dump trailers. The dirt bottom dumps put Euclid on the map of the earth-moving industry and dozens of different models were produced, in varied sizes and capacities. When GM purchased Euclid in 1953, the largest dirt bottom dumps being offered by the firm were the 17 and 18LDT-105W (Cummins) models, first introduced in 1950, rated at 25-cubic-yard capacity. The smallest bottom dumps were the 89W, 13-cubic-yard trailers, and the 122W, 17-cubic-yard units, already mentioned in connection with the early six-wheel scrapers. The Euclid Division's engineering efforts were focused on larger-capacity units utilizing various LDT tractor models. Between 1958 and 1959, Euclid introduced the first of its 30-cubic-yard dirt bottom dumps, the 34 and 37LDT-137W, both with GM Diesel engines. These were followed by the 34LDT-141W (GM Diesel) and 41LDT-141W (Cummins), each with 40-cubic-yard capacities, in 1961. In 1962, Euclid introduced the first of the B-63 bottom dumps, models 36LDT-144W (Cummins) and 49LDT-144W (GM Diesel), both rated at 42 cubic yards, with a 63-ton maximum payload. In 1965, both of these B-63 bottom dump

The big Tandem TSS-40 (53LDT-65SH-66SH) was rated at 80 cubic yards struck and 104 cubic yards heaped, with a 250,000-pound (125-ton) load limit. The TTSS-40 shown here is working in October 1964 in Modesto, California, on the San Luis Canal aqueduct project, which was the first job site on which all five of the scrapers first worked.

models received upgraded 147W trailers that offered hydraulic controls instead of the previous 144W unit's air system. Payload ratings were unchanged. The largest of the Euclid Division-designed dirt bottom dumps were the B-100 models: 45LDT-146W (GM Diesel), introduced in mid-1963; and 46LDT-146W (Cummins), introduced in 1964. These units were rated at 60 cubic yards, with a payload rating of 100 tons. The majority of the B-100 bottom dumps produced were equipped with the GM Diesel 16V-71N, two-cycle, 16-cylinder engine, rated at 580 gross horsepower and 555 fhp, with six-speed Allison CLBT-6061 Torqmatic transmission. This was the same engine and transmission combination found in the Euclid TTSS-40 scraper, but with a slightly different power curve.

Euclid's next class of bottom dumps were the coal haulers, which date back historically to 1935, when the first unit designed to carry coal was built. Like the dirt bottom dumps, dozens of coal-hauling trailers had been built before GM entered the picture. The first of the smaller-capacity coal haulers to be introduced by the Euclid Division in 1955 were the 76FDT-121W (Cummins) and the 77FDT-121W (GM Diesel), both with 25-ton load capacity ratings. These models replaced the 70FDT-121W (Cummins) version that had been in service since 1950. Larger models in service were the 40-ton-capacity 17 and 18LDT-118W (both Cummins), introduced in 1950. These models were replaced in 1958 by the 28LDT-133W (GM Diesel) and the 33LDT-133W (Cummins), both

The first of the B-63 (36LDT-147W) bottom dumps to feature hydraulic controls for the trailer was this 36LDT-147W model from November 1964. This version was powered by a Cummins NVH, 12-cylinder, diesel engine rated at 450 gross horsepower and 421 fhp. The hopper had a rated capacity of 42 cubic yards struck and 64 cubic yards heaped, with a 63-ton load rating. An optional 70-ton capacity unit was also available. The B-63 bottom dump was officially released in 1965.

The largest bottom dump model produced by GM Euclid Division was the B-100 (45LDT-146W), first introduced in July 1963. The 45LDT-146W was equipped with a GM Diesel 16V-71N engine rated at 580 gross horsepower and 555 fhp. The hopper's capacity was 60 cubic yards struck and 78 cubic yards heaped, with a 100-ton load limit. Fully loaded, and on level ground, the B-100 was capable of attaining a 47-mile-per-hour top speed.

One of Euclid's most popular large bottom dump coal haulers was the 51-ton-capacity 24TDT-128W, introduced in 1954. The 24TDT tractor was powered by a Cummins Model NVH, 12-cylinder, diesel engine rated at 380 gross horsepower. The 128W coal hopper was rated at 67 cubic yards struck and 94 cubic yards heaped. This 51-ton coal hauler, shown in January 1963, was built for the Gibraltar Coal Corporation, located near Central City, Kentucky. This was one of the nicest-looking and most-colorful versions ever produced by Euclid Division.

The 10-ton-capacity Euclid R-10 (1UD) was the smallest regular-production rear dump hauler to be manufactured by Euclid. The 1UD model of the truck was first introduced in June 1948, and was in production until early 1963. Pictured is an R-10 hauler working in November 1957, powered by a GM Diesel 4-71 engine rated at 132 gross horsepower.

with 40-ton capacities. The largest coal haulers in service for Euclid, before GM entered the picture, were the 47-ton-capacity 11TDT-124W (Buda), introduced in 1952, and the 44-ton-rated 9TDT-125W (Cummins), offered in 1953. New models introduced by the Euclid Division were the 51-ton capacity 24TDT-128W (Cummins), in 1954, and the 47-ton 29TDT-128W (Cummins) in 1957. Euclid replaced its previous 51-ton coal hauler with the newer model 36LDT-138W (Cummins), in 1958. It was also rated at a 51-ton capacity.

Euclid Rear Dump Haulers

As far as the Euclid product line was concerned, the rear dump haulers were the industry standard in design and function. After 1934, they had become synonymous for what an off-road truck should look, sound, and perform like.

The Euclid rear dump haulers were divided into six categories; UD, FD, TD, LD, FFD, and LLD model lines. The smallest of these was the UD range of trucks, rated between 10- and 13-ton capacities. The first of these was the 1UD, introduced in mid-1948. The little 10-ton-capacity 1UD was powered by a GM Diesel 4094, two-cycle, four-cylinder engine rated at 125 gross horsepower,

with a Fuller Model 10-E-650, 10-speed transmission. The 1UD might have been small, but it shared many of the heavy-duty design features found in its larger brethren, such as a forged I-beam front axle, three-stage double-acting hydraulic hoist, super-strong frame, and Euclid's own double-reduction planetary rear drive axle. Even though the 1UD had been released before the GM purchase, it was kept on the market for some time. In its last few years of production, the 1UD, now called the R-10, was powered by a GM Diesel 4-71, two-cycle, four-cylinder engine rated at 132 gross horsepower. Other than that, the truck looked the same as it did when it was released in 1948.

In early 1963, the R-10 hauler was replaced by the improved R-12, model 3UD, rear dump. The R-12 had a rated payload capacity of 12 tons, in either its standard or quarry dump body. It was powered by a GM Diesel 4-71 engine, rated at 148 gross horsepower and 143 fhp, connected to a Fuller 5-CW-650, five-speed transmission. The R-12 also featured a newly designed cab and sheet metal, offering a much-improved working environment for the operator. The 3UD model of the R-12 was in service until 1965, when it was upgraded to the 4UD

The last of the "UD" model haulers to be built by Euclid was the 13-ton-capacity R-13, first introduced in May 1966. The R-13, model 5UD, was powered by a GM Diesel 4-71N engine rated at 160 gross horsepower and 154 fhp. The R-13 replaced the previous R-12 hauler that had been in the product line since 1963.

version. New to the 4UD was an independently sprung front suspension. Gone were the old leaf springs, replaced by large coil springs and shock absorbers. The new ride was light-years ahead of the old version for ride quality and control. The truck also featured an improved hydraulic system for the hoist and steering system; drivetrain and power ratings remained unchanged. The last version of the UD to be released was the

The 22-ton-capacity 46TD hauler, shown here in 1956, was a very popular model for Euclid while in production from 1950 to 1962. The 46TD was powered by a Cummins NHRS diesel engine rated at 300 gross horsepower. The 46TD came from a long line of 22-ton-capacity trucks built by the company, dating back to 1945. Starting in 1957, all of the 22-ton haulers in the product line, including the 46TD, were referred to as R-22 series rear dumps.

R-13, model 5UD, in late-1966. Improvements of the new model over the older R-12 were a more-powerful GM Diesel 4-71N engine, now rated at 160 gross horsepower and 154 fhp. The transmission was the same as the unit found in the 4UD. A new "V-profile" chute-type dump body was now standard, with an increased 13-ton payload capacity. All other major specifications remained unaffected.

The next-biggest model class of Euclid haul trucks were the FD rear dumps. The FD trucks were the company's oldest model line, dating back to the first 15-ton capacity 1FD in 1936. The longest-running truck that shared the characteristic three-section windshield and square cab design found in even the earliest 15-ton models, was the 80FD (Cummins), which was finally discontinued in 1958. This model served as the simple "bread-and-butter" truck for customers where reliability and low cost were preferred over more-complex designs. Basically, if you've seen one of the old-styled FD haulers, you've seen them all.

Other 15-ton-capacity trucks in operation, but designed prior to the GM acquisition, were the 82FD (GM Diesel), 84FD (GM Diesel), 85FD (GM Diesel), 86FD (Cummins), and 87FD (Cummins). These versions were all released in 1950, with the exception of the 86FD, which was introduced in 1952. The 82FD shared the older body style of the 80FD, while the other models were of a more-modern design that was first introduced with the 55FD (GM Diesel) in 1948. The Euclid Division replaced these older model trucks with the 91FD (GM Diesel), in 1955, and the 94FD (Cummins), in 1958. The 91FD was powered by a GM Diesel 6-71, rated at 218 gross horsepower, with a Fuller Model 5F-1220, five-speed transmission. In later 91FD versions, the power output was increased to 227 gross horsepower. The 94FD was equipped with a Cummins NH-6-BI, rated at 220 gross horsepower. The transmission remained unchanged. Both of these trucks were classified as R-15 units, rated at 15 tons. But if equipped with the optional larger tires with the higher ply rating, the payload increased to 18 tons. These versions were known as R-18 rear dumps.

In late 1962, Euclid replaced the R-15/R-18 haul trucks with the R-20, models 95FD (GM Diesel) and 96FD (Cummins), both with 20-ton payload ratings. The 95FD was powered by a GM Diesel 6-71 engine rated at 239 gross horsepower and 226 fhp, connected to a Fuller 5GT-1220, five-speed transmission. The engine offered in the 96FD was a Cummins NH-250 rated at 250 gross horsepower and 232 fhp, with the same transmission as the 95FD. Also new was an updated operator's cab and hood sheet metal. In early 1965, both of these models were upgraded to the 97FD (GM Diesel) and 98FD (Cummins). These new versions featured independent coil spring and shock absorber front suspensions, instead of the previous leaf spring suspension. All other major features remained unchanged. Optional versions of these models were the 99FD (GM Diesel) and 100FD (Cummins). These models featured an Allison CLBT-4460 Torqmatic, six-speed, full power shift transmission, replacing the old manual Fuller unit found in all of the previous R-20 trucks. Horsepower ratings were unchanged.

Shown working in August 1962 is a Euclid R-27 (66TD) rear dump with a special 30-ton-capacity "T-1" dump body. The 66TD model was normally rated with a 27-ton payload capacity. The 66TD was powered by a Cummins NRTO-6-BI "Turbo-Diesel," rated at 335 gross horsepower. The R-27 truck line was officially upgraded into the series R-30 haulers in mid-1962, with the model 70TD taking the place of the previous 66TD version.

The next step in the evolution of the Euclid FD haulers was the R-22, models 101FD (GM Diesel), in mid-1966, and the 102FD (Cummins), in late 1966. The 101FD was powered by a GM Diesel 6-71N engine rated at 239 gross horsepower and 225 fhp, with a Fuller 5GT-1220, five-speed transmission. The 102FD was equipped with a Cummins NH-250 diesel engine rated at 250 gross horsepower and 232 fhp, using the same transmission found with the GM-engined unit. These trucks utilized a new "V-profile" dump body and redesigned engine hoods. Both units were rated at 22-ton capacities. Optional versions of these models, the 103FD (GM Diesel) and 104FD (Cummins), were virtually the same as the other trucks except for the use of an Allison CLBT-4460 Torqmatic, six-speed transmission, instead of the standard manual Fuller gearbox.

The second-oldest Euclid rear dump model lines in the series were the TD haulers, first introduced in March 1944. Many model variations of the TD haulers were produced over the years, with several types in service before GM bought Euclid Road Machinery, and continuing into the Euclid Division era. These included the 31TD (Cummins),

1951-'56; the 36TD (Cummins), 1951-'61; the 46TD (Cummins), 1950-'62; the 59TD (GM Diesel), 1953-'54; the 60TD (GM Diesel), 1954-'60; the 62TD (Waukesha), 1953-'55; and the 63TD (GM Diesel), 1954-'60. All of these models were 22-ton-capacity haulers, like most of the early TD variations. Only the very first models, 1TD through 7TD (except for the 3TD), had lower payloads than 22 tons. In 1957, the 22-ton TD trucks started to be referred to as R-22 rear dumps. These were not the same as the R-22, FD models from 1966, since both types were not in production at the same time. The TD, R-22 nomenclature was finally retired in 1962.

The next TD model in capacity was the Euclid R-27, officially introduced in late 1957. Two versions of the R-27 were produced, the 65TD (GM Diesel) and the 66TD (Cummins). The 65TD was powered by a GM Diesel 6-110, two-cycle, six-cylinder engine rated at 336 gross horsepower, with a four-speed Allison CLBT-5640 transmission. The 66TD housed a Cummins NRTO-6-BI, four-cycle, six-cylinder diesel, rated at 335 gross horsepower, mated to the same transmission as in the GM-powered model. Payload capacity for both versions was

The popular 35-ton-capacity Euclid R-35 rear dump was introduced in April 1965, and was considered one of the company's finest haulers. The model 74TD, shown here in March 1967, was powered by a GM Diesel 12V-71N engine rated at 434 gross horsepower and 394 fhp. The 75TD version of the R-35 was the Cummins NTA-380 Turbo-Diesel-engined model, with a power output of 380 gross horsepower and 350 fhp.

The 45-ton-capacity Euclid R-45 (11LD), shown working in August 1962, was also a very popular hauler for the company. The 11LD model was powered by a Cummins V12-525 diesel engine rated at 525 gross horsepower and 492 fhp. The 10LD version of the R-45 was the model with the GM Diesel 16V-71 engine rated at 530 gross horsepower and 496 fhp.

27 tons. In 1962, the R-27 was upgraded to the R-30, now with a 30-ton load rating. Models included the 69TD (GM Diesel), the 70TD (Cummins), and the 71TD (GM Diesel). The 69TD was powered by a GM Diesel 6-110, two-cycle, six-cylinder engine rated at 336 gross horsepower and 317 fhp. The 70TD was equipped with a Cummins NT-335 "Turbo-Diesel," four-cycle, six-cylinder engine rated at 335 gross horsepower and 306 fhp. The 71TD had the most powerful engine of the group, the GM Diesel 12V-71, two-cycle, 12-cylinder diesel rated at 370 gross horsepower and 348 fhp. Transmissions for the 69TD and 70TD trucks were the full power shift Allison CLBT-5660, six-speed, while the 71TD utilized a six-speed Allison CLBT-5860 unit. In 1963, the R-30 received numerous mechanical and detail refinements, including a redesigned cab. The drivetrains in all three truck models remained unchanged. Model designations and payload capacities were also unaffected.

The last TD haulers to be designed by the GM Euclid Division were the R-35 haulers, models 74TD (GM Diesel) and 75TD (Cummins). The 74TD was powered by a GM Diesel 12V-71N, two-cycle, 12-cylinder engine rated at 434 gross horsepower and 394 fhp. The transmission of choice was the six-speed Allison CLBT-5860, full power shift unit. The 75TD made do with a Cummins NTA-380 "Turbo-Diesel," four-cycle, six-cylinder engine rated at 380 gross horsepower and 350 fhp; the transmission was the same as in the 74TD. The R-35 featured a "V-profile" dump body, rated at a 35-ton capacity, and an independent front-wheel suspension. The R-35 was well-engineered, and sales reflected that. It was tough and reliable, exactly what a "Euc" was all about. The R-35 model line also had the distinction of including the 20,000th Euclid rear dump manufactured, a 74TD model, in 1966.

The largest two-axle production haulers built by Euclid were the model LD rear dumps. This line of trucks dated back to February 1942, when the first 1LD was built. Additional LD models were manufactured between 1944 and 1949, the 2LD through 8LD, all rated at 30 tons capacity. None of these trucks was built in large numbers though, with most being of a special-order nature. It was not until 1960 that Euclid started testing a new two-axle LD rear dump, the model 10LD, eventually to be known as the R-45. Early prototype versions of the 10LD were known as R-40 trucks, since their payload capacity at the time was rated at 40 tons. The prototype 10LD was powered by a GM Diesel 12V-71 rated at 432

The R-50 series of haulers were introduced by Euclid in October 1965, and included two models, the GM-powered 12LD and the 13LD Cummins version. Even though both models were announced at the same time, the first 13LD variation was not built until June 1966. The 50-ton-capacity 12LD, shown working in June 1966, was powered by a GM Diesel 16V-71N engine rated at 635 gross horsepower and 609 fhp.

A 40-ton-capacity Euclid R-40 (9FFD) waits at the St. Clair plant shipping yard for the next train out of Cleveland in 1957. The 9FFD model of the R-40 was powered by two GM Diesel 6-71T, turbocharged engines rated at 470 gross horsepower and 450 fhp. The first GM-powered R-40 was introduced in January 1957, but the first Cummins-engined 10FFD model wasn't built until November 1957. *John G. Addams*

fhp. The final production versions of the 10LD utilized a GM Diesel 16V-71, two-cycle, 16-cylinder engine rated at 530 gross horsepower and 496 fhp. The transmission for the big 16-cylinder was a six-speed Allison CLBT-5960, full power shift unit. Even though this 16-cylinder version of the 10LD was offered in early 1962, factory records seem to indicate that the final production unit wasn't available until the first part of 1963. An 11LD model of the R-45 was offered; it was powered by a Cummins V12-525, 12-cylinder diesel engine rated at 525 gross horsepower and 492 fhp. The transmission was the same unit found in the 10LD version. This model of the R-45 was released in 1962. Both production versions of this hauler were rated at 45 tons capacity. In 1963, both models also received new operator's cabs, replacing the older rounded-edged versions.

In 1965, Euclid released an upgraded version of the R-45 called the R-50, with models 12LD (GM Diesel) and 13LD (Cummins). The R-50 featured an independent front coil spring suspension, replacing the front leaf springs used on the R-45. Tire and wheel sizes were also increased, and matched the rears. The R-45's front tires were always smaller than its rear set, giving the truck a sort of hot rod look. The R-50 also was equipped with a newly designed chute-type dump body, now rated at 50 tons capacity. The 12LD version was powered by a GM Diesel 16V-71N, two-cycle, 16-cylinder engine rated at 635 gross horsepower and 609 fhp. The 13LD was equipped with a Cummins VT-12-635, 12-cylinder diesel engine rated at 635 gross horsepower and 600 fhp. A six-speed Allison CLBT-6061 Torqmatic was the only transmission available for both models.

In 1966, the Euclid Division was hard at work on a larger LD model two-axle rear dump, in the 60- to 65-ton range, to round out its product line. This truck would occupy a position just above the R-50 and was not meant

to replace that series of haulers. The pilot version of this truck was the 14LD, referred to as the R-60. The 14LD was ready for preliminary testing in May 1966. The R-60 looked a bit like the R-50 on steroids. The pilot model's dump body was made of aluminum for high strength and low weight, and had a capacity rating of 60 tons. The 14LD was powered by a GM Diesel 16V-71T engine. Horsepower ratings for this engine in the 14LD were not made available since the unit was still in the prototype stage. The pilot version also featured an experimental operator's cab that was entered from the front, through a combined door and front windshield. In 1967, an improved version of the prototype 14LD was introduced called the R-65, model 16LD. This model was powered by the same 16-cylinder engine found in the 14LD, with power ratings of 700 gross horsepower and 654 fhp. This was connected to a six-speed Allison DP-8860, full power shift transmission. Gone were the experimental cab, replaced by a more-traditional unit, and the aluminum dump body, replaced by an alloy steel version. The payload capacity was now up to 65 tons. For whatever reason, Euclid decided that the R-65 was not to be sold in the United States, but instead was to be built by Euclid (Great Britain) Ltd., in Scotland, and geared exclusively toward the overseas market. The hauler was still called the R-65, but the model designation was changed to the B16LD. Factory records indicate that the first unit built at the Motherwell plant was shipped in April 1968. An improved version of the R-65, called the R-70, was announced in early 1968, with an increase in payload capacity to 70 tons, which was achieved through tire and transmission upgrades. But none of the R-70 versions were ever shipped carrying the Euclid name.

Along with the two-axle rear dump haulers, Euclid also offered two model lines of tandem-drive, three-axle trucks, referred to as FFD and LLD. The FFD haulers were classified as 34- to 45-ton capacity trucks, while the larger LLD models were rated at 50 to 62 tons. The first of the tandem-drives to go into full production was the twin-engined 1FFD, introduced in February 1949, which was discussed in chapter 2. Other FFD models were to follow and not all of these utilized the twin-power concept. The 2FFD and 3FFD versions were both powered by a single Cummins NVH, 12-cylinder, diesel engine. The 2FFD was equipped with a 10-speed Fuller 10-F-1220 transmission. The 3FFD used a five-speed Fuller 5-F-1220 unit. Both haulers were rated at 34 tons capacity. The 2FFD was released in 1950 and the 3FFD in 1951. Both models were special order only and were tailored to a customer's particular needs. The one advantage these versions had over the 1FFD was in price. The 1FFD retailed for $54,655 and the single-engined models averaged $39,800 apiece. A saving of $14,855 was a mighty big incentive in 1950. The downside was a poorer-performing truck that was not very operator-friendly and required very expensive replacement parts for the big 12-cylinder engine.

In mid-1961, the Euclid R-40 series was upgraded into an R-45 version by the use of a larger but lighter dump body. Engine and power ratings remained unchanged from the two previous different-engined models. Shown working in May 1962 on a railroad relocation project in Somerset, Kentucky, is a model 9FFD with the 45-ton-capacity R-45 series body.

In early 1951, Euclid introduced the 4FFD twin-engined Cummins version of the original 1FFD that used GM Diesels. Both models shared the same overall design, except the 4FFD was powered by two Cummins Model NHB, four-cycle, six-cylinder diesel engines, totaling 400 gross horsepower. The 4FFD Cummins version enjoyed a slight power advantage over the GM-powered 1FFD until 1956, when the two GM Diesel 6-71 engines were upgraded to 436 gross horsepower. With the engine covers in place, it was almost impossible to tell the difference between the two models, except by the sound of their engines. Except for redesigned operator's cabs in late 1954, both models looked virtually the same until 1957, when the updated Euclid R-40 rear dumps, models 9FFD (GM Diesel) and 10FFD (Cummins), were released. The 9FFD was powered by a pair of GM Diesel 6-71T, two-cycle, six-cylinder engines, rated at 470 gross horsepower and 450 fhp combined. The 10FFD was equipped with two Cummins Model NT-6-BI "Turbo-Diesel," four-cycle, six-cylinder engines, rated at 500 gross horsepower and 481 fhp. Each truck used a pair of three-speed Allison Torqmatic TG-609 transmissions, with Allison TC-544 torque convertors. Rated payload capacity for each version was 40 tons. In mid-1961, an upgraded version of the R-40 called the R-45 was introduced. The 9FFD and 10FFD

This specially prepared Euclid 9FFD tractor is on its way to the Iron Ore Company of Canada's Wabush mine in New-foundland in April 1962. The 9FFD tractor version utilized the same two GM Diesel 6-71T, turbocharged engines found in the regular rear dump model.

model identifications remained unchanged, as did the drive-trains of both trucks. The new 45-ton rating was achieved through the use of a redesigned dump body made from alloy steel. It was stronger and lighter than the previous body, giv-ing the hauler a greater payload capacity. These two models

The first 5LLD model of the 55-ton-capacity R-55 series of tandem-drive haulers was introduced in November 1959. The 5LLD shown working in March 1960 is one of 21 series R-55 rear dumps purchased by American Smelting & Refining for its mining operation in Tucson, Arizona.

became the last of the twin-engined FFD haulers, when they were both discontinued at the end of 1963.

In late 1960 and early 1961, Euclid offered three single-engined, tandem-drive haulers, R-40 models 11FFD (GM Diesel) and 12FFD (Cummins), and an R-45, 13FFD (Cummins), which few in the marketplace even noticed.

Then in 1962, Euclid introduced the 14FFD (GM Diesel) and 15FFD (Cummins) models, both classified as R-45 rear dumps. The 14FFD was powered by a single GM Diesel 16V-71, two-cycle, 16-cylinder engine mated to a six-speed Allison CLBT-5960 Torqmatic transmission. Power ratings were 530 gross horsepower and 496 fhp. The 15FFD was

The LLD assembly line was in full swing at the St. Clair No. 1 Plant in December 1959. The trucks being assembled are R-55 series, 5LLD haulers, rated at 55 tons capacity.

equipped with a Cummins V12-525, four-cycle, 12-cylinder diesel rated at 525 gross horsepower and 492 fhp. The transmission was the same as the GM-engined 14FFD. Each truck's rated payload capacity was 45 tons. Except for newly designed operator cabs and engine hoods, these models looked pretty much like any other R-40 or R-45 tandem-drive Euclid hauler. By this time, two engines were no longer needed to power the FFD haulers, with more and more of the powerful 16- and 12-cylinder diesels being produced. Only one engine and transmission were now needed. But at the same time, the capacity ratings of the two-axle haulers were equaling and surpassing those of the tandem-drive units. Almost overnight, the FFD haulers had become the dinosaurs of the Euclid product line.

The Euclid FFD tandem rear dumps were also offered as tractors, minus their dump body and outfitted with a fifth wheel. Not many of these FFD tractors were produced, but the ones that did get built were used for pulling coal, haulers, iron ore side-dump trailers, or working as logging trucks. The most popular of these was the 9FFD tractor. Most 9FFDs had the more-powerful twin GM Diesel 6-71T engines, rated at 470 gross horsepower and 450 fhp combined. The total number of Euclid FFD trucks built was 843 units, and the model breakdowns are as follows: 1FFD, 373 produced; 2FFD, 42; 3FFD, 5; 4FFD, 175; 9FFD, 152; 10FFD, 36; 11FFD, 1; 12FFD, 0; 13FFD, 6; 14FFD, 8; and 15FFD, 45. The last of these models built, a 15FFD unit, was shipped from the factory on March 17, 1966. Some Euclid records mention additional 5FFD, 6FFD, 7FFD, and 8FFD models, but factory build sheets indicate that none were ever produced as serial-numbered units.

The largest of Euclid's tandem-axle, twin-engined, rear dumps were their LLD haulers, produced from 1951 to 1964. The first of these trucks, the 1LLD, was discussed in chapter 2, but other models were to follow.

In August 1955, Euclid produced a 2LLD model, equipped with GM Diesel 6-110, two-cycle, six-cylinder engines, with Allison TG-607 transmissions, but this particular model was built specially for the GM Powerama as part of the Euclid Division display. The 2LLD was considered an experimental model, and it was basically a 1LLD with a new cab design and GM diesel engines. Only one was ever produced.

The next models of the Euclid LLD line to go into production were the 3LLD (GM Diesel) and 4LLD (Cummins) haulers, introduced in mid-1957. The 3LLD was powered by two GM Diesel 6-110 engines, each rated at 336 gross horsepower, totaling 672 gross horsepower and 632 fhp. This time around, two Allison CLT-5640 Torqmatic, four-speed transmissions were installed, which were big improvements over the older TG-607 units. The 4LLD was equipped

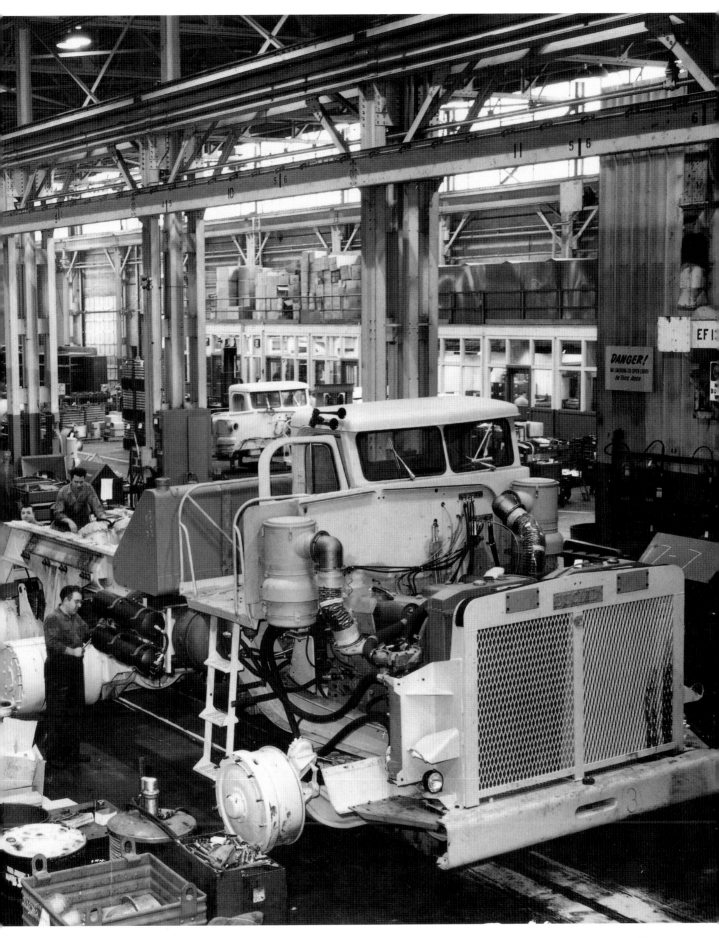

In January 1961, the R-55 model line was upgraded into the R-62 series. The extra capacity was made possible by a redesigned dump body that increased the payload rating to 62 tons. Shown working at Kennecott Copper Company's Ruth Mine, in Ely, Nevada, is a 5LLD model, powered by two GM Diesel 6-110 engines rated at 672 gross horsepower and 632 fhp. These Kennecott trucks were some of the first R-62 haulers to be put into service.

with two Cummins Model NRTO-6-BI "Turbo-Diesel," four-cycle, six-cylinder engines, rated at 335 gross horsepower each, totaling 670 gross horsepower and 613 fhp. Transmissions were the same units found in the 3LLD. These models also featured the new operator's cab, first shown on the 2LLD, and a revised hood and front grille assembly.

In early 1959, the 3LLD and 4LLD, now referred to as Euclid R-55 rear dumps, had their payload capacity

rating increased to 55 tons through the use of improved Allison CBLT-5640 transmissions and new gear ratios in the two Euclid-built rear axles. Power ratings remained unaffected. The R-55, 3LLD was upgraded to a 5LLD (GM Diesel) model, in November 1959, which was followed by the 4LLD being replaced by the 6LLD (Cummins), in February 1960. Other than the chassis being reinforced and a little more overall weight, the trucks

The last major design changes made to the R-62 tandem-drive hauler line occurred in May 1963 with the release of this GM-powered 5LLD model. This version featured many mechanical upgrades, such as new Allison transmissions and a redesigned operator's cab. In October 1963, the Cummins 6LLD version also received these improvements, which brought the weight of the R-62 up to 118,100 pounds, without payload. The last R-62 hauler to be built, a 6LLD model, was shipped from the Euclid St. Clair plant on June 11, 1964.

The first of the redesigned Euclid R-X haulers, model 10LLD, started on-site testing at a Duval Corporation copper mine in Tucson, Arizona, in February 1967. The 10LLD model of this truck originally evolved from the earlier prototype 7LLD versions of the R-X. The 105-ton-capacity 10LLD was powered by a single GM Diesel 12V-149T, turbocharged engine rated at 1,000 gross horsepower and 912 fhp. Overall weight of the R-X was 137,000 pounds empty.

were virtually the same as the previous R-55 versions. By early 1961, a more significant upgrade was in store for the 5LLD and 6LLD, when their payload capacities were increased to 62 tons, making them R-62 haulers. The extra payload can be attributed to a newly designed dump body, which was made stronger and lighter than the former unit through the increased use of high- and low-strength alloy steels. The weight savings of the body alone totaled 10,000 pounds.

The last major upgrade to the R-62 haulers was introduced in May 1963, first with the 5LLD, then followed a few months later in October by the 6LLD version. Both models received a newly designed operator's cab, beefed-up chassis, and new six-speed Allison CLBT-5660 Torqmatic full power shift transmissions. The GM Diesels in the 5LLD remained unchanged, but the two engines in the 6LLD were replaced with different Cummins NT-335, four-cycle, six-cylinder units. Horsepower ratings did not change between the two different types of Cummins engines. Even though Euclid offered the R-62 hauler line in late 1964, factory records indicate that the last unit delivered, a 6LLD model, was shipped on June 11, 1964. No more of these trucks were sold after this date. The total number of tandem-drive LLD trucks manufactured was 145 units, and individual numbers per model type are as follows: 1LLD, 46; 2LLD, 1; 3LLD, 7; 4LLD, 7; 5LLD, 55; and 6LLD, 29.

In the 1960s, the Euclid Division faced a serious threat to its hold on the off-road hauler market. Between 1961 and 1965, Euclid actually found itself falling behind the rest of the industry in the over-60-ton class of haulers. Also to Euclid's dismay, Caterpillar had launched

its own line of haulers, first in the 35-ton class with its model 769, then in the 50-ton range with the 773. Companies such as WABCO (with its 65-ton hauler in 1961), Unit Rig (with its 85-ton-capacity diesel-electric M-85 in 1963), and KW-Dart (with its 110-ton-capacity DE-2771 in 1965), dominated the large mining-truck field. During this time, Euclid had nothing in its product line that could counter these threats. To top it off, Caterpillar was announcing the introduction of its own diesel-electric 85-ton hauler, the 779, in 1965. The Euclid Division would take a unique approach to this dilemma by creating a new line of haulers that covered the 85- to 105-ton market segment, all based on a single truck platform. The "magic bullet" truck would eventually be called the "R-X," an engineering extravagance that did not quite live up to Euclid's expectations.

The R-X hauler actually started out as the Euclid R-90, model 7LLD rear dump, in mid-1964. Its design features were meant to be trendsetting, and not to be seen as a "me too" catch-up copy of existing trucks in the industry. The 7LLD hauler concept was based around its articulated frame, which allowed the truck to pivot steer, much like Euclid's own wheel loaders and overhung scrapers. This enabled the hauler to have unmatched maneuverability in the most difficult of working conditions. Add to this four-wheel drive, dual-mounted tires on all wheels, rubber-disc packed suspension struts, and a single engine and transmission package. The dual wheels in the front and the articulated steering movement provided the hauler with a very distinctive personality. It definitely looked as if it could get the job done.

One of the more popular logging trucks produced by Euclid was its 64TD model, taking a load of timber out of the Potlatch Forests in Idaho in 1957. The 64TD was powered by a GM Diesel 6-110 engine rated at 300 gross horsepower. The logging trailer pulled by the truck was not built by Euclid, but was supplied by one of the various outside manufacturers.

The first 7LLD was shipped up to the GM Milford Proving Grounds for field engineering evaluations that were carried out in early 1965. Early on, the handling characteristics of the articulated design were in question. To solve this, the unit was shipped back to the Euclid factory in Cleveland, for a complete teardown and evaluation of the pilot truck. The frame design was modified, and a host of other improvements were made. The truck was completely rebuilt and readied for its unveiling at the American Mining Congress show in October 1965. At this point, the reference to the truck as the R-90 was dropped in favor of the new designation, "R-X."

The concept of the R-X was a hauler with different capacity ratings based on combinations of engines, transmissions, tire sizes, gear ratios, and dump bodies from which customers could chose to suit their particular needs. Four versions of the R-X were initially announced, rated at capacities of 85-, 90-, 100-, and 105-tons. The 85- and 90-ton trucks would be powered by a GM Detroit Diesel 16V-71T, two-cycle, 16-cylinder engine rated at 700 gross horsepower and 650 fhp. The

transmission would be a six-speed Allison DP-8860 full power shift unit. The 100- and 105-ton R-models would use the GM Detroit Diesel 12V-149T, two-cycle, 12-cylinder, rated at 1,000 gross horsepower and 912 fhp, utilizing a six-speed Allison DP-8960 transmission. The first R-X field study truck was put into service at Kennecott Copper's Bingham Canyon Mine, Utah, in January 1966. After these early evaluation tests, it was apparent that more changes would be needed to bring the hauler up to production standards.

In January 1967, the next step in the evolution of the R-X hauler program was ready. This version was a 105-ton-capacity R-X carrying the model identification of 10LLD. It was powered by the GM Detroit Diesel 12-cylinder engine mentioned earlier. The 7LLD pilot trucks had used the 16-cylinder diesel engines. This truck featured a redesigned frame, dump body, and front end. By the time the 10LLD model of the R-X was ready, customer interest in the smaller versions evaporated. The concept of ordering a haul truck the way a consumer would order a car was a little more than the industry could handle. In the

One of the early preproduction C-6 dozers equipped with a Gar Wood Dozecaster and hydraulic side-mounted cylinder blade controls. The hydraulic control did not make it into final production. This dozer was specially built for use at the GM Powerama held in August and September 1955 at Soldier Field in Chicago.

end, only one version of the R-X was produced, but it was the best of the bunch, the 105-ton-capacity 10LLD. Most of the early R-X models that utilized the 16-cylinder engines were converted to full 10LLD-specification trucks. Factory records indicate that the GM Euclid Division built a total of only 18 R-X haulers before the truck line was acquired by White Motor Company, where an additional 97 haulers, now renamed the R-105 (201XD), were produced between 1969 and 1976.

The early preproduction C-6 crawler tractor was powered by a GM Diesel 6-71 engine rated at 218 gross horsepower and 207 fhp. The headlight treatment was similar to other Euclid model designs that were being built at the time, but the C-6 would never go into full production with it. The C-6's big brother, the TC-12, can clearly be seen in the background at Euclid's Clinton Road factory yard in 1956.

Euclid Log Haulers

Euclid hoped its success in the off-road hauler market could be applied to the logging industry as well. In 1954, Euclid offered a 36TD Log Hauler truck and trailer outfit, specially built for demanding off-road forestry and logging operations. After encouraging early field tests, the smaller R-15 (91FD) was also added to the logging hauler line in late 1956. In 1957, both of the early models were replaced by the R-18 (93FD) and 64TD Euclid models. In March 1960, a specially modified Euclid 67TD Log Hauler was built to take the place of the 64TD model. The 67TD was basically a standard model 65TD with its frame extended 4 feet. Though these truck and trailer outfits performed extremely well, their high cost compared to trucks the industry was used to purchasing kept them from making any real dent in that market. This forced Euclid to abandon the project by the early 1960s. An FFD tandem-drive tractor truck was also tested as a logging hauler, but was found to be too large and heavy for the haul roads that were cut into the forests. It was never officially released for sale.

Euclid Crawler Dozers

While Euclid's hauler and scraper models were well established in the marketplace, it was now up to the company's engineers to do the same with the crawler dozer product line. The TC-12 was the first crawler offered by Euclid, but a single-engined model was well under way by the time the first twin-powered dozer was introduced. The new model would be called the Euclid C-6. The "C" stood for crawler and the "6" represented a six-cylinder diesel engine. The first experimental prototype C-6 started testing in May 1955. It was the main test bed for the drivetrain and undercarriage, with only a basic sheet metal skin covering the tractor's components. A more-refined version of the C-6 was first shown publicly at the GM Powerama in Chicago, on August 31, 1955. At this point, the dozer was still in its preliminary testing program, which included 30 trial machines to be put into service to find out how the C-6 would perform under various working conditions. The preproduction C-6 dozer was powered by a single GM Diesel 6-71, two-cycle, six-cylinder engine rated at 218 gross horsepower and 207 fhp, driving a three-speed Allison CRT-5532 Torqmatic transmission. The sheet metal design at this stage in the crawler's life resembled the TC-12 dozers, with its many rounded corners, rear-mounted radiator, and twin headlight enclosure built into the unit's front end. The crawler looked great, but like the TC-12's early design, the front end would have to be redesigned and strengthened to survive the rigors of heavy bulldozing work.

In 1958, the first production Euclid C-6-1 dozers were introduced. The new front end on the C-6-1 may not have been as nice to look at as the preproduction model, but it was much more practical for installing a cable-wind to control the bulldozer blades' up and down motion. Basic components were the same in the C-6-1 model as in

NO SMOKING,
MATCHES OR
OPEN LIGHTS
IN THIS AREA

Dri-Zit

PREVIOUS PAGE: A line of crawler tractors makes its way down the C-6 assembly line at the Hudson plant in July 1960. The Euclid C-6 was formerly built at the Clinton Road facility, before crawler and scraper operations were transferred to the new Hudson factory in 1959.

The first production C-6-1 crawler dozers were introduced in mid-1958 with a completely redesigned front end. This C-6-2, in 1960, was powered by a GM Diesel 6-71 engine rated at 227 gross horsepower and 213 fhp (211 fhp in earlier versions). Both early models of the C-6 looked almost exactly alike.

The improved C-6-3 was officially introduced in November 1961, with redesigned front and rear ends. Power ratings were listed at 227 gross horsepower and 213 fhp.

the previous version, except for redesigned final drives for the crawlers. The power ratings for the GM diesel were now listed at 218 gross horsepower and 202 fhp. About a year after the dozer's introduction, the power output was increased to 227 gross horsepower and 211 fhp. In late 1959, an upgraded C-6-2 version of the dozer was released, with revised power ratings of 227 gross horsepower and 213 fhp. Most of the improvements were of a fine-tuning nature, in hopes of increasing the dozer's reliability. The drivetrain, however, was unchanged.

In late 1960, the C-6-2 became the first Euclid dozer to get the optional Gar Wood single-hydraulic-cylinder blade control, mounted on the center of the front end in place of the standard cable control mount. This single-cylinder design, plus the rear-mounted radiator, eventually became the most widely recognized design features of Euclid crawler dozers. The single-cylinder-controlled blade system offered five key advantages over more conventional two-cylinder designs: greater lifting capacity, less maintenance, better visibility, better tractor balance, and equalized lifting of the blade. The competition would argue the validity of these benefits for years to come. In fact, the system worked quite well, but old buying habits are hard to break. Customers often took the attitude that if one cylinder is good, then two must be better.

During the next few years, many improvements were being made on the C-6 crawler that required new models to be released almost yearly. In November 1961, the first C-6-3 version rolled out of the factory, now wearing new sheet metal, both front and rear. The dozer could be factory equipped with either the cable blade control or the single hydraulic-strut model. The major operating specifications of this version were the same as the previous C-6-2. By the time the paint was dry on this model, the C-6-4 version was released in June 1963. The previous C-6-3 crawler introduced the new look of the model line, while its replacement, the C-6-4, was the unit with the major mechanical changes. Improvements made to the GM 6-71 diesel engine increased power output to 238 gross horsepower and 224 fhp. Changes made to the undercarriage included a new mounting of the equalizer bar to the track frames, and new high-performance, high-reduction rear planetary final drives. The C-6-4 held a 10 percent overall performance gain over the old C-6-3 model. The C-6-4 was a popular unit with customers and Euclid was very proud of it. So much so, the company displayed the dozer, along with other Euclid equipment, at the 1964 New York World's Fair as part of the GM Futurama exhibit.

Around the time the C-6-4 was introduced, the division of the Gar Wood company that produced all of the blade and ripper attachments, including all of their necessary control units, was being acquired by GM. On July 1, 1963, the Euclid Division assumed the manufacturing and sales responsibility of all of the Gar Wood-designed crawler attachments. After the acquisition, the Gar Wood name was dropped entirely, replaced by the Euclid name.

In May 1965, Euclid introduced yet another updated version of its six-cylinder-engined crawler, the C-6-5. This model's improvements were mostly concentrated in the undercarriage and crawler sections of the dozer, which included new bench-adjustable rollers, new roller seals, improved track tensioning, and heavier gearing. Power ratings were revised slightly, and were listed at 239 gross horsepower and 225 fhp. By this time, almost all C-6 dozers ordered were equipped with the single-hydraulic-cylinder blade control.

The C-6 name of the popular Euclid dozer was retired at the end of 1965 and replaced with the new "82-series"

The operator of this C-6-3 dozer, working in a stone quarry in Tulsa, Oklahoma, in March 1962, probably wished he could be doing something else. Before ROPS cabs became standard, most operators were left out in the open, which wasn't the best place to be if you happened to be operating in a dusty gravel pit.

nomenclature, with the crawler now being referred to as the 82-30. The first version of the Euclid 82-30 (EA) was actually unveiled in Boca Raton, Florida, in December 1965, but the model was not officially released until the following month. The new 82-30 (EA) dozer was basically a C-6-5 with a different model number. In June 1967, the

82-30 (FA) version was released with a bit more to talk about. This model was equipped with the improved GM Diesel 6-71N engine and Allison CRT-5534 Torqmatic transmission. Power figures were unchanged from the previous version. The C-6/82-30 crawler dozers built by Euclid were very popular models in the marketplace,

In January 1966, Euclid officially changed the designation of the C-6 crawler line to the 82-30 series. Pictured undergoing testing in Boca Raton, Florida, in December 1965 is an 82-30 (EA) model powered by a GM Diesel 6-71 engine rated at 239 gross horsepower and 225 fhp. The first 82-30 model was almost identical to the last C-6-5 version produced.

The C-260 dozer (shown here in prototype form) was completed in December 1964, and featured a front-mounted cable control unit. A single hydraulic cylinder replaced the cable unit in May 1965. The C-260 was the engineering prototype of the Euclid 82-40 crawler model.

though they still did not sell in the numbers like their Caterpillar and International counterparts. Part of this can be blamed on the uniqueness of the dozer's design and the marketplace's slow response to new ideas and new ways of thinking. Even so, the dozer carved out a nice niche for itself, with many years of life still ahead for it.

To help bridge the gap in the model line between the C-6 and TC-12 dozers, Euclid started developing an eight-cylinder-engined model that would fall somewhere in between the two existing crawlers as far as power was concerned. The first prototype of this dozer, called the Euclid C-260, was completed in December 1964. That first C-260 was equipped with a cable-controlled front-mounted blade, which was replaced with the single-hydraulic-cylinder blade control in May 1965. From then on, the new dozer line was only offered with this latter type of setup for use with all available bulldozing blade options. The name of the new crawler was changed from the C-260 to the 82-40 when it was introduced in Boca Raton, with the 82-30 model. The Euclid 82-40 (AA) was officially released in January 1966. This first series was powered by a single GM Diesel 8V-71N, two-cycle, eight-cylinder engine rated at 290 gross horsepower and 275 fhp, connected to a three-speed Allison CRT-6030 Torqmatic transmission. The 82-40 and 82-30 looked very much alike, with the 82-40 being a bit bigger and having a more squared-off front end design. The 82-40's radiator was still mounted in the back, like all other Euclid crawler dozers before it. In

Euclid introduced its new 82-40 dozer model line in January 1966. The first 82-40 (AA) version was powered by a GM Diesel 8V-71N engine rated at 290 gross horsepower and 275 fhp.

February 1967, an upgraded version of the 82-40 (BA) was released with an improved Allison CRT-6031 Torqmatic transmission and better brakes. By mid-1968, another upgraded version of the dozer was released, the model 82-40 (CA). This version contained only minor changes that were basically aimed at addressing some reliability concerns. These last two models' power output and basic specifications were the same as the original 82-40. Though the 82-40's stay as a Euclid model would be brief, it would continue on for a few more years in production, but this time with the TEREX name on its side.

Euclid Front-End Loaders

The Euclid Division's rubber-tired wheel loader program actually dates back to two experimental vehicles, built during the Euclid Road Machinery days. These were the four-wheel-steer and -drive 1FPM wheel dozer/grader, built in November 1949, and the rear-wheel-steer 1TPM military wheel dozer, introduced in June 1953. The engineering knowledge gained from these early creations would eventually lead Euclid into developing its own complete line of articulated-front-end wheel loaders, with most of the early experimental and prototype machines being built at the old Euclid Chardon Road facilities.

The smallest of the early Euclid Division front-end loaders was the Euclid L-7 (1QPM), sometimes referred to as the little "Q-P Doll" loader. The first pilot model of the unit was built in June 1956, and was rated at 0.7 cubic yards, or 19 cubic feet. It shared the same sheet metal design philosophy first introduced with the TC-12 dozer,

including dual headlights mounted in a single "Cyclops-eye" bezel. This light-mounting design would be a prominent fixture in the early loader program, and gave the machines a unique look, one not shared with any other manufacturer's products. The first L-7 was powered by a Waukesha FC series gasoline engine that was replaced by a 49-horsepower Continental F-162 gasoline-powered unit in the production version first introduced in July 1957. The engine, mounted in the rear of the unit, drove the front two wheels and used the small rear wheels to steer. In design, the production L-7 looked just like the original prototype, except the headlights were removed and replaced with a blanked-out panel with the "Euclid" name cast into it. The 1QPM was classified as a small utility loader and was in production until 1962.

The first rubber-tired front end loader built by Euclid of the articulated steering type was the 3UPM wheel loader. The first pilot model of this loader was built in early 1956, and was rated at 1.5 cubic yards. It was powered by a GM Diesel 3-71, two-cycle, three-cylinder engine rated at 107 horsepower, mated to a three-speed Allison CRT-3331 Torqmatic transmission. The 3UPM had all four wheels driven, and steered by means of an articulated frame, just in front of the operator's seating area. This gave the unit maneuvering characteristics that were far superior to the more common rear-wheel-steering loaders then available. After early engineering evaluations, a redesigned 3UPM loader was finally released as a preproduction model in mid-1958 as the Euclid L-20. This loader, still considered a 3UPM model, was still powered by the same GM 3-71 diesel engine found in the

Euclid produced its first prototype 0.7-cubic-yard front end loader, the 1QPM, in June 1956. The little loader was powered by a Waukesha FC series gasoline engine, which powered the front drive wheels. The 1QPM steered by means of its rear wheels, which were not powered. The headlight assembly seen here was only in the pilot stage and did not make it into production.

Euclid introduced the 1QPM as the L-7 series in July 1957. The L-7 was the first production front end loader to be released by the company, and was powered by a 49-horsepower Continental F-162 gasoline engine. The L-7 (shown here at the Euclid St. Clair plant in 1959) was often referred to as the little "Q-P Doll" loader.

prototype. Its capacity was also up a bit, and was now rated at 2 cubic yards. Another model called the 4UPM was also offered, and it was originally powered by a Waukesha 195GK series gasoline engine that was later replaced by a 101-horsepower Continental M-330, four-cycle, gasoline-powered unit. The 4UPM loaders looked the same as the diesel-powered 3UPM models.

As Euclid was releasing the first preproduction L-20 loaders, a slightly larger L-30 (5UPM) front end loader, rated at 2.5 cubic yards, was introduced in mid-1959. The 5UPM model looked very much like the early L-20, but was powered by a GM Diesel 4-71, four-cylinder engine, instead of the three-cylinder unit found in the 3UPM.

After months of testing of the 30 preproduction field units of the L-20 and L-30, extensive changes were made to the frame and axle mountings to help eliminate some odd handling characteristics when loading on uneven ground. Also, the outsides of the loaders were redesigned to keep in step with the rest of the product lines. Gone were the Cyclops-eyed headlight housings, replaced by a more traditional squared-off look. The first prototype of the new Euclid L-20 (7UPM) was finished in June 1961, and it was released officially in January 1962 as the first full-production, articulated-front-end loader built by the Euclid Division. The 7UPM model of the L-20 was rated as a 2.25-cubic-yard bucket machine powered by a single GM Diesel 3-71 rated at 109 gross horsepower and 105 fhp. The transmission was the same unit used in the earlier 3UPM model.

Introduced at the same time as the L-20 (7UPM) loader was its bigger 3-cubic-yard brother, the Euclid L-30 (9UPM), first manufactured in January 1962. The 9UPM model was powered by a GM Diesel 4-71 engine rated at 152 gross horsepower and 144 fhp. This was connected to the same type of Allison transmission found in the L-20 model.

Euclid introduced two new models of front end loaders in February 1964, targeted at rounding out its

loader product line. The smallest of the new loaders was the Euclid L-15 (2UPM), rated at 1.75 cubic yards. The 2UPM was powered by a GM Diesel 3-53N, two-cycle, three-cylinder engine rated at 101 gross horsepower and 93 fhp. The transmission was a two-speed Allison TT-2220 Torqmatic unit. The next loader released and positioned between the existing L-20 and L-30 models was the 2.5-cubic-yard Euclid L-25 (8UPM). This unit was powered by a GM Diesel 4-71 engine rated at 127 gross horsepower and 119 fhp and used the same transmission as the L-20 and L-30.

The one thing that makes identifying Euclid loaders difficult is that they all looked alike. If you were to cover up the model name, it would be almost impossible to tell which version was which. Things became even more confusing when upgraded models of the L-20, L-25, and L-30 were released in early 1965. The new L-20 (15UPM) was now rated as a 2.25-cubic-yard machine powered by a GM Diesel 4-71 engine rated at 128 gross horsepower and 119 fhp. The L-25 (16UPM) was classified as a 2.75-cubic-yard loader rated at 156 gross horsepower and 147 fhp from its GM 4-71 engine, which was connected to a new three-speed Allison CRT-3630 transmission. The L-30 (17UPM) was rated as a 3.25-cubic-yard model powered by a GM Diesel 6V-53N, two-cycle, six-cylinder rated at 180 gross horsepower and 171 fhp. Its transmission was the same Allison unit found in the new L-25.

Just when all of the Euclid salespeople and dealers were getting used to the new loaders, it was time to change the model names. In January 1966, the new "72-series" nomenclature went into effect for all loader models. The L-15 loader became the 72-10; the L-20 became the 72-20; the L-25 became the 72-30; and the L-30 changed to the 72-40. All specifications remained unchanged, but even this change would not last long.

By the end of 1966, Euclid was ready to release upgraded versions of its complete front loader product

The first experimental prototype Euclid 3UPM front end loader, built in July 1956 and featuring the articulated pivot-steering design. This 1.5-cubic-yard capacity machine was powered by a 107-gross horsepower GM Diesel 3-71 engine that drove all four wheels.

In mid-1958, Euclid released the first of the preproduction pivot-steer L-20 wheel loader field units, based on the redesigned 3UPM model from 1956. The new version, still referred to as a 3UPM model, was rated at 2 cubic yards, instead of the prototype's 1.5-cubic-yard capacity. This early L-20 is working in Sidney, Ohio, in May 1960.

Just after the release of the L-20 loader, Euclid introduced a slightly larger preproduction version called the L-30 series in mid-1959. The first model released, the 2.5-cubic-yard capacity 5UPM, was powered by a GM Diesel 4-71, four-cylinder engine, as opposed to the L-20's GM 3-71, three-cylinder unit.

After two pilot models of the L-X wheel loader were built, engineering test data provided by both units led directly to the production of the 72-80 model. Pictured in January 1968 at Euclid's St. Clair facilities is the first 72-80 front end loader, now classified as a 9-cubic-yard machine. The big loader was powered by a GM Diesel 12V-71T, turbocharged engine rated at 465 gross horsepower. This model did not become officially available until February 1969, when it was released as the Terex 72-81.

line. In October 1966, the first Euclid 72-21 was introduced, filling the 2-cubic-yard bucket class in the model line. The 72-21 was powered by a GM Diesel 3-71N engine rated at 115 gross horsepower and 107 fhp, mated to a two-stage Allison Hydro Power Shift TT-2220 transmission. In the next class up in size was the 2.5-cubic-yard Euclid 72-31, released in September 1966. The 72-31 was powered by a GM Diesel 4-71N, rated at 145 gross horsepower and 134 fhp, connected to a two-stage Allison Hydro Power Shift TT-2420 transmission. Next in line was the 3-cubic-yard Euclid 72-41 loader, introduced in November 1966. This model was also powered by the GM 4-71N engine, but one rated at 163 gross horsepower and 151 fhp. The transmission was a three-speed Allison CRT-3630 Torqmatic unit. The largest loader in the new line was the 3.5-cubic-yard Euclid 72-51, released in November 1966. The 72-51 was powered by a GM Diesel 6-71N engine rated at 202 gross horsepower and 191 fhp, connected to a two-stage Allison Hydro Power Shift TT-4420 transmission.

Comparing the old loader line and the new, the 72-21 replaced the 72-10; the 72-31 replaced the 72-20; the 72-41 replaced the 72-30; and the 72-51 replaced the 72-40. Once again, all of the models looked basically alike, and from a distance, it was almost impossible to tell one from another.

To help broaden Euclid's customer base for its pivot-steer wheel loaders, various optional pieces of equipment were made available that would enable the machines to perform a wide variety of additional tasks. Among the most popular of these options was the Drott 4-in-1 Bucket. Because of the hydraulically powered hinged bucket design, it could perform four basic earth-moving

Euclid officially introduced the full production version of its pivot-steer L-20 front end loader in January 1962. The production 7UPM model looked totally different from the early 3UPM version, and was now rated as a 2.25-cubic-yard loader. The engine was the same unit found in the early test units, with new power ratings of 109 gross horsepower and 105 fhp. Pictured at the Hudson plant in December 1962 is an L-20 wheel loader equipped with the optional Warner & Swasey Snap-Mount Backhoe attachment.

The Euclid L-X (18 UPM) front loader project was the company's first step toward entering the large front end loader market. The first 18UPM model, simply referred to as the Pilot No. 1 machine, was classified as a 6-cubic-yard class loader. The first unit built rolled out of the factory in May 1966, and was shipped to the GM Milford Proving Grounds to start its engineering evaluation testing. The L-X is pictured shortly after arriving at the Proving Grounds in June 1966.

In November 1966, Euclid released its new 72-51 series front end loader that took the place of the previous 72-40 version. The 72-51 was rated as a 3.5-cubic-yard machine, powered by a GM Diesel 6-71N engine rated at 202 gross horsepower and 191 fhp. The 72-51, shown in December 1967, loads a 12-ton capacity Euclid R-12, model 4UD rear dump, and is equipped with the optional larger tire and wheel combination.

jobs with one attachment. It could be utilized as a dozer, a scraper, a clamshell, and of course, a bucket loader.

If even more versatility was needed, the Warner & Swasey Snap-Mount Backhoe attachment could turn your ordinary wheel loader into a backhoe digging

tractor, and this attachment could be put on or removed in minutes. This attachment was first offered in 1963 for use with the L-20 and L-30 front end loaders. Other popular options included GABCO logging forks, and various forklift attachments, available for all of the wheel loader models.

The four loader models in the Euclid line were placed at the low end of the capacity scale, where sales volumes were high. Once these machines had established themselves in the marketplace, Euclid began work on much larger front end loaders in a program called the "L-X" project. The first experimental Pilot No. 1 Euclid L-X

(18UPM) wheel loader rolled out of the factory in May 1966. This first machine was immediately shipped to the GM Milford Proving Grounds for engineering evaluation testing. While it was there, in April 1967, a second pilot L-X model was finished. Both of these early loaders were 6-cubic-yard class machines. The engine in the L-X Pilot No. 2 version was a GM Diesel 8V-71T, two-cycle, turbocharged, eight-cylinder engine. Records do not indicate what engine configuration was in the L-X Pilot No.1.

After months of field testing of both prototype Euclid L-X loaders, a major redesign of the L-X loader was launched to increase power, capacity, and front

lifting arm strength. The fruits of this labor were unveiled in January 1968, as the 9-cubic-yard Euclid 72-80 wheel loader, which was followed by a second preproduction 72-80 in May 1968. The 72-80 was a big loader, and was a major engineering step for the designers at Euclid. It was powered by a GM Diesel 12V-71T, two-cycle, turbocharged, 12-cylinder engine connected to a three-speed Allison CRT-6033 Torqmatic transmission. But the 72-80 would never be sold as a Euclid model. A few months later this 9-cubic-yard loader would be released not as the Euclid 72-80, but as the Terex 72-81.

The Earth-King and the Return of the Haulers

During the time of General Motors ownership of the Euclid Division, the earth-moving industry had undergone major changes, in both the marketing of machines and the technology built into these products. Euclid always depended on the strength of its hauler and scraper sales to maintain the company's profits while new product lines were being designed and tested. Launching the new tracked dozer and wheel loader model lines, not to mention the factory expansions required to build them, was a very expensive endeavor.

At the same time, Euclid's competitors in these areas, such as Caterpillar and International Harvester (IHC), were selling their dozers and loaders in very large numbers. And when these companies introduced their off-road rear dumps, Euclid started to feel the heat. While Euclid was trying to play catch-up, or reach an equal footing with its newer product lines, the other companies were out making big profits. This was not to say that Euclid was not profitable, just not as much as GM thought it would have been when it purchased the company back in 1953. For GM's investment of 305,137 shares of unissued stock, valued at about $20 million, to purchase Euclid Road Machinery, there were probably expectations of the Euclid Division becoming the next Caterpillar. After all, GM controlled around 50 percent of new auto sales in the United States and had virtually unlimited resources to draw on. This fact did not go unnoticed by other manufacturers in the industry, but that's life in a free market society. Or was it? Good old Uncle Sam didn't think so, and decided to poke the giant automaker in the side with a big legal stick to get its attention.

On October 15, 1959, the Department of Justice, under Attorney General Robert Kennedy, issued an antitrust civil suit against General Motors Corporation in U.S. District Court in New York City, under Section 7 of the Act of Congress of October 15, 1914, entitled "An Act to Supplement Existing Laws Against Unlawful Restraints and Monopolies and for Other Purposes," better known as the Clayton Act.

The federal government felt that GM posed too great a threat of controlling the off-road hauler market and would force its competitors out of business. Of course, GM denied these charges and fought the government, and for the next eight years, this suit lingered behind the scenes of normal division and company operating procedures. To most, it was business as usual. But it was soon becoming clear to GM that the federal government was not going to back down on this issue.

General Motors confirmed on January 19, 1967, that it had held exploratory discussions with the White Motor Corporation, located in Cleveland, Ohio, regarding a possible sale of a portion of the assets of the Euclid Division to White. But these discussions were discontinued when an agreement in principle, satisfactory to all parties, including the Justice Department, could not be reached. On August 1, 1967, GM announced that it would again reopen negotiations for the proposed sale of certain assets of the Euclid Division, now that it had worked out an agreement in principle on settlement terms with the Department of Justice. These details included the sale of Euclid's manufacturing plants in Euclid, Ohio, including certain equipment that was part of the original Euclid Road Machinery Company in 1953. This included the rear dump haulers, bottom dump trailers and their tractors, an option for a license to produce scrapers, and all logo and trademark symbols relating to the "Euclid" brand name. Also included in the proposed settlement was an arrangement under which the buyer would initially be required to franchise the off-highway haulers being acquired from GM to its Euclid Division dealers, both in and outside the United States.

White Motor Corporation was once again interested in part of the Euclid Division, now that an agreement had been reached with the Department of Justice. On February 5, 1968, White officially announced that it

Shown working at Marmoraton Mining, located in Marmora, Ontario, on May 18, 1971, is the first 150-ton-capacity Terex 33-15 diesel-electric-drive hauler to go into service. This truck was considered pilot No. 2. A pilot No. 1 test truck was built in September 1970, but was soon scrapped. The first pilot was basically an experimental test bed and never went into service. The 33-15 was powered by a GM Detroit Diesel 16V-149TI, rated at 1,600 gross horsepower and 1,445 fhp.

The Terex 33-22 hauler was one of the carryover Euclid Division designs that could be built by the Diesel Division in Canada. The 33-22 was powered by a GM Detroit Diesel 6-71N engine rated at 238 gross horsepower and 226 fhp, and carried a payload capacity of 22 tons. The 33-22 was essentially an old Euclid R-22, model 103FD. The truck was sold at first in Canada as the Terex R-22, then in July 1971 it was changed to the Terex 33-22. After July 1, 1972, the hauler was offered in the United States as the Terex 33-03. Same truck, just different forms of identification. *GM Diesel Division Archives*

had purchased the off-highway hauler product lines from GM's Euclid Division for $24 million in cash and notes. With the sale, GM agreed not to build or sell a competing hauler product, or parts associated with these products in the United States, for four years, from July 1, 1968, to July 1, 1972. GM retained the right to build and market haulers from its factories in Canada and at the Motherwell plant in Scotland. These machines just could not be imported for sale in the United States.

White Motors also agreed to offer GM equipment dealers franchise agreements for three years, ending June 30, 1971, and to accept, under certain conditions, orders for haulers necessary to meet the requirements of dealers during the fourth year of the GM ban. This would give the GM dealers a truck line to sell, along with their other products. This also gave Euclid, Inc. the new name for the White Motors subsidiary, a temporary dealer network in the United States. On the down side, Euclid, Inc. would lose its

The Terex R-65 (16LD) was another of the older Euclid-designed models later built by the Diesel Division in Canada. The R-65 was powered by a GM Detroit Diesel engine rated at 700 gross horsepower and 654 fhp. The truck's payload capacity was 65 tons. In July 1971, the hauler's model identification was changed to the Terex 33-65. One of the first Terex R-65 haulers to be produced in Canada is shown at the Diesel Division plant in London, Ontario, in September 1969. *GM Diesel Division Archives*

The smallest rear dump hauler built by Terex was the R-17, which was in production from 1968 to 1984. The 17-ton-capacity hauler was built in Scotland, and was offered with two engine choices, a GM Detroit Diesel 6-71N, rated at 238 gross horsepower and 224 fhp, or a Cummins N-855-C220 diesel, rated at 220 gross horsepower and 212 fhp. The R-17 model was not offered in the United States. *Terex Equipment, Ltd.*

entire international dealer network, since this still belonged to GM. This would have to be rebuilt from scratch.

Once the announcement was finalized, the Euclid Division's white-collar office workers were given the choice of staying with GM or joining Euclid, Inc. The majority of the hourly workers in St. Clair plants No. 1 and No. 2 automatically became Euclid, Inc. employees. GM workers at the Hudson plant were unaffected.

To many, it did not make sense for the government to pursue GM as it did over a purported monopoly in the haul truck field. Almost all of Euclid Division's competitors now had their own haul truck lines. Many in the industry felt at the time the suit was really because of the type of engines that were being installed in the majority of GM equipment—mainly GM's own Detroit Diesel engines—with Cummins diesels offered as alternates. Before 1953, the vast majority of engines in Euclids were Cummins units. Whatever the reason, what was done is done.

In the wake of the suit, it was time for GM to concentrate on the business of developing and selling new earth-moving machines. In 1967 and 1968, earth-moving equipment sales as a whole for the industry were down. This was even more pronounced at the Euclid Division, where the antitrust suit played havoc on sales, marketing, and most important, customer confidence. Now that GM no longer had the use of the Euclid name, an entirely new

corporate identity was required. As of July 1, 1968, the Earthmoving Equipment Division of General Motors would serve as the new product name, at least until marketing had the time to come up with something better. By August 1968, the selection of a new product identification name was finally reduced to three possibilities, Ram, Husky, or Terex. After a series of test logo designs was tried on different pieces of equipment at the factory, it was decided that Terex, from the Latin words terra, meaning earth, and rex meaning king, would be the new product line name. In October 1968, after three months of having no name for its machines, Terex became the new brand name for the equipment, but the corporate division name would still remain the Earthmoving Equipment Division of GM. It was not until July 1, 1970, that the division name was officially changed to the Terex Division. Though the name was new, the Hi-Lite green paint color would remain, with only a slight change in the shade.

Terex Rear Dump Haulers

With marketing well in hand, it was now the Terex engineers' turn to do something about designing an entirely new hauler line from the ground up. Even though GM was not allowed to sell or promote haulers in the United States, it could still engineer and test prototype units during the design phase of the program.

The 40-ton-capacity hauler in the Terex product line was the 33-07, officially introduced on July 1, 1972, along with the other new 33-series trucks that were being released at the same time. The 33-07 was powered by a GM Detroit Diesel 12V-71T, rated at 525 gross horsepower and 493 fhp. The first pilot model of this truck was built in May 1971.

During the early planning stages of the new models, it was up to the other GM plants in Canada and Scotland to supply rear dumps in their respective markets. These trucks were the same models being built previously by the Euclid Division. In a way, Euclid, Inc. was now building the same R-series haulers that Terex was also producing in Canada and Scotland. It would not be until 1969, that Euclid, Inc. would design new front grilles, hoods, and fenders for its R-series, giving them a more distinctive appearance.

The haulers available from the Diesel Division, General Motors of Canada, Ltd. were the R-22 (101FD and 103FD); R-35 (74TD); R-45 (10LD and 11LD); R-50 (12LD); and R-65 (16LD). At General Motors Scotland, Ltd., production was maintained on the R-17, R-22, R-25, R-35S, R-35, R-45, and the R-65 rear dump haulers. The R-X model line was never built outside of the United States, so all manufacturing rights were transferred to Euclid, Inc. where the truck eventually became known as the R-105.

The first of the new "33-series" models to reach prototype stage was the Terex 33-05, in September 1970. Though this hauler was initially referred to as the 33-27 (AA) during its early design phase, it was decided that the tonnage rating should be taken out of the model designation to simplify the model line nomenclature, because capacity ratings would inevitably change. The "33" in the model's identification was the engineering number assigned to the rear-dump product line. The 33-05 was but the first of the 33-series trucks that were being designed simultaneously by Terex engineering. In March 1971, the first pilot Terex 33-07 hauler was built. This was followed by the 33-11 in August 1971. In Canada, the Diesel Division was responsible for the development of the new diesel-electric drive truck line. The first truck, the Terex 33-15, was officially put into service at a Canadian mining operation in May 1971, for evaluation testing. All of the new trucks carried the distinctive "keystone" front ends, a design feature that would come to symbolize Terex equipment worldwide. The haulers were very handsome designs that were a complete departure from the Euclid Division days. Even though pilot trucks were built and in various prototype testing stages, the mechanical drive haulers built in Ohio could not be offered for sale because of the moratorium on U.S. truck sales, as stipulated by the antitrust settlement agreement. However, the 33-15 diesel-electric drive hauler being built in Canada was allowed to be sold, just not in the United States. In fact, the 33-15 was displayed at the AMC mining show in Las Vegas in

Terex introduced a new truck model, the 33-09, into its hauler line in April 1974. The 33-09 was a 55-ton-capacity rear dump, powered by a GM Detroit Diesel 16V-71T, rated at 665 gross horsepower and 624 fhp. The first pilot model of this truck was completed in November 1972.

October 1971. This was permitted, as long as it was stated on the truck and in any sales literature, that the unit was not for sale in the United States. After the show, the display truck was shipped back to Canada.

The testing of the original seven pilot trucks was crucial to the success of the new Terex model line. GM had given the division a blank check to develop the trucks, allowing the engineers to build the best, most-modern truck, from the ground up. They had to be right from the very beginning. There were three pilot models of the 33-05 hauler built. The 33-05 pilot truck No. 1 spent most of its testing time at the GM Milford Proving Grounds in Michigan. Pilot No. 2 was shipped from the Proving Grounds to Johns Manville Asbestos Corporation's Reeves Mine, west of Timmins, Ontario, for field testing. Pilot No. 3 was used for stress check tests at the Terex Division's Engineering & Research Center in Hudson, Ohio. From there, it was shipped to the Proving Grounds, then off to a customer's site for field testing. The 33-07 pilot truck No. 1 worked at National Steel Corporation of Canada, Ltd.'s Moose Mountain mine in Capreol, Ontario. The 33-07 pilot truck No. 2 was also placed at the Moose Mountain mine after a brief stay at the Proving Grounds. The 33-07 pilot truck No. 3, after completing a series of stress

checks at the Hudson engineering center, was shipped to the Proving Grounds in Michigan.

The single 33-11 pilot truck was first tested at the Proving Grounds, then shipped to a Cleveland Cliff's mine in Temagami, Ontario, in May 1972. All the pilot trucks were put through extensive, and sometimes brutal testing and working scenarios. Engines were changed, transmissions swapped, haulers torn down, inspected, rebuilt, and torn down again. Nothing was left to chance. The working availability of the pilot models proved to be excellent. Terex felt it had a winner.

The Terex Division could re-enter the off-road truck market on July 1, 1972. To prepare for this, fabrication of production bodies and frames started in April 1972. These early parts were considered subassemblies, and were allowable under the settlement; Terex just could not begin final line assembly of a truck.

The official "closing date" in the sales agreement with White Motors was June 28, 1968, at 10 A.M. In theory, Terex could start assembling its trucks at 10:01 A.M., on June 28, 1972. Eventually, it was decided to start the final line assembly on July 3, 1972, which was the first working day of the month. The new mechanical drive haulers were to be built at the division's Terex-West

Shown working at a mine site in Ontario, Canada, in August 1973 is one of the first production versions of the 80-ton-capacity Terex 33-11 series haulers. The 33-11 was powered by a GM Detroit Diesel 16V-71TI engine rated at 800 gross horsepower and 758 fhp. The first pilot model of the 33-11 was built in August 1971.

plant, in Brooklyn, a suburb of Cleveland. The 760,000-square foot facility was acquired by Terex in December 1969 from the GM Fisher Body Division. The plant would also build scrapers and large wheel loaders. This facility had formerly been used by Euclid Division in the 1950s. The first haulers to be produced were limited-production units that were followed closely by Terex sales and engineering teams. Initial build numbers of these special units were: 23 of the 33-05 haulers in July 1972; 25 of the 33-07 haulers in August; and 10 of the 33-11 haulers in September. Full production commenced about six months later, in early 1973.

Instead of going to the expense of duplicating tooling costs to build the diesel-electric-drive 150-ton capacity 33-15, the truck was imported into the United States from the Diesel Division in Canada. A reciprocal trade agreement between the two countries permitted duty-free shipments of haulers in both directions. Terex was also going to continue building the old R-series trucks in Canada for as long as there was a demand for them. To bring them more into the family of the new 33-series haulers, the model designations were officially changed in July 1971 to

33-22 (from R-22), 33-35 (R-35), 33-45 (R-45), and 33-65 (R-65). The 33-22 was also sold in the United States as the 33-03. The R-50 model was discontinued.

The older haulers being built in Scotland would still be referred to as R-series trucks. Model types for the most part were the same as the units in Canada and older GM Euclid Division designs, with only minor specification differences. But a few models were built in Scotland exclusively for the U.K. market. The smallest of these was the 17-ton-capacity Terex R-17 rear dump, originally introduced in May 1968 as a Euclid model. When the first R-17 unit was shipped in August 1968, GM had already divested itself of the Euclid name in the United States, and the Terex name had not yet been put in place. To top it off, the old GM business name of the overseas company, Euclid (Great Britain), Ltd. was not changed until December 1968, when it became General Motors Scotland, Ltd. It is probably best to refer to these early trucks as Terex units, since it is less confusing than just calling them GM R-17 rear dumps.

The R-17, model B15FD, was powered by a GM Diesel 6-71N, two-cycle, six-cylinder engine rated at 238 gross horsepower and 224 fhp. The R-17, model B16FD, was equipped with a Cummins N-743-C220, four-cycle, six-cylinder diesel, rated at 220 gross horsepower and 208 fhp. The R-17 was a steady seller to smaller quarry operations, and to customers where a "low-tech" truck was preferred to a more complicated and expensive model. The little green truck was in the Terex product line as late as 1984, so it must have been doing something right to justify its 16-year production life span.

The next model built in Scotland, aimed primarily at developing countries, was the Terex R-25, announced at the same time as the R-17. What was previously said about the R-17's name heritage also goes for the R-25, as the first unit of this model was shipped in October 1968. The R-25 hauler's history actually dates back to the Euclid 22-ton-capacity model B1TD from October 1953. The R-25 was still available as a model B1TD when it became a Terex unit. Except for a new cab design in the early 1970s, the truck looked like it did back in 1953. The model B1TD was powered by a Rolls Royce C6SFL, four-cycle, six-cylinder, supercharged diesel engine rated at 275 gross horsepower and 260 fhp. The B3TD was the Cummins-engined version of the R-25. This model utilized a Cummins NT-855-C335, four-cycle, six-cylinder "Turbo-Diesel," rated at 305 gross horsepower and 290 fhp. A GM-powered version of the R-25 was introduced in November 1973, model B18TD, with a GM Diesel 8V-71N, two-cycle, eight-cylinder engine. In 1975, the model identification nomenclature was dropped and the trucks were simply known as Terex R-25 rear dumps, with only the Cummins-engined version being offered in 1975. This hauler was in the European product line as late as 1982. After a 29-year production run, the oldest design of any Euclid/Terex truck still being built was finally retired.

The 33-14 was the largest-capacity mechanical-drive rear dump hauler ever built by the Terex Division. The prototype 33-14 was officially introduced at the American Mining Congress Convention, in Las Vegas, Nevada, in October 1978. Production versions of the truck were powered by a GM Detroit Diesel 12V-149TI engine rated at 1,200 gross horsepower and 1,092 fhp. The payload capacity of the early 33-14 hauler was 120 tons. In 1988, the last year of production for this model for Terex, the 33-14B version was rated as a 138-ton-capacity hauler.

This publicity shot at the Terex 33-15 was taken at an open house event held at the Diesel Division in London, Ontario, in late 1971. The truck featured a redesigned front end and better ladder placements, though the keystone wings on either side of the ladder steps did not make it into final production. Even though this truck is equipped with the box-type Farr-designed air cleaners, most 33-15 haulers went into service with the round Donaldson units. The few that did make it into the field with the Farr air cleaners were soon retrofitted with the Donaldson units. The 33-15 stood 18 feet, 7 inches to the top of the spill guard, was 41 feet, 9 inches in length, and rode on six 36.00x51, 58PR tires. Total weight of the hauler was 235,000 pounds, and 535,000 pounds with a payload. *GM Diesel Division Archives*

General Motors Scotland, Ltd. produced two types of 35-ton-capacity rear dumps. The Terex R-35 was based on the older Euclid Division designs and there was very little difference between the two truck types. The Terex R-35S was an upgraded-capacity R-30, once again dating back to the GM Euclid years. The R-35S front suspension was a leaf spring, I-beam affair, just like the one that was found on the old R-30. The dump body was also of the old style, as opposed to the V-profile unit on the R-35. The R-35S was used as a Terex price leader in that capacity range.

A similar situation was also true for the Terex R-50, introduced in 1972. The R-50, model B19LD, was simply an improved R-45, with a more powerful GM Diesel 16V-71N engine rated at 580 gross horsepower and 546 fhp, and five tons more capacity. This R-50 is not the same as the GM Euclid Division-built model from 1965. The R-50 built in Scotland retained the old leaf spring front suspension and dump body design found on the R-45 version.

The largest of the older R-series haulers to be built was the Terex R-70, model B21LD. This model was an upgraded R-65, powered by a GM 16V-71NT, two-cycle, 16-cylinder diesel engine rated at 700 gross horsepower and 654 fhp. The major differences between the two trucks, besides an increase in capacity to 70 tons, was a redesigned operator's cab and a larger tire-and-wheel combination, with increased ply ratings. Even

though the R-70 was introduced in 1968 as a Euclid model, the first unit actually built was shipped in June, 1972. Records seem to indicate the counterpart to the R-65 being built in Canada, the 33-65, was never upgraded into a production 70-ton version.

During the 1970s, the Terex Division in the United States had a very impressive hauler product line consisting of nine different 33-series hauler types, including both rear

and bottom dump offerings. Three of the nine models were built by the Diesel Division in Canada, the smallest of which was the Terex 33-03. After July 1, 1972, the 22-ton capacity 33-03 was allowed to be imported into the United States to round out the new Terex hauler line. The hauler had previously been sold in Canada as the R-22, then as the 33-22, before finally becoming the 33-03. All were direct descendants of GM Euclid Division's R-22 rear

Shown working in 1979 at a Kaiser Steel Corporation's mine in Raton, New Mexico, is one of the first 34-11C coal haulers to be put into service. The 150-ton-capacity bottom dump trailer was pulled by a modified 33-11C hauler powered by a GM Detroit Diesel 16V-92TA, turbocharged and aftercooled engine rated at 880 gross horsepower and 840 fhp. The total length of the 34-11C was 76 feet, 5 inches.

dump—and were, in fact, virtually the same truck. The 33-03 was powered by a GM 6-71N, two-cycle, six-cylinder diesel engine rated at 238 gross horsepower and 226 fhp. This was matched with a six-speed Allison CLBT-4460, full power shift transmission. Major dimensions were the same as that for the GM Euclid R-22. In other words, the two trucks looked exactly alike. In 1978, an upgraded version was introduced as the 33-03B, also produced in Canada. The first European 33-03B was built at the Terex Luxembourg plant and shipped in December 1977. The Canadian-built 33-03B continued to use the same GM diesel engine found in the previous model, but power ratings were 228 gross horsepower and 215 fhp. The former six-speed transmission was changed to a five-speed Allison CLBT-750, semi-automatic unit. On the outside, the truck sported a new hood and "keystone" grille front end. Its capacity remained unchanged. The 33-03B was the last of the old R-series-based designs produced in Canada. All of the other older haulers had been dropped from the product lines by 1974.

The smallest Terex 33-series rear dump hauler built in the United States was the 33-05, which carried a rated capacity of 28 tons when first released. The 33-05 was powered by a Detroit Diesel 8V-71T, two-cycle, eight-cylinder engine rated at 350 gross horsepower and 321 fhp. The transmission was a five-speed Allison CLBT-750, semi-automatic unit. In 1975, an improved 33-05B version was released, with a new payload capacity rating of 30 tons. The drivetrain remained unchanged except for new optional drive axle ratios. The "B" model improvements did not affect the look of the truck, since most were in areas of reliability and a general "fine-tuning" of existing components.

The Terex 33-07 was released at the same time as the 33-05. The 33-07 was classified as a 40-ton-capacity

hauler, powered by a Detroit Diesel 12V-71T, two-cycle, 12-cylinder engine rated at 525 gross horsepower and 493 fhp. This was mated to a proven six-speed Allison CLBT-5960 transmission. During the next few years, the truck only received minor component improvements, in line with normal product development. The 33-07 was a very popular truck and was basically the right design from day one.

When Terex released its first three U.S.-built haulers in 1972, plans were well under way to add an additional model in the 55-ton-capacity class, to be known as the 33-09. The first pilot 33-09 was built in November 1972, and performed for months in preproduction engineering evaluation testing. In April 1974, the final prototype version was approved for full production. The 33-09 had a visually longer nose than previous Terex trucks to accommodate its Detroit Diesel 16V-71T, two-cycle, 16-cylinder engine, which was rated at 665 gross horsepower and 624 fhp. This was teamed up with a six-speed Allison CLBT-6061 transmission. Like the 33-07 before it, the 33-09 received only minor improvements not requiring a new model designation while being built by Terex Division.

The Terex 33-11 was the third model produced of the early 33-series mechanical drive rear dumps. The 33-11 was rated at 80 tons capacity, one of the most competitive payload classes for haulers in the industry. This 33-11 was equipped with a Detroit Diesel 16V-71TI, two-cycle, 16-cylinder engine rated at 800 gross horsepower and 758 fhp, connected to a six-speed Allison DP-8961 automatic transmission.

In 1975, an improved 80-ton-capacity 33-11B model was introduced, featuring a Detroit Diesel 16V-92T, two-cycle, 16-cylinder engine rated at 860 gross horsepower and 800 fhp, utilizing the same Allison transmission. In 1976, the 33-11B received an increase in capacity to 85 tons. This was achieved mainly through a larger dump body, brake, and tire-and-rim upgrades.

More changes were in store for this model when the 33-11C version was released in 1978. More power was available from the Detroit Diesel 16V-92TA engine, rated at 880 gross horsepower and 840 fhp, due mainly to an aftercooler being added to the turbocharged 16-cylinder diesel. Transmission and capacity ratings remained unchanged. An optional larger tire package was also made available. The 33-11C was also available with a Philippi-Hagenbuch coal body, rated at 90 tons capacity. The competition of the class was evident by how often manufacturers update a particular model, to get the upper hand in making a sale. And this 85-ton class was the most crowded of all, so Terex again had to up the ante by introducing a 33-11D model in May 1980. This model now featured an oil-cooled disc brake system, offering increased braking capacity, improved retarding capabilities for long downhill hauls, and extended component life. All other specifications were unchanged from the 33-11C, which remained in the product line to offer customers a choice between the two different types of braking systems.

The largest of all 33-series mechanical drive haulers produced by Terex was the 33-14, introduced at the October 1978, American Mining Congress Convention, held in Las Vegas, Nevada. The prototype truck was assembled at Terex Division's Engineering and Research facility in Hudson, Ohio. About the only thing that the 33-14 shared with its small brothers was the environmental operator's cab and the paint color. The 33-14 was a beefy design, rated at 120 tons capacity. The hauler was powered by a Detroit Diesel 12V-149TI, two-cycle, 12-cylinder engine, originally rated at 1,350 gross horsepower and 1,240 fhp, in the first prototype truck. Production versions had their power outputs lowered to 1,200 gross horsepower and 1,092 fhp. The 12-cylinder diesel was mated to a six-speed Allison CLBT-9680, fully automatic transmission, with a hydraulic dynamic braking retarder. The hauler also featured nitrogen-over-oil suspension, considered the best system for large mining trucks.

The "big-boys" in the Terex hauler line were the two diesel-electric-drive trucks built by the Diesel Division, General Motors of Canada Ltd., in London Ontario. These were the 150/170-ton-capacity Terex 33-15 and the monstrous 350-ton-rated Terex 33-19 Titan hauler. Since the Titan is a story in itself, it will be covered separately in chapter 6.

The 33-15 hauler was originally introduced with the three original, smaller 33-series haulers in 1972. The first pilot model, nicknamed "Fat Albert," started testing in September 1970. The Fat Albert 33-15 hauler was never put into active service and was soon scrapped. The second pilot prototype truck went into service at Marmoraton Mining, a division of Bethlehem Steel, in Marmora, Ontario, in May 1971. It was later moved to the Pine Point Mine, in the Northwest Territories, Canada, in October 1971. The production 33-15 model was rated at 150 tons payload capacity in its 85-cubic-yards struck and 115-cubic-yards heaped dump body. The 33-15 was powered by a Detroit Diesel 16V-149TI, two-cycle, turbocharged and intercooled 16-cylinder engine rated at 1,600 gross horsepower and 1,445 fhp. The 33-15 did not rely on the use of a mechanical type of transmission found in the smaller Terex trucks, but instead utilized an electric-drive system. In this type of system, the engine drives an AC generator. A solid state rectifier bank then converts the AC output of the generator to DC, which is supplied to the two GM D79, direct current traction motors located in the rear axle. The traction motors were similar to the same units being used on locomotives, except for the way they were mounted. These same motors also acted as dynamic brakes, capable of developing 2,700 horsepower (2,014 kilowatts) of braking energy produced by the rotating rear wheels. This energy was converted to electrical power by the traction motors operating in generator mode. The power was then conducted to fully fan-blown grids and dissipated as heat.

The truck would be brought to a full stop by the operator applying the normal service brakes. This system was best utilized when the hauler was going down steep grades, thus extending the life span of the regular braking system. The front radiator housing was in the characteristic Terex keystone shape, and it also contained two ladders for mounting and dismounting of the truck. Because the built-in ladders in the front were vertically mounted, operators found them a bit on the treacherous side. A modified front end was made available in late 1971 that mounted the ladders at an angle on either side of the radiator shroud, which helped reduce the chances for injury.

In January 1975, Terex introduced an improved 33-15B model. The 33-15B version now carried a payload capacity of 170 tons. Other than updated GM D79-CFA traction motors, most of the other major specifications remained unchanged. In 1980, the hauler received a redesigned dump body, and its Donaldson SRG air filters on the front of the truck were rotated 90 degrees to provide better operator visibility and for easier maintenance. Tonnage capacity remained unchanged.

Terex Division also offered a coal bottom dump tractor/trailer combination in the form of the 150-ton-capacity Terex 34-11C. The 34-11C project actually started with a pilot model built by Terex called the CH-125, dating back to December 1973. This 125-ton-capacity prototype was tested, but never went into production. The basic design of the CH-125 was used as the pattern for the 150-ton unit. The 34-11C concept was announced in August 1977, with the first unit assembled in late 1978. This was the first of three such units ordered by Kaiser Steel Corporation, Raton, New Mexico. The tractor portion of the bottom dump was a modified 33-11C hauler. Changes were made mainly to the exhaust, hydraulics, and air systems. The engine, transmission, and power ratings were the same as those of the standard rear dump model. The coal hopper itself was rated at 180 cubic yards struck and 205 cubic yards heaped. Total gross weight, including payload, was 480,000 pounds (240 tons). Terex had also announced plans in May 1980 to introduce a 120-ton-capacity 34-09 dirt bottom dump hauler, based on the 33-09 truck. But no 34-09 bottom dump was ever built by the GM Terex Division.

Terex had made plans for two other ultra-large-capacity haulers in the late 1970s. The first was a 240-ton-capacity coal bottom dump trailer to go with a tractor version of the 33-15B. The trailer was designed in 1976 and Terex was initially prepared to build three units for use in the United States or Canada. But for whatever reasons, the tractor/trailer combination was never produced. The second hauler proposed but never built was the Terex 33-17, 200-ton-capacity diesel-electric drive rear dump. This truck was originally announced in September 1978, with availability scheduled for sometime in 1980. Unfortunately, a soft market and worsening worldwide economic conditions caused the cancellation of the 200-ton hauler project.

The World's
Largest Truck

While Terex Division was busy planning its new hauler line in late 1968 and throughout 1969, an eye was cast further down the road as to where the large open pit and surface mines might be in terms of scale.

The Terex people involved with new product market research, relying on data obtained through mathematical modeling and computer analysis of the economics of scale in high-volume material handling systems, determined that a hauler of great capacity would be needed to fill the projected needs. Terex was already well into the development stages of the 33-15 project to meet the mining industry's current needs. But what about a few years down the road? If current trends were any indication, a truck with double the capacity of the 33-15 unit was going to be sought after. The Terex Division was determined to be there first with a field-tested hauler ready to take on all comers. Terex wanted to show the industry that it could do more than just catch up with everyone else, that it had the engineering and design might to become the leader in the haul truck field.

Early projections of an ultra-large rear dump hauler, built with technology currently available, put the payload capacity in the neighborhood of 250 tons. This was based on two major areas of component availability, an engine of suitable power, and tires of an adequate size to handle the power and carry the load. The largest tires then available from more than two suppliers were the 36.00x51, 58PR-sized units. Terex determined that a three-axle configuration using 10 tires would be needed instead of a two-axle truck with only six tires.

During the early planning stages of the big truck, the competition was coming to market with haulers that were aimed at the same market. Between 1970 and 1971, prototype large-capacity trucks were put into operation by a number of manufacturers. These were the Unit Rig Lectra Haul M-200, the Dart DE-2991, and the WABCO

Haulpak 3200. These were all initially 200-ton capacity rear dumps, with the Haulpak 3200 being upgraded from a 200- to 235-ton machine shortly after it was introduced. One hauler being tested by Peerless, the 250-ton-capacity VCON 3006, was right in line, as far as capacity, with what Terex was considering. But the actual field tests of these units gave the engineers at Terex a chance to see how a hauler of this type would perform in the real world. It was soon evident that the tires were the shortcomings of many of these early trucks. These haulers all utilized the 36.00x51 tires (33.00x51 on the Haulpak 3200). In the case of the Unit Rig and Dart two-axle trucks, these tires kept them from attaining their rated payload. On paper, the tires should have worked, but in real mining conditions, they were not up to the task. If Terex was going to build its truck, it would need a tire larger than the 36.00x51 to do it.

Tire manufacturers were not blind to the shortcomings of the then-available haul tires for large mining trucks. A larger tire was in the works to address many of the problems these haulers were experiencing. This tire, the 40.00x57, would be one of the most important developments in the design of Terex's ultra-large truck. With the availability of this new class of tire, a new target capacity of 350 tons could be reached. In essence, Terex designed the 33-19 "Titan" hauler, as it was now called, around these tires.

The 350-ton-capacity hauler would use a diesel-electric drive system, like the one used in the 33-15. But the largest Detroit Diesel engine that GM had available was the 16V-149TI model, rated at 1,600 horsepower. This was nowhere close to the power that was going to be needed to haul a 350-ton load. So GM looked to another of its divisions, the Electro-Motive Division (EMD), to supply the necessary powerplant. EMD produced a family of 645-cubic inch (ci) per cylinder displacement, "V" type locomotive engines that were available in 8-, 12-, 16-, and 20-cylinder configurations. The engine that achieved Terex's power-to-weight ratios for off-highway use was the 10,032-ci (169.5-liter) EMD Model 16-645E4. This was a two-cycle, turbocharged and aftercooled 16-cylinder engine rated at 3,300 gross

This image of the 33-19 Titan was taken just a few days before the official opening of the American Mining Congress Convention, October 7–10, 1974, in Las Vegas, Nevada. Again, the size of the truck is put into perspective by the small boy standing by one of the front tires of the hauler.

The models on the 350-ton-capacity Terex 33-19 Titan hauler, shown on June 5, 1974, at the Diesel Division plant, in London, Ontario, Canada, provide a clear size reference of just how big the 33-19 actually was. It measured 25 feet, 7 inches wide and 66 feet in length. *GM Diesel Division Archives*

horsepower and 3,000 fhp at 900 rpm, with an idle speed of only 315 rpm. The locomotive engines, with their peak power outputs available at such low rpm, were some of the most reliable and longest-lasting diesel engines. The one big drawback was their weight. In a locomotive, where they were intended to be used, this wasn't a big concern. But in a haul truck, that weight steals from payload capacity and puts a larger strain on the front steering axle. But for the Terex engineers, it was this engine or none at all. There simply was not a higher-revving, lighter diesel engine available at the time.

With the drivetrain, tires, axle configuration, and capacity established, it was now time to put all systems together. By October 1971, design specifications for the 350-ton-capacity 33-19 "Concept No. 2" hauler were finalized; it was to be built by the Diesel Division, General Motors of Canada, Ltd. in London, Ontario. The 33-19 diesel-electric-drive system functioned in the same way as the system used in the 150-ton-capacity 33-15 hauler. The big EMD V-16 engine was directly coupled to an EMD AR10-D14 alternator with built-in three-phase full-wave rectification, rated at 1,250V DC. A power take-off at the back end of the main alternator was used to drive the hoist pumps, and the front and rear steering pumps. The alternators' primary function was to

supply power to the four rear D79CFA series-wound DC traction motors, two of which were mounted inside each axle housing. Each motor powered one wheel through a pinion and bull gear arrangement to outboard-mounted planetary gears. At 2,700 traction motor rpm, top speed of the hauler was 30 mph.

Three braking systems were utilized. As in the 33-15 hauler, the traction motors in the rear axles could be used as generators to help stop the hauler on steep downhill grades by means of dynamic retarding. The power the motors generated was conducted to grid resistors, where the energy was dissipated as heat. The operator could modulate the braking effect by use of a separate brake pedal, and bring the unit to a complete stop by applying the regular service brakes. The engine was cooled by means of two large radiators mounted on the left and right sides of the front end. Each section had its own hydraulically driven, thermostatically controlled, 68-inch-diameter fan to keep temperatures in an acceptable operating range. The cooling controls would open the radiator shutters and fully engage the fans when temperatures rose above 185 degrees Fahrenheit, and close the shutters and de-energize the fan motors when 175 degrees Fahrenheit was reached. The entire system was designed to operate in 120 degrees Fahrenheit maximum ambient outside temperature, an operating range the hauler was working in quite often early on in its field testing. The entire engine assembly was fully enclosed and pressurized with filtered air to keep the powerplant as clean as possible. Walkways on either side of the engine compartment allowed maintenance engineers to gain access through a series of hinged doors. Additional access doors were located in the nose of the truck, between the two large radiator housings. The complete power module assembly was suspended in the truck frame on three suspension points. This permitted easy removal of the unit, either out through the front of the truck, or straight up, after removal of a bolted-on top portion of the front axle cross-member.

The axles and suspensions on the 33-19 were each designed to address separate problems that affected the handling of the unit. The rear-drive tandem-axles had the ability to turn five degrees, an action controlled by the amount and direction the front wheels were turned. A 15-degree steering trip point for right and left front turns would trigger the rear steering axles. This system helped lessen the tendency of the tandem-drive truck to understeer, or "snow-plow." As originally installed, the system would steer the rear axles in one of three positions: full right, full left, or dead center. In its first years of operation, an optional proportional control system was also added. This was done to test the merits of one system over the other in actual operating conditions. The operator could select either steering mode by means of a selector switch. This system worked well in slow-speed turns, but in full-power minimum-radius turns at speeds over 10 mph, the truck exhibited severe understeer

During the AMC show in Las Vegas, the dump body of the Titan was raised periodically to reveal five GM automobiles secured in the back of the giant truck. At this point, the cars were at a 55 degree angle to the parking lot, with the top of the spill guard some 56 feet in the air.

behavior caused by the driving characteristics of the DC series drive motors. This was corrected by means of a front axle steering angle sensor to control the electrical disconnect of one of the two inside motors during a turn. Engine horsepower levels remained the same, with the power of the disconnected motor being absorbed by the other three drive units, two outside and one inside. When the truck was originally built, its rear suspension was equipped with a pair of single-rate ride struts with a rubber pad spring media. In 1976, these were replaced with a new, fully hydraulic system for rear axle load equalization. This system would maintain equal tire loads on both sides of the truck while the truck moved over the haul road.

The scale of the Terex 33-19 Titan hauler was, to say the least, huge. At 66 feet, it was almost 16 feet longer

The 33-19 Titan hauler was shipped to its first working assignment at Kaiser Steel's Eagle Mountain iron ore mine in southern California at the end of December 1974, and was officially turned over to Kaiser personnel in March 1975. The hauler, shown in April 1975, is having 350 tons of material loaded into its massive dump body.

The 33-19 Titan hauler was powered by a huge 169.5-liter GM EMD Model 16-645E4 diesel locomotive engine rated at 3,300 gross horsepower and 3,000 fhp at 900 rpm. The operating net weight of the 33-19 truck was 520,000 pounds, and fully loaded it grossed 1,220,400 pounds, or 610.2 tons. Shown sitting alongside an Eagle Mountain mine haul road in March 1976, the Titan carries a full 350-ton load on its back.

than its nearest rival, the WABCO Haulpak 3200 (and 12 feet longer than the 3200B model). It was also wider than the big WABCO. The Titan's width was 25 feet, 7 inches, as compared to the 3200's 24-feet girth. Only the Peerless/Marion VCON 3006 was wider than the Titan, measuring a healthy 28 feet across.

The Titan's dimensions added up to a truck that weighed in empty at 520,000 pounds, and with its 350-ton payload, topped the scales at 1,220,400 pounds (610 tons) fully loaded. GM's marketing departments would highlight the size of the Titan hauler whenever they had the opportunity. The Titan shined a bright light on the Terex Division, and on the entire GM Corporation. The truck was a GM publicist's dream come true.

On June 5, 1974, at the Diesel Division plant in London, Ontario, the 350-ton hauler was pulled out of the factory and into the sunlight for its first series of promotional photos. At this point in the truck's life, it was still just referred to as the 33-19. A few weeks after these initial images were taken of the hauler, it was decided to add the word "Titan" to the name in preparation for the AMC show in October, where the 33-19 would officially be introduced. These first photos taken at the factory were probably the best-remembered of all images produced of the unit. The 33-19 was posed in different situations, with various GM personnel, a Pontiac Firebird, and an EMD locomotive, proudly displaying the CN logo of the National Canadian Railways, on its nose. It was a perfect showcase for what GM of Canada was capable of. After the shoot, the hauler underwent further tests before being disassembled and shipped to Las Vegas, Nevada, for its world premiere.

The Titan arrived in Las Vegas by means of eight railroad cars and was assembled in the parking lot of the convention center. The American Mining Congress convention

was held October 7–10, 1974. All of the major mining equipment manufacturers were in attendance, but there was little doubt in the minds of the show attendees who the star of the event was. The only thing the press was really interested in seeing was the Titan, and it did not disappoint. The 33-19 was officially christened on opening day by GM Vice President Roger Smith and his wife, Barbara. To make sure that all eyes were on the mammoth hauler, the dump body was raised periodically to reveal five GM automobiles fastened down in the hauler's bed. When the bed was fully raised, the cars were at a 55-degree angle to the parking lot, with the top of the spill guard of the dump body a full 56 feet in the air. If that wasn't enough, Al Hirt and his New Orleans Jazz Band played on a podium directly in front of the Titan at its christening ceremonies to make sure that the crowds that waited in line to get on the hauler were properly entertained. They also played at the Terex exhibit inside, where a 33-11 hauler and an 82-50 dozer were on display. When the band was not playing, a magician entertained the crowds. Every visitor who went up to see the Titan was presented a button that read, "I just saw the 350 ton Terex—World's Largest Hauler."

The Terex Titan display at the AMC show was a complete marketing success for GM. Not only were images of the hauler being reproduced in magazines and newspapers worldwide, the most popular photos contained the GM automobiles in the dump bed. After all, GM's primary goal in life was to sell cars, wasn't it?

The display of the Titan was a high point for GM in 1974, since the company was still suffering, as were all domestic car manufacturers, from the effects of the Arab Oil Embargo that had started a year earlier. The embargo would have a far-reaching effect on how cars—not to mention earth-moving equipment—would be produced

In late 1978, the Terex Titan was shipped to Kaiser Resources' Balmer mine near Sparwood, British Columbia, Canada. Shown here in spring 1984, the Titan 33-19 is painted in the colors of Westar Mining, its owners at the time. The hauler had just undergone a complete overhaul and was ready to rejoin the Westar truck fleet at the Balmer pit. Note the extended sideboards on the dump body that were originally installed when the truck was commissioned at the mine. They were necessary for times when the truck would sometimes haul coal, which was a lighter material that took up a much larger volume of space to attain the load rating of the truck. It was during this rebuild program that the Terex name was removed from the front of the hauler and replaced with simply the Titan identification. *Bruce Kurschenska*

in the United States. Big cars with big engines were out. Fuel efficiency was in. Even in large machines, fuel economics were now a major concern for buyers, since these purchases usually gulped diesel fuel that was measured in the hundreds of gallons per shift. And the big Terex hauler carried 960 gallons of diesel fuel to quench the thirst of its 169.15-liter V-16 engine. Average fuel consumption for the Titan was 550 gallons every 8 hours.

Interest was there for the truck, but potential buyers, concerned over the energy markets, assumed a wait-and-see attitude. The Titan was designed and built for large-scale mining operations that did not yet exist. A mine is a materials-removal system, of which the Titan was to be one part. The shovels that would be properly matched to this size of a hauler were yet to be built. The fuel crisis was but one bump in the road in the development of these ultra-large mining systems. The roller-coaster ride for the industry—and the fate of the Terex Titan—was just beginning. In mid-December 1974, the Terex Titan was dismantled in Las Vegas and shipped in truckloads to its first home, at Kaiser Steel's Eagle Mountain iron ore mine in the eastern desert region of southern California's Riverside County. The mine entrance was 12 miles north of Desert Center, midway between Indio and Blythe, on Interstate 10. The iron ore produced by the mine was intended primarily for use at the Kaiser Steel Corporation steel mill in Fontana, California, and the remainder was exported to Japan. The Titan was joining a fleet of Terex 33-15 haulers already in operation at the site. After the assembly of the hauler and some initial testing by Terex, the 33-19 Titan was officially handed over to mining officials in March 1975; the hauler spent the better part of the next three years operating at Eagle Mountain.

Kaiser did not actually buy the Titan, but had leased the unit from Terex on a trial basis. During the first two years of operation, many modifications were made to the hauler that frequently took the truck out of service. This was expected, since the hauler was still classified as a prototype model. One design change resulting from early field testing was a shift in the body pivot points to reduce the weight load on the front end while on steep downhill road hauls. This corrected excessive heating caused by flexing of the front tires.

Visually, the Titan looked as it did when it was on display in Las Vegas, with only minor additions. A pair of work lights were mounted to the front of the hauler to help illuminate the front engine access panels between the radiator housings. Also, a warning beacon light was mounted on top of the operator's cab. It was broken sometime in late 1976, and removed altogether in 1977. A pair of splash guards was added to the front of the lower dump body to control debris being splashed on the access steps on the left side of the truck and the fuel tank on the right. Sometime in mid-1976, the hauler lost one of its rear right splash guards, which had been damaged by the truck being repeatedly backed into the loading bench. By late 1977, the left guard joined the right one in the scrap yard.

The hauler had logged about 7,000 hours of operating time when Kaiser officials decided that the hauler did not fit in well with the existing mine layout. It was decided to ship the Titan up to British Columbia, Canada, to the Kaiser Resources open pit coal mine for further evaluations. While at Eagle Mountain, the 33-19 Titan hauled 3.5 million tons of material, even with frequent downtime. That's equivalent to about 10,000 truckloads.

The new home for the Terex Titan was Kaiser Resources' Balmer mine, near the town of Sparwood, in the Kootenay region of the Canadian Rocky Mountains, in British Columbia. The Balmer operation was one of the largest open pit coal mining operations in North America.

The hauler arrived in late 1978 and spent the entire month of October being assembled and repainted. Modifications were few, but some are worthy of mention. Sideboards were added to the dump body to increase load-volume capacity for the lighter material being loaded at the mine. Additional safety railings were added on top of the nose of the truck, around the front engine maintenance panels. The "Kaiser Resources" name was painted on both sides of the over-spill guard and large "GM" logos were placed on each outside radiator housing and on the front and the door of the operator's cab. The truck was assigned haul truck mine number 175, which was painted on the front upper sides of the dump body. Throw in a fresh set of Goodyear tires for good measure and the Titan was ready to go back to work. After the 33-19 completed its mandatory brake code testing on November 3, 1978, the hauler was turned over to Kaiser personnel. In 1979, for some unexplained reason, the Titan name was painted over on the spill-guard and on either side of the dump body. The 33-19 nomenclature, and GM and Terex logos were left untouched.

By the end of 1980, the Titan had accumulated just over 13,000 hours of operation, including its 7,000 hours from Eagle Mountain. But it was soon to get a new owner. B.C. Resources had bought all of Kaiser's mine property in 1980 and by the end of 1980, had renamed the operation B.C. Coal, Ltd. The name of the Balmer pit where the Titan operated remained unchanged. But this was a hard time for the coal industry, and with the worldwide recession now in full swing, change was the order of the day.

In 1983, confusion over the B.C. Coal name in the marketplace led to the company being renamed Westar Mining, Ltd. Same company, only a different name. It was during this time that Westar management felt the Titan was starting to show its age and that something would soon have to be done to address the truck's problems. Westar's studies showed that the truck was still cheaper to run per bank cubic yard than the Lectra Haul M-200 haulers, the next-largest units at the Balmer mine. Westar, up until this point, had been leasing the truck from the GM Diesel Division. When Westar approached GM about buying the truck outright, GM was more than happy to strike a deal. Westar agreed to pay $200,000 for the hauler, a new set of tires, and $1 million worth of spare parts. In short, the

"Baby, that's a lot of Iron!"

Television commercials whose subject matter relates to heavy earth-moving equipment are very rare. And such a commercial with a celebrity spokesperson is even rarer still. Yet in 1976, discussions between Terex management and the division's advertising agency, Griswold-Eshleman Company, on how to increase the awareness of the Terex name concluded that a television spot might be just the thing to get the job done. Expensive advertising time for this type of product was just about unheard of. That in itself would attract a certain amount of attention. But something else would be needed if viewers were to remember what they had just seen.

In July 1977, Terex marketing asked the agency to come up with a concept for a TV commercial. The following month, the agency presented a concept that had world-renowned golfer Jack Nicklaus and the world's largest truck, the Terex Titan, together in the same commercial. Terex officials liked what they heard and the project was given the go-ahead.

Jack Nicklaus was an excellent choice as spokesperson for the Terex Division. GM had worked with Nicklaus before in various golf-related events, and felt that his image was the one that would best relate to the audience they were seeking. The Titan hauler spoke for itself. It was the one piece of equipment that was sure to capture one's attention.

Terex and agency officials met with representatives of Nicklaus' management company, Golden Bear, Inc. in mid-August in Dallas and again at the P.G.A. Tournament at Pebble Beach, California, to finalize Nicklaus' role in the commercial. There was only one day available in the golfer's schedule for a complete day of location shooting—one day and one day only. These are surely some of the most dreaded words an art director can hear. With Nicklaus signed on to the project, it was time to get the Titan ready.

At the time, the 33-19 Titan was working at Kaiser Steel's Eagle Mountain iron ore mine in southern California. Since the location of the commercial shoot was predetermined by where the giant hauler was working, logistics teams were sent out to start getting the other Terex equipment needed for the spot. At the same time, a preproduction outing to the Kaiser site was made in early September by members of the agency and film crew to find a suitable filming location within the mine area. The location finally picked was in a difficult area to get to. Access was poor at best, so a short road had to be built to the shooting area. Once this was accomplished, the freshly painted Terex machines could be moved into position. The 33-09 hauler, 72-71 loader, and 82-50 dozer were brought in from Phoenix, Arizona. The TS-14 scraper was shipped all the way from Casper, Wyoming.

On September 24, with all of the Terex machines in place, the film crews set up their equipment. Operators of the Terex equipment were briefed on what they would be doing and the Titan's dump body was filled with rock, which was to be covered later by a layer of sand to simulate a golf course sand trap. While the sand was being spread in the back of the truck, a technician noticed that the sand being used did not look like the golf course variety. So a mad scramble was on to find sand that looked like the fine, yellow or white type usually found in a real sand trap. If that wasn't enough, during early video tests, a pile of rocks in the background was disrupting the visual composition framed in by the camera. The closest dozer on hand was the pristine Terex 82-50. Soon the rocks were history and somebody who didn't have very much to do was putting a new coat of paint on the gouged-up dozer blade of the 82-50.

Some suitable sand was located and spread on top of the old sand. Camera rehearsals were held using a stand-in for Nicklaus, and things seemed to be going well, until, that is, the western desert winds kicked up and blew a good portion of the precious yellow sand out of the back of the Titan. After numerous panic-stricken telephone calls, the last bags of yellow sand had been located. Arrangements were made to have all available bags brought to the shooting site. But to be on the safe side, the new sand was left bagged until final filming began.

On the morning of September 28, a private jet carrying Nicklaus and other officials of Golden Bear, Inc. touched down on an old army airstrip built by Gen. G. S. Patton at Desert Center in 1942. As officials went to pick up Nicklaus and friends, the order was given to get the sand trap up to par—or else.

Pro golfer Jack Nicklaus, getting ready to climb into the back of the Terex Titan to start the filming of the first part of a TV commercial on September 28, 1977.

Nicklaus drove golf balls out of the specially prepared sand trap in the Titan's dump body during numerous takes to get one that was just right for the opening sequence of the Terex commercial.

Once at the mine site, Nicklaus looked over his script, studied the test video tapes, and climbed onto the Titan. At 8:40 A.M., the cameras started rolling. All Nicklaus had to do was drive a golf ball out of the sand trap in back of the Titan, which he did, 30 times. Once the thirtieth ball sailed over some executives' heads some 100 yards away, the film crew decided they had all of the images needed from on top of the truck. It was on to the second and last scene of the day.

The last part of the filming had Nicklaus talking to the camera as the other four pieces of Terex equipment converged on him. As Jack would say his last lines of script, the dozer would pull in right behind him and drop its blade with a loud "clank." Just as this happened, Nicklaus flinched just a bit just before delivering his last line of dialogue, "And baby... that's a lot of iron." This was not faked. Even though additional takes were made of the shot, the one with the flinch was the best of the bunch. It was perfect.

By 11:30 A.M., the second part was finished. After lunch, Nicklaus and his associates were driven back to the airstrip, where another private jet was waiting. The camera crew's equipment was broken down and packed away, while the Titan backed up to a spoil pile and dumped its load of sand and rock. The hauler was back to work by the end of the day, and the last grains of the troublesome yellow sand blew out into the desert.

The 30-second spot was scheduled to play during key sporting events in December 1977, and through the first four months of 1978. The first airing of the spot was during an AFC playoff game on NBC on December 24. It would also run on CBS and ABC. The Terex TV commercial opens with a close-up of Nicklaus driving a golf ball out of a sand trap. As the camera pulls back, it becomes apparent he is not on a golf course, but instead, is in back of the Terex Titan. The scripted dialogue was as follows: "I've played out of some monsters before, but this one is something else. This monster is the Terex Titan, the world's largest truck. It's the Big Daddy in the Terex line of off-highway equipment, equipment used worldwide for mining, logging, and for heavy construction. Whether it's playing golf or moving mountains, you need to use the right iron. And baby... that's a lot of iron."

The one-and-only 33-19 Titan as it looks today after being put on display in Sparwood, British Columbia. After the truck was officially retired from its working duties in 1991, it was saved from being scrapped by the efforts of the Sparwood Chamber of Commerce, which saw to the truck's eventual restoration and creation of the display area just off of Highway 3. *Bruce Kurschenska*

amount of money paid covered the cost of the tires, and the truck and parts were thrown in for good measure.

Now that Westar had clear ownership of the 33-19, it could let its engineers and maintenance crews make the necessary modifications to the hauler. When the modification program finally got under way in December, the Titan had been idle for most of the second half of 1983 due to a cracked rear axle housing. A complete rebuild program was started on the hauler, with four major areas needing special attention: the frame, rear steering axles, hydraulic hoists, and the relocation of some vital components, such as the filtering systems. The frame was strengthened in strategic areas that were prone to fatigue. Because of the length of the hauler's frame, the Titan suffered severe load-shifting characteristics when traveling at top speed on uneven haul roads. So much so, in fact, that the truck would get into a "pitching motion" between the high and the low points in a poorly maintained haul road, causing the payload weight to transfer to the rear axles, momentarily pulling the front wheels off the ground. It was this seesawing action that put massive amounts of strain on areas of the frame that weren't suppose to receive such punishment. This situation led directly to the next problem area, the rear steering axles.

The load-shifting problem was causing excessive wear to the rear drive axles, along with normal dumping cycles. When the dump body was raised, a good portion of the hauler's payload weight was supported by the rearmost rear axle. It was determined that these two conditions caused the crack in the rear housing. This problem was so serious that Westar management almost had the Titan scrapped earlier in 1983. The back axle housing was shipped to Vancouver where it was welded, then returned to the Balmer mine. During this rear end repair, the hydraulic hoists for the dump

body were completely rebuilt, and all of the high-pressure hosing was replaced. While repairs that needed engineering changes were commencing, other standard components were rebuilt, such as the four traction motors in the rear axles, and the front and rear suspensions. About the only thing on the Titan that wasn't rebuilt was the EMD engine. Over the years, this engine proved to be one of the most reliable aspects of the hauler. Except for routine maintenance, replacements of normal wear-and-tear components such as turbochargers, and scheduled rebuilding requirements, this powerplant was just about as bullet-proof as they came.

The rebuild program was completed in early spring, 1984. The 33-19 Titan's original Terex Hi-Lite green was replaced by Westar's corporate colors of blue, cream, and red-orange. The Terex name had also been removed from the nose of the truck, replaced by the Titan name only. The 33-19 nomenclature was still carried on the sides of the dump body spill-guard hood.

For the next six years, the 33-19 Titan was worked hard by the mine, with the truck at times reaching an availability record of almost 70 percent. That was considered excellent for a truck of this vintage. But the hauler couldn't hide its age forever. All of the times that the Titan carried loads greater than its rated 350 tons were now catching up to it. The hauler routinely carried loads in the 400-ton range. But it was those times the truck was loaded with 450–500 tons of overburden that probably did the most damage. Westar knew the truck's days were numbered and wanted to get as much tonnage hauled as possible.

To help prolong the hauler's life, it was moved from carrying overburden to coal hauling. Even with the added sideboards on the dump box, it was impossible to overload the Titan with the lighter-weight coal. But the hauler's number was up in mid-1990, when the trouble-some rear drive axle cracked again. This time it was for good. Maintenance staffers looked the truck over and determined that it was beyond repair without millions of dollars being spent on the project. The Titan's working days were over. In 1991, Westar officially removed the 33-19 from the active truck duty roster.

After almost 16 years of service, it was no surprise when the 33-19 was officially retired. After all, it was living on borrowed time as it was. The truck was taken to the main truck maintenance facility to see what was salvage-able on the unit. The EMD diesel engine was removed and sold. The tires could still be used on existing haulers at Westar, so they too were removed. When Westar Mining went into bankruptcy in 1992, the prospects of any part of the truck being left intact were bleak, to say the least.

In December 1992, Teck Corporation became the new owners of the Balmer operation of Westar, now renamed Elkview Coal Corporation, with the Balmer pit now being referred to as the Elkview mine. Elkview realized the histori-cal value of the 33-19, and in late 1993 offered it to the town of Sparwood as a monument to the coal mining region of the area. All the town would have to do is come up with the funds necessary to dismantle the hauler the rest of the way, trans-port it into town, and then reassemble it. This, of course, was easier said than done. Alternatives to completely dismantling the Titan to get it into Sparwood were discussed. Because the bridge into town was too narrow for the hauler to cross, it was thought that maybe it could be towed through the creek instead. But the logistics of towing a 260-ton truck through the mud, and controlling its momentum on dry land were more than anyone wanted to deal with. Funding would have to be based on the dismantling of the unit.

In November 1993, the Sparwood Chamber of Commerce established a "Save the Titan" committee to raise the necessary funds to have the truck restored. Large donations were received from the District of Spar-wood, $200,000 (Canadian); the BC-21 (Provincial Grant), $113,000 (Canadian); and $7,500 (Canadian) from the B.C. Heritage Trust. The remainder of the pro-jected $450,000 (Canadian) needed came from corpo-rate donations, local fund raising, and volunteer work.

Once all of the necessary funds were in hand, work started on the dismantling of the truck at the mine site and its piece-by-piece transport into Sparwood. In the summer of 1995, most of the work on the truck was completed. Today, the Terex-33-19 Titan resides alongside Highway 3 in downtown Sparwood. The truck was restored to its orig-inal Terex green paint scheme, with extra railings installed on the upper deck for safety reasons. The problem of the tires going flat over time due to air loss or vandalism was solved by filling the tires with concrete. About the only major component missing is the engine. Since the original unit was sold, an effort was made to find a used or possibly a damaged EMD 16-645 series engine. There were some available, but the costs involved outweighed the benefits, since the entire engine would have been fully enclosed and

out of sight. The money could be better spent elsewhere.

In the summer of 1996, the landscaping and lighting system of the grounds was completed. The "world's largest truck" now had a permanent home, with no fear of being cut up for scrap. A piece of earth-moving his-tory lives on, as it does also for Terex. There might have been other 170-ton GM Titan haulers, but there was only one 350-ton, Terex 33-19 Titan truck.

When one looks back on the history of the 33-19 and why only one unit was built, the answer has more to do with the world economics at the time and less with how the truck actually performed. In fact, the hauler per-formed very well, especially after the prototype received early modifications while operating in California. But the mining expansion that Terex and the rest of the industry had anticipated did not happen, at least not when they thought it would. The oil embargo was the first of a series of economic hiccups that slowed mining expan-sions, with many anticipated new projects put on hold.

GM had made several proposals to Kaiser manage-ment on purchases of 33-19 haulers. One of the last was made to B.C. Coal, Ltd. in early 1981. This involved the proposed purchase of seven 33-19 haulers and one truck provided by the Diesel Division as a standby unit. These Titans were also to be equipped with 3,800-gross-horse-power engines, as opposed to the prototype's 3,300-horse-power rating. But the price of the trucks was quoted at $3,405,000 (Canadian), a staggering amount for the day. In 1980, the hauler was quoted at $2,880,000 (Canadian). Three things were making impossible long-term pricing estimates on the production of 33-19 haulers: the world economy was in a recession; runaway inflation, which was reflected in the truck's pricing; and double-digit interest rates. Add to this B.C. Coal management's shock at the news of GM selling the Terex Division to IBH in Ger-many. Even though the diesel-electric-drive haulers pro-duced at the GM Diesel Division in Canada were not part of the deal, B.C. Coal was concerned about GM's long-term commitment to the large hauler industry. Also, the coal company's plan to increase mine output was put on hold because of the unstable economic market. When all of these situations and concerns were added together, they spelled doom for any possible sales of 350-ton haulers.

Today, the Terex Titan still holds the title of the world's largest-capacity hauler, but one day that crown will have to be given up. The largest haulers to come within shouting distance of the 33-19, in terms of capac-ity, are the Komatsu Haulpak 930E, rated at 310 tons; the Unit Rig Lectra Haul MT-4400, rated at 280–300 tons; the Kress CH-300 bottom dump, rated at 300 tons; and the Caterpillar/MEGA CH-290 coal hauler, rated at 290 tons. New trucks currently in the design phase are all rated at between 320–340 tons. It would be nice if the Terex Titan's capacity record could make it to the year 2000. Then it could always be known as the largest hauler of the twentieth century. Whatever happens, its place in the his-tory of earth-moving is ensured.

Nothing is
Forever

The General Motors Terex Division thrived in the 1970s. Production, research, and market expansions were all happening at record paces. The production of Terex equipment was becoming more international as new markets were opened up. To better serve these new interests, manufacturing plants were established in key marketplace areas.

In 1971, GM Luxembourg, S.A., a 172,000-square foot factory, was established to build Terex loaders and haulers. In 1972, Hindustan Motors, Ltd. became a Terex licensee in Madras, India, for the production of Terex loaders, haulers, scrapers, and dozers. In 1973, GM Terex do Brasil, S.A. was established in Brazil to manufacture Terex scrapers, loaders, and haulers. In 1978, Tierra Factors Corporation, in Manila, Philippines, also became a Terex licensee to produce Terex haulers, dozers, and loaders. GM plants in South Africa and Australia were building Terex attachments such as bulldozer blades, loader buckets, rippers, and dump bodies. The plants in Scotland were also expanding, and by 1979 totaled 807,300 square feet of manufacturing space. But the two U.S. plants were still the center of the Terex universe. Terex-West was up to 843,171 square feet of plant space by 1976, and the massive Hudson facilities, which included the 238,626-square foot Engineering and Research Center and the main plant, totaled 1,074,480 square feet by 1976. To help keep all of GM's earth-moving endeavors organized, "Terex Worldwide" was established in September 1974 as a single international organization for the manufacturing and marketing of products under the Terex name. Terex was now truly a world player in the international marketplace.

Terex manufactured four principal lines of earth-moving equipment: the 33-series haulers, the 72-series wheel loaders, the 82-series crawler dozers, and the S and TS scraper lines. All other product lines were derivatives of these four categories. The wheel loader, dozer,

and scraper product lines that first bore the Terex name had all previously been Euclid Division designs. At first, the only difference between the old Euclid models and the Terex versions was a decal. The 33-series haulers were the exception to this, as covered in detail in chapter 5. But new designs and products were moved quickly in the manufacturing pipeline for Terex, forcing some old favorites from the Euclid days into retirement.

Terex Scrapers

Terex continued to offer single- and twin-engined, over-hung scrapers, continuing the success story started with these machines when they carried the Euclid name. But the tractor-pulled scrapers, such as the SS-28 and SS-40, were discontinued because Euclid, Inc. had the rights to the tractor, while Terex held the scraper designs. Euclid, Inc. was allowed to buy licensing rights to the Terex scraper units to continue building six-wheeled tractor scrapers if it wanted to, but it didn't.

In 1969, Terex introduced the twin-hitch concept, called the "Helpmate," for use with many of its larger all-wheel-drive scraper models. In the Helpmate system, each scraper is equipped with a hook on the rear of the scraper and a cushioned push plate assembly on the front, which incorporated an air-actuated loop. In operation, the lead scraper is assisted in loading by the rear unit, which acts as a pusher. When the lead scraper is loaded, it pulls the rear scraper to assist in loading that unit. The scrapers then unhook and operate independently on the haul, dump, and return cycles, and re-enter the working area and begin a new loading cycle. This pushing and pulling method often eliminated the need for a push dozer. But in extremely hard loading materials, a push dozer could still be used, since the Helpmate hitch in no way interfered with the normal operation of the scraper.

The smallest of the single-engined scrapers offered by Terex was the S-7 (4UOT-26SH). The S-7 carried over from the Euclid to the Terex unit with no changes, but its stay would be brief. The lack of demand for a conventional 7-cubic yard scraper in the marketplace led Terex to phase the S-7 out of production by the end of 1969.

The front end loader assembly line at the Hudson plant, in 1968. All loaders were built at this factory, with the exception of the two largest Terex models, the 72-71 and 72-81 models, which were produced at the re-acquired Clinton Road facilities, by then referred to as Terex-West.

The Terex S-24 (39LOT-76SH) was the next-largest scraper in the product line powered by one engine. No major changes were made to the Euclid design of this unit until 1969, when the Terex S-24, model 49LOT-76SH was introduced. The 49LOT tractor of the S-24 was powered by a GM Detroit Diesel 12V-71T, a two-cycle, 12-cylinder engine rated at 465 gross horsepower and 423 fhp. A new six-speed Allison CLBT-5965 transmission topped off the drivetrain changes. Capacity ratings remained unchanged at 24 cubic yards struck and 32 cubic yards heaped. In 1975, Terex made some minor upgrades to the S-24, which included a new 425 fhp rating from the V-12 engine and a different six-speed Allison CLBT-5865 transmission. The engineering model designation did not change.

In 1977, Terex introduced the S-24B "Loadrunner," the replacement for the aging S-24, as model 023-024. A key element to the design of the scraper was its front axle suspension. Since this design was first introduced on the S-24B's twin-engined counterpart, the TS-24B, it will be discussed in greater detail with that unit's features. The S-24B was powered by a Detroit Diesel 12V-71T, a two-cycle, 12-cylinder engine rated at 500 gross horsepower and 475 fhp. This was connected to a six-speed, fully automatic Allison CLBT-5865 transmission. Payload capacity ratings were 24 cubic yards struck and 34 cubic yards heaped, with a maximum 81,500-pound load limit. Compared to the previous model, the S-24B offered a larger standard tire package and many standard features that were once optional equipment.

Terex released the first prototypes of the redesigned TS-14B (17UOT-97SH) scraper, featuring the distinctive keystone grille assembly, in November 1971. The TS-14B was powered by two GM Detroit Diesel 4-71N engines rated at a combined 320 gross horsepower and 288 fhp, and it had a payload capacity of 14 cubic yards struck and 20 cubic yards heaped. The TS-14B pictured is shown working in August 1972.

A pair of Terex TS-24 (43LOT-78SH) scrapers utilizing the Helpmate twin-hitch attachments in July 1971. This hitch enabled the two scrapers to be hooked together while working, pushing, and pulling each other, providing faster loading times.

The twin-engined TS-18 (33TOT-92SH) scraper was released by Terex in early 1971. The TS-18 was powered by a GM Detroit Diesel 8V-71N engine in the tractor and a Detroit Diesel 6V-71N in the scraper unit. Combined, the two units produced 556 gross horsepower and 517 fhp. The scraper was rated at 18 cubic yards struck and 24 cubic yards heaped. The two TS-18 units, working in June 1973 in Parker, Colorado, utilize the Helpmate hitch system, which basically turns the scrapers into a single eight-wheel-drive machine for loading purposes.

The largest of the single-engine scrapers offered by Terex was the S-32. Again, this model was initially carried over from the Euclid line as is without change. In 1971, the GM Detroit Diesel 12V-71T was revised with a new power curve, now rated at 525 gross horsepower and 482 fhp. The transmission was the same unit as the one used in the Euclid version of the S-32. The S-32 was phased out of the Terex product line by the end of 1973.

The 1970s was the decade of the all-wheel-drive, twin-engined scrapers. Interest in the single-engine types was waning, with buyers wanting more productive machines that could go it alone in the most difficult of conditions. When these scrapers were hooked together, or were push-loaded by high-powered dozers, they were an unbeatable combination for high-volume material moving applications in difficult loading situations.

The smallest all-wheel-drive scraper produced by the Terex Division in the United States was the TS-14. This unit was carried over from the Euclid line virtually unchanged and only received minor updates that did not affect any of the machine's major systems specifications. In November 1971, the first TS-14B (17UOT-97SH) scraper preproduction model was built, and featured the keystone front radiator housing. The TS-14B's front and rear engines were the same Detroit Diesel 4-71N, two-cycle, four-cylinder units rated at a combined 320 gross horsepower and 288 fhp. Each also utilized the same six-speed Allison CLT-3461, full power shifting transmissions. The scraper was rated at 14 cubic yards struck and 20 cubic yards heaped, with a payload capacity of 47,000 pounds. The TS-14B went into full production in 1972. In 1976, the TS-14B was issued the new engineering model number of 053-054, but major specifications remained unchanged. In late 1977, a more-powerful version of the TS-14B (20UOT-104SH), featuring turbocharged DD 4-71T engines, was built but never went into production because of its high costs.

In September 1978, a more-powerful TS-14B (071-072) was offered with a pair of Detroit Diesel 6V-53N, two-cycle, six-cylinder engines rated at 372 gross horsepower and 342 fhp. Both front and rear powerplants used five-speed Allison CLT-654 automatic transmissions. Payload capacities were unchanged. This model, originally called the TS-14B "Plus" (19UOT BZ-102SH BZ) when first built in 1977, was only offered for a brief time, and was soon removed from the U.S. product line. The unit eventually went into full production as the GM Brazil-built Terex TS-14B (611-612), intended for South American markets. The model built in Brazil was powered by identical Detroit Diesel 6V-53N engines rated at a combined 324 gross horsepower and 294 fhp. Transmissions were the same Allison units found in the U.S.-built TS-14B (053-054) scraper model.

Another Brazil-built model was the single-engined Terex S-14, introduced in 1983, during the IBH years. The rear scraper bowl in this unit was essentially a TS-14B model, without the engine, with a tractor specially designed to accept the 304-fhp Cummins NT-855C-335 engine.

Terex continued to offer the old Euclid-designed Tandem-14 (13UOT-82SH-83SH) twin-bowl scrapers in 1968 and 1969. The only difference between the Terex and Euclid versions was the name decals. The Terex Division had no sales of Tandem-14 scrapers in the United States during the time the unit was offered. The last three units built in the United States were shipped from the Hudson plant in March 1968, as Euclid Tandem-14 (13UOT-82SH-83SH) scrapers. The only factory-produced Terex Tandem-14 scrapers were built at the Motherwell plant, in Scotland, as British units. The last and only production runs of these units were the GM 4-71-engined, British model B12UOT-B16SH-B13SH versions, shipped in June 1969.

Terex built its first prototype TS-24B "Loadrunner" (58LOT-110SH) scraper in November 1975, and the model was officially released in 1977. The TS-24B was powered by a GM Detroit Diesel 12V-71T engine in the tractor, and a DD 6V-71T in the rear scraper, producing a combined 750 gross horsepower and 717 fhp. The TS-24B was the production version that evolved from the Terex 979 (50LOT-95SH) scraper project. The single-engined model of the TS-24B was the S-24B Loadrunner. It was basically the same unit, except it was powered by the tractor only, since it had no engine in its rear scraper unit.

The second-largest-volume coal scraper built by Terex was its TS-46B Loadrunner, first announced in May 1978. The first prototype versions of this model were put into service in early 1980. The TS-46B (035-036) was rated at 46 cubic yards struck and 56 cubic yards heaped. The drivetrains and engine power ratings were the same as those in the TS-24B Loadrunner model. Shown in 1982 is a new IBH/Terex TS-46B, which was identical to the GM-produced version.

The improved and updated TS-32B twin-engined scraper replaced the previous TS-32 model, which had been in the product line since Terex started up. The scraper was powered by a GM Detroit Diesel 12V-71T engine in the front tractor, and a DD 8V-71T in the rear scraper unit, totaling 875 gross horsepower and 807 fhp. Payload capacity was 32 cubic yards struck and 43 cubic yards heaped.

The next-largest model in the Terex product line for its all-wheel-drive scrapers was the TS-18 (33TOT-92SH). The Terex TS-18 had nothing in common with the earlier Euclid model carrying the same name. This Terex version was an entirely new model for the company. The TS-18 started out as the TS-17 scraper when the unit was in its prototype testing stages in November 1969. By June 1970, the first preproduction TS-18 rolled out of the factory for field testing, and the unit was officially introduced in early 1971. The 33TOT tractor of the TS-18 was powered by a Detroit Diesel 8V-71N,

The S-35E (47LOT-90SH) was the largest elevator-type scraper offered by Terex. The scraper was powered by a single Detroit Diesel 12V-71T rated at 500 gross horsepower and 457 fhp. The scraper elevator was hydraulically powered. Payload capacity was 35 cubic yards heaped. A struck capacity rating was not applicable for elevator-type scrapers. This S-35E works on an expansion project of the Tucson Airport in June 1975.

two-cycle, eight-cylinder engine rated at 318 gross horsepower and 292 fhp. The 92SH scraper was equipped with a Detroit Diesel 6V-71N, two-cycle, six-cylinder engine rated at 238 gross horsepower and 225 fhp. The total combined power ratings were 556 gross horsepower and 517 fhp. Each engine had its own six-speed Allison Torqmatic CLT-4465 transmission. The rated capacity for the TS-18 was 18 cubic yards struck and 24 cubic yards heaped.

The TS-18 was a very modern design, with a low, wide bowl design and roll-out ejection system. The scraper also featured a newly designed gooseneck and the characteristic Terex keystone front end.

In 1978, an upgraded version of the TS-18 (021-022) was released. Both front and rear engines were the same Detroit Diesels, but the power rating for the front unit was now 318 gross horsepower and 295 fhp, so total output was now rated at 556 gross horsepower and 520 fhp. The big change was in the transmissions, which were five-speed automatic Allison CLT-750 units, both front and rear. Capacity ratings were unchanged. The TS-18 model line was withdrawn from the product line in late 1982.

Rocker trailers for scraper front tractor units were becoming fairly rare in the 1970s, but a small demand still existed. To fill this need, Terex offered the TS-18, 33TOT tractor, combined with an Athey-built T2233R Rocker rear dump trailer, rated at 66,000 pounds or 33 tons, in 1973. This type of unit was well-suited for work in quarries, dams, and tunnel construction, where their short wheelbases made them extremely maneuverable in confined working situations.

The most popular scraper model line for Terex in the 1970s was the 24-cubic-yard, 80,000-pound capacity TS-24. It was a star performer in the field and was well-liked by contractors who used it. The TS-24 (43LOT-78SH) was carried over unchanged from the last Euclid model version. In 1971, the TS-24 power ratings for both of its engines were revised. The 43LOT tractor's Detroit Diesel 12V-71N was now rated at 434 gross horsepower and 394 fhp. The 78SH scraper's Detroit Diesel 6-71N, was rated at 238 gross horsepower and 219 fhp. Total output thus became 672 gross horsepower and 613 fhp.

In 1976, the TS-24 (57LOT-109SH) received new front and rear transmissions. The tractor's unit was a

Shown in 1969, the first twin-engined Terex 82-80 (DA) crawler to be equipped with the factory produced, side-by-side-mounted Terex 4000 Series Hydraulic Control Unit. The hydraulic cylinders were the same units found on the 82-30 and 82-40 dozers. The old-style cable-control unit was still offered, but few customers wanted it, opting for the more-modern hydraulic system.

This Terex 82-80 (DA) dozer is a special coal-stockpiling version, destined for work at Detroit Edison in June 1970. The crawler is equipped with a coal "U" bulldozer blade that measures 22 feet across and 6 feet, 1 inch high. The optional environmental comfort cab was needed to protect the operator from the hazards of coal dust.

These Terex 82-80 (DA) dozers are working in Providence, Kentucky, in August 1971. The "DA" model of the 82-80 was the most powerful of all of the TC-12-derived Twin-Power crawlers produced. The dozer was powered by two GM Detroit Diesel 6-71N engines rated at 476 gross horsepower and 440 fhp at 2,100 rpm. When the big dozer was finally discontinued in 1974, a total of about 901 of the TC-12/82-80 crawlers had been built, with the last 125 units being the DA model.

six-speed, Allison CLT-5860 power shift transmission, while the scraper's was a five-speed Allison CLT-750 automatic unit. Engine output for the rear DD6V-71N had also increased slightly to 238 gross horsepower and 225 fhp. New combined power ratings for both engines were 672 gross horsepower and 619 fhp, and payload capacity ratings were unchanged. A new front end, with the now-familiar Terex grille shroud, finally replaced the older Euclid design that had been with the unit since 1963. In 1977, the model identification nomenclature was changed on the TS-24 to 007-008. Major specifications were unchanged. This older model type of the TS-24 scraper was offered in the product line until 1986, when it was quietly phased out of production.

Terex officially introduced a new member to the TS-24 family of scrapers in 1977: the TS-24B "Loadrunner" (035-036). The standout feature of the Loadrunner model line was the use of a suspension system on the front tractor portion of the scraper. The system utilized a nitrogen-over-oil suspended front axle, which dampened the loping motion an over-hung type scraper often gets itself into when at speed. It also absorbed shocks better and provided a smoother ride than non-suspended machines, resulting in less pounding on the scraper structure, and less operator fatigue. The roots of the development on this type of scraper for Terex dated back to September 1971, when the first pilot version with such a suspension was built as the TS-24 "Plus" (50LOT-95SH). In February 1973, this same model was briefly introduced as the Terex 979 scraper. The "979" carried the same model identification as the TS-24 "Plus." The number 979 was the engineering in-house product number issued to this model while it was being developed, but at the time of its release, marketing had not yet issued new sales product identification for the unit.

The Terex 979 scraper's front 50LOT tractor was powered by a Detroit Diesel 12V-71T, two-cycle, 12-cylinder engine rated at 500 gross horsepower and 460 fhp, connected to a six-speed Allison CLT-5865 transmission. The rear 95SH scraper used a Detroit Diesel 6V-71T, two-cycle, six-cylinder engine rated at 250 gross horsepower and 237 fhp, mated to a six-speed Allison CLT-4465 transmission. Total power output was 750 gross horsepower and 697 fhp. The capacity rating of the unit was 24 cubic yards struck and 32 cubic yards heaped, with an 80,000-pound load limit. The first Terex 979 was built in June 1973. The picture on the specification sheet released in February 1973 was actually an image of the pilot TS-24 Plus. The Terex 979 only went into very limited production, and was basically considered a preproduction model of the first prototype TS-24B Loadrunner that was built in November 1975, as the model 58LOT-110SH. The full production TS-24B (035-036 model number as of September 1976) was powered by a Detroit Diesel 12V-71T, rated at 500 gross horsepower and 475 fhp, with a six-speed Allison CLT-5865 transmission in the tractor. The rear scraper used a Detroit Diesel

The 82-30B (GA) dozer replaced the previous 82-30 (FA) model when it was introduced in June 1973. The 82-30B was powered by a GM Detroit Diesel 8V-71T engine rated at 277 gross horsepower and 245 fhp. The new 82-30B, shown here in April 1974, had just been delivered to a job site in Harrisburg, Pennsylvania.

6V-71T, rated at 250 gross horsepower and 242 fhp, connected to a five-speed Allison CT-750 unit. The total rated power output was 750 gross horsepower and 717 fhp, and the load capacity was 24 cubic yards struck and 34 cubic yards heaped, with a maximum load rating of 81,500 pounds. The Loadrunner featured the new gooseneck design first seen in the TS-18. Other features included a power-down bowl and push-out ejection system for fast and easy unloading of material. The Loadrunners were probably the best scrapers ever developed by the Terex Division, and their design features served as the basis for all subsequent large scraper models.

The TS-24 line of 24-cubic-yard scrapers was not unique to just the North American market. Several models built at the Motherwell plant in Scotland, by General Motors Scotland, Ltd., had features and specifications that were only found on the British-made machines. The Terex TS-24 (B4LOT-B7SH) had been on the market since 1963, when it was a Euclid model. Its front and rear engines were both Cummins NT-855-C310, four-cycle, "Turbo-Diesel," six-cylinder units, each rated at 280 gross horsepower and 267 fhp, for a total output of 560 gross horsepower and

534 fhp. Each engine had its own four-speed Allison CLT-5640/1 Torqmatic transmission. The payload capacity was 24 cubic yards struck and 32 cubic yards heaped, with a maximum load rating of 80,000 pounds.

This model was replaced by the TS-24 (B9LOT-B20SH) model in 1970, which was upgraded into the TS-24 Mk IV (B9LOT-B21SH) in 1971. These versions were powered by matching Detroit Diesel 8V-71N, two-cycle, eight-cylinder engines, each rated at 290 gross horsepower and 272 fhp. The total combined power output was 580 gross horsepower and 544 fhp. Both transmissions were four-speed Allison CLT-5640/1 Torqmatic units. The coal-loading version of the TS-24 MK IV was the TS-40c MK IV (B9LOT-B23SH). The TS-40c was identical to its dirt-loading counterpart mechanically, except for the extended side boards on the B23SH scraper bowl that increased capacity volume to 40 cubic yards struck and 49 cubic yards heaped for the lighter coal material. In May 1975, a new TS-24 Mk V (B10LOT-B26SH) was introduced with significant changes that set it apart from its predecessors. The TS-24 Mk V used the same Detroit Diesel 8V-71N engines found in the Mk IV version, but more power was now available,

This Terex 82-30B (GA) is shown working in Roseburg, Oregon, in June 1975. These types of working conditions would really put the crawler's undercarriage to the test. Starting in 1976, more power was available from the dozer's DD 8V-71T engine, which was rated at 277 gross horsepower and 260 fhp.

with each unit now rated at 318 gross horsepower and 300 fhp, totaling 636 gross horsepower and 600 fhp. The increased power was due mainly to the use of new Allison CLT-5660/1 Torqmatic transmissions, both front and rear, and repositioned air cleaners. The TS-24 Mk V also featured the Terex keystone front and rear radiator shroud designs found on U.S.-built Terex machines. The front sheet metal design on the British model was a bit more squared-off, but there was no mistaking the distinctive Terex family look. This model also had a coal-loading counterpart, the TS-40c Mk V (B10LOT-B26SH) and, like the previous version, had a larger-capacity scraper bowl with sideboards. Volume and payload ratings were unchanged from the older Mk IV model.

The largest and most-powerful regular production scraper produced by the Terex Division was the TS-32 (47LOT-80SH). Like other Terex scrapers that were once sold as Euclid models, the big TS-32 was carried over virtually unchanged. Specifications were the same as for the last Euclid version offered.

In early 1971, the TS-32 received revised power ratings for its engines. The front Detroit Diesel 12V-71T was now rated at 525 gross horsepower and 482 fhp and the

rear DD 8V-71T was rated at 350 gross horsepower and 326 fhp. Total output was now 875 gross horsepower and 808 fhp. Capacity and payload ratings remained consistent with earlier models at 32 cubic yards struck and 43 cubic yards heaped. The maximum payload rating was 104,000 pounds. In 1978, an upgraded Terex TS-32B version was introduced. The "B" model now featured the Terex keystone grille design along with other overall improvements. Because of upgraded Allison automatic power shift transmissions, the power rating was changed to 807 fhp. Slow sales, due to the drop in demand for large-capacity scrapers and the high prices they carried, forced Terex to withdraw the TS-32B from the product line in early 1980.

In the 1970s, the Terex Division offered several models of coal scrapers based on standard production units already being built. The TS-24 coal scraper was offered in late 1968 and had its sales model name changed to the Terex TS-36 in 1969.

The TS-36 was the same as the TS-24, model 43LOT-78SH, except the scraper bowl had sideboards to increase its volume capacity to 36 cubic yards struck and 46 cubic yards heaped. The payload rating was 80,000 pounds, which was the same as its dirt-scraper counterpart. The drivetrains were the same in both units. When the TS-24 was upgraded in 1976, its coal-scraper counterpart, the TS-36, also received the same changes. Capacity ratings were the same as the previous units. The TS-32 was also offered in a coal-scraper version in late 1968, which became the Terex TS-50 coal scraper in 1969. The same standard TS-32, model 47LOT-80SH, was used as the basis for the coal unit. The scraper bowl had sideboards, which increased its coal-carrying volume to 50 cubic yards struck and 59 cubic yards heaped. The payload weight of 104,000 pounds was the same as the TS-32. All major specifications were shared between the two units. In 1978, an upgraded TS-32B coal scraper was announced, but records seem to indicate that none was ever built.

The popular Terex TS-24B Loadrunner had two different coal scrapers based on its components. These were the TS-38B and TS-46B Loadrunner coal scrapers, first announced in May 1978. Both units were basically TS-24B, model 035-036, machines, with modified rear scraper bowls. The TS-38B used a standard 036 scraper bowl, but with sideboards to increase its volume to 38 cubic yards struck and 46 cubic yards heaped. The TS-46B coal scraper had the same 036 bowl as the TS-24B/TS-38B, but in addition to getting sideboards, the scraper bowl itself was lengthened by 2 feet 4 inches. This increased the coal volume capacity to a whopping 46 cubic yards struck and 56 cubic yards heaped, with the same payload rating of 81,500 pounds found in all of the Loadrunner scrapers. All three models shared the same basic mechanical and drivetrain specifications. The first prototypes of both the TS-38B and TS-46B coal scrapers were placed into early testing duties in 1980, but production records indicate that the first true, full-production version of the TS-46B was not delivered until 1982.

Shown at the Hudson plant in July 1973 is the first production unit of the Terex 82-20 series of crawler dozers. The 82-20 was powered by a Detroit Diesel 6V-71T engine rated at 208 gross horsepower and 180 fhp. In 1976, this model was upgraded into the 82-20B version, with power ratings of 232 gross horsepower and 205 fhp.

Terex Elevator Scrapers

Following the introduction of the first elevating scraper, the Euclid S-7 Hancock, Terex expanded the model line in the 1970s. The S-7 Hancock continued on as a Terex S-12E (4UOT-12E2) as a stopgap measure until its replacement, the Terex S-11E (16UOT-94SH), was introduced in mid-1969. The S-11E was an entirely new model, utilizing an 11-cubic-yard heaped Hancock-built elevator-type scraper with hydraulic elevator drive. This was preferred to the old system used in the S-7 Hancock unit, which used a rear-mounted engine to drive the elevator. The S-11E's tractor was powered by a Detroit Diesel 4-71N, two-cycle, four-cylinder engine rated at 160 gross horsepower and 144 fhp. This was connected to a five-speed Dana P5-400, full power shifting transmission.

In 1973, an upgraded S-11E Series B (18UOT-101SH) was released with an improved rear elevator unit. The scraper bowl was reinforced on the outside with the addition of steel side plating, and a more powerful, variable-speed hydrostatic drive motor drove the elevator. Power ratings for the tractor engine and scraper capacity were unchanged from the previous version. The little S-11E Series B never quite found the buying audience it was looking for and was removed from the product line by 1977.

In 1972, Terex officially introduced a mid-sized elevator-type scraper in the form of the 23-cubic-yard-capacity S-23E (33TOT-H-93SH). The prototype of the S-23E started engineering field testing in September 1970, and it was really put to the test before being released for sale. The S-23E's 33TOT-H tractor, which was borrowed from the TS-18 scraper, was powered by a

Detroit Diesel 8V-71N, two-cycle, eight-cylinder engine rated at 318 gross horsepower and 292 fhp. This was mated to a six-speed Allison VCLT-4465 Torqmatic transmission. The rear 93SH Hancock-designed elevator scraper was hydraulically powered. The capacity rating was 23 cubic yards heaped, with a 53,000-pound load limit. In 1973, an improved version of the S-23E was released with minor modifications to the standard engine and an upgraded torque convertor for the Allison transmission, which increased power output to 333 gross horsepower and 310 fhp. The elevator scraper unit remained unchanged. The S-23E was removed from the Terex product line in 1983.

The largest elevator-type scraper offered by Terex was the S-35E. This model actually got its start as a Euclid-developed model dating back to 1966, when the concept was first tested as the prototype Euclid S-24 Hancock scraper. This early unit was found to be lacking in power, so a redesigned unit called the Euclid S-32 Hancock was built in April 1968. It officially became the S-35E (47LOT-335E) in August 1968. The S-35E used the same tractor front as the Terex S-32 scraper, and was powered by the identical Detroit Diesel 12V-71T engine rated at 495 gross horsepower and 451 fhp. The transmission was a six-speed Allison VCLBT-5965 Torqmatic unit. The rear elevator scraper was a hydraulically powered, Hancock-built model 335E with hydrostatic elevator drive, rated at 35 cubic yards heaped, with a 84,000-pound load limit.

In 1970, an upgraded version of the S-35E (47LOT-90SH) was released with more power from the DD 12V-71T, now rated at 500 gross horsepower and 457 fhp. Except for some improvements to the hydraulic elevator drive, the unit was basically the same as the previous model. A new model of this scraper, the Terex S-35E B, was built in 1980, utilizing the new tractor front of the TS-32B. But while the scraper was still undergoing early engineering testing, the model line was canceled in 1981 because it was too costly to produce.

Terex Crawler Dozers

Like most of the other model lines that were formerly Euclid Division designs, the three crawler dozers, 82-30, 82-40, and 82-80, became Terex units with little or no change at first. In the case of the twin-engined Terex 82-80 (DA) dozer, the only addition made to the crawler was the availability in 1969 of twin, side-by-side-mounted Terex 4000 Series Hydraulic Control Units to control the front bulldozing blade. These cylinders were the same units as those found on the 82-30 and 82-40. This was the only difference between the Euclid 82-80 (DA) and the Terex version. The 82-80 stayed in the Terex product line until 1974, when the last batch of 15 units was produced. In total, there were 125 Euclid and Terex 82-80 (DA) dozers built, with about 80 of the Terex units equipped with the twin hydraulic cylinder blade control unit. In total, 901 units of the TC-12/82-80

The Terex 82-40 (DA) crawler dozer was introduced in May 1969. The 82-40 (DA) version was powered by a GM Detroit Diesel 8V-71N engine rated at 290 gross horsepower and 275 fhp at 2,100 rpm. The U.S.-built 82-40 model line was phased out of production in 1973.

twin-engined dozers were manufactured between 1954 and 1974, including prototypes.

In its day, the TC-12 dozer was GM's most technologically advanced and powerful crawler. During its career, the reliability of the model was always in question. Even though the major drivetrain components were mass-produced and parts were widely available, keeping them all operating at the same time and in the proper state of repair was something that some owners were not especially good at. If the dozer was well-maintained and serviced regularly, it was fairly reliable. But fall behind in your maintenance of the unit and it would come back to haunt you. This was especially true if both engines, transmissions, and torque converters had to be rebuilt. The costs involved were not for the squeamish. This situation was most notable in used machines that were on their second or third owner. The large contractors who first bought large fleets of the TC-12 could afford to maintain them, but smaller outfits that didn't have the best-trained mechanics on staff often found themselves with a "basket case" on their hands. Sometimes, you can be too technically advanced for your own good. This was the case of the TC-12/82-80 program.

It is a shame that this cloud lingered over the twin-engined dozer most of its life, because as far as its productivity was concerned, it was an excellent performer. It was a good bulldozer for pushing large amounts of material. It was an excellent ripping dozer, one that few other machines could match in its day. But as a push-dozer, for helping scrapers load faster, it was unmatched for its ability to put all of its massive power to the ground, and none could question the incredible maneuverability of the unit. Dozers come and go through the years, but the TC-12/82-80 is still remembered today as one great machine. It takes a dozer with personality to be remembered after its working days are over, and that is one thing the twin-powered super-dozer had plenty of.

One of the other dozers to be carried over from the Euclid product line was the 82-30 (FA) crawler. This unit was performing well in the marketplace, so no immediate changes were initiated right away. But Terex released a special turbocharged version of the 82-30 in 1969 that would retain its full rated power output in high altitude and high ambient temperature applications. The Terex 82-30 (FAT) turbo actually started life as a Euclid prototype model in June 1968, but the unit was too early in its engineering evaluation testing to be released at that time. The 82-30 (FAT) was powered by a single GM Detroit Diesel 6-71T engine rated at 239 gross horsepower and 25 fhp. These were the same power ratings as those found in the standard 82-30 (FA) version.

In June 1973, Terex introduced the 82-30B (GA) dozer model that replaced both the standard and turbo 82-30 versions built at the Hudson plant. The first pilot model of the 82-30B (GA) version was built in August 1970, and the second pilot model was the unit announced in June 1973. The new "B" version featured a more heavy-duty undercarriage and redesigned front and rear ends, giving the unit a more squared-off look. The 82-30B was powered by a single GM Detroit Diesel 8V-71T, two-cycle, turbocharged, eight-cylinder engine rated at 277 gross horsepower and 245 fhp. This was connected to a three-speed, full power shifting Allison CRT-6031 transmission.

In 1976, an upgraded 82-30B model was released with revised power ratings of 277 gross horsepower and 260 fhp from the original GM 8V-71T engine. In 1982, the 82-30B nomenclature was changed to the Terex D750. Mechanically, the two models were identical. The last D750/82-30B dozer to be produced in the United States was built in 1984, but wasn't shipped from the Hudson plant's remaining inventory until April 1989.

The Euclid 82-40 (CA) dozer joined the Terex model line unchanged, but a new version was already being planned for a 1969 release. The upgraded Terex 82-40 (DA) model rolled out of the Hudson plant in May 1969, and featured many improvements over the former CA version. Some of these upgrades were a lengthened track frame, beefed-up track and undercarriage components, and a doubling of the air cleaner capacity. Power ratings were unchanged from the previous model. A turbocharged version, the 82-40 (DAT), was also offered at the same time as the standard DA model. The first prototype of the turbo version was built as a Euclid model in March 1968, but was never released as such. Power ratings for the 82-40 (DAT) were 308 gross horsepower and 290 fhp from the GM Detroit Diesel 8V-71T engine. Both of these versions of the Terex 82-40 were available until 1973, when they were both withdrawn from the U.S. product line.

Just after the release of the 82-40 (DA) dozer, Terex was already hard at work on its replacement. The first pilot version of the 12-cylinder-engined Terex 82-40 (EA) model was finished in February 1970. After early trial testing, a complete rebuild program was started on the undercarriage in January 1971, with the finished unit being put back into field testing duties as the Terex 972 crawler tractor. The Terex 972 was the engineering model number of the dozer while it was being developed, and at this point in the crawler's evolution, was still part of the 82-40 (EA) program. This prototype version was powered by a GM Detroit Diesel 12V-71N, two-cycle, 12-cylinder engine rated at 335 fhp, mated to a three-speed, full power shifting Allison CRT-7031 transmission. Early field trials indicated a need for more power from the Terex 972's engine, and a need for further modifications to the undercarriage. Design changes were made to the crawler track assemblies and a turbocharger was added to the engine in early 1973. This turbo version of the dozer would be the one that would go into production, but not as an 82-40 model. Marketing felt that the new crawler was so far removed, design-wise, from the old 82-40 series, that new model identification nomenclature was needed. It was finally decided

that the new model would be called the Terex 82-50. The 82-50 dozer identification had been used once before on a prototype Euclid model developed in 1967, but never released for sale. It sounded good then, so why not use it now?

The first Terex dozer carrying the 82-50 identification was introduced in August 1973. This model was powered by a GM Detroit Diesel 12V-71T, two-cycle, turbocharged, 12-cylinder engine rated at 415 gross horsepower and 370 fhp. The transmission was the same Allison unit found in the Terex 972 version of the dozer. In 1976, the 82-50 received numerous component improvements, with all major specifications remaining unchanged. The last version of the 82-50 dozer, referred to as the Terex D800, was introduced in September 1982. Power output from the 12V-71T engine was rated

at 350 fhp on this model, with all major drivetrain components the same as those used in the previous 82-50. Design-wise, this model featured twin, front-mounted dozer hydraulic cylinders, sealed and lubricated tracks, and redesigned outboard planetary rear final drives. The front end of the D800 was painted black, which gave the illusion that a radiator was now in the front, but in fact it was still mounted in the rear like all other Terex U.S.-designed and -built crawler dozers. The last D800 produced came off the assembly line in 1986 and was, in fact, the last Terex crawler dozer to be built by the company. The final unit stayed in inventory at the Hudson plant until it was finally sold in April 1989.

The smallest production crawler dozer offered by the GM Terex Division was the 82-20 model. The first pilot version of this model rolled out of the factory in

In August 1973 Terex introduced the 82-50 heavy crawler dozer, which would eventually replace the 82-80 as the largest model in the crawler line. The 82-50 was powered by a Detroit Diesel 12V-71T, rated at 415 gross horsepower and 370 fhp. This 82-50 works in Northampton, England, in July 1976. As equipped, the dozer weighed in at about 90,000 pounds.

July 1971. After months of engineering testing, the first production 82-20 was unveiled in July 1973. The Terex 82-20 was powered by a GM Detroit Diesel 6V-71T, two-cycle, turbocharged, six-cylinder engine rated at 208 gross horsepower and 180 fhp, connected to a three-speed Allison CRT-5434 transmission. In 1976, an upgraded 82-20B version was released, with increased power ratings of 232 gross horsepower and 205 fhp now available from the DD 6V-71T engine. Both versions of the dozer shared the same basic design features that were found in the larger Terex 82-30B and 82-50 crawlers, only in a smaller package. In 1982, the model identification of the 82-20B was changed to the Terex D700A.

Crawler dozers were also produced at the Motherwell plant in Scotland, and closely resembled their American cousins. Models produced included the C-6, 82-30, 82-30B, and the 82-40. The Scottish plant did not produce the larger 82-50 and 82-80 dozers, nor the smaller 82-20 versions. Most model releases were in step with the same versions being made in the United States. Exceptions to this include the Euclid/Terex 82-30 (FA) dozer and the Terex D750P pipelayer. Even though the Terex Division in the United States replaced their 82-30 (FA) model in 1973 with the 82-30B, General Motors Scotland, Ltd. continued manufacturing the older 82-30 crawler until about 1986. General Motors Scotland, Ltd. also produced the 82-30B model, shipping their first unit in March 1979. A special-purpose crawler tractor built in Scotland and also not available in the U.S. market was the Terex 82-30B/D750P pipelayer, made available around 1985, rated at 43 tons lifting capacity at 4 feet.

Terex Front-End Loaders

The fourth major product line carried by Terex was the rubber-tired front end loaders, consisting of the former Euclid Division machines that were available in 1968. All of the Euclid loaders were carried over into the Terex line, including the Euclid 72-80, which was released as the Terex 72-81.

The smallest U.S.-built front end loader carried by Terex was the 72-21. This model was unchanged from the previous Euclid version when it became a Terex machine. In 1970, Terex released a 72-21S version, which was marketed as a basic loader to which the customer could add optional equipment for the particular job requirements. The 72-21S was the "economy" loader in the product line. In 1971, the standard 72-21 power ratings were revised for its GM Detroit Diesel 3-71N engine, and showed 109 gross horsepower and 115 fhp. In 1974, the loader received an upgraded two-speed Allison TT-2221 dual-range transmission. The bucket capacity range for the 72-21 was from 2 to 3 cubic yards. The 72-21 model was removed from the loader product line at the end of 1975. It would be a couple of years before its replacement, the 72-21B, was ready for release. In 1979, the 72-21B was officially introduced with a bucket capacity range of 2 to 2.25 cubic yards. The 72-21B was powered by a GM Detroit Diesel 3-53T, two-cycle, turbocharged engine rated at 125 gross horsepower and 115 fhp. The transmission was a three-speed Clark 18326 full power shift unit. In late 1982, the name of the 72-21B was changed to the Terex 40C wheel loader. It remained this way until the unit was removed from the product line in 1985.

Like the 72-21, the Euclid 72-31 became a Terex model with no major changes and a bucket range of 2.5

The Terex 72-61 front end loader was one of the most thoroughly tested models the company ever produced. The first proto-type of the 72-61 was built in March 1973, but the production machines were not officially released until mid-1976. The loader was powered by a Detroit Diesel 8V-71T engine, with a power output of 343 gross horsepower and 307 fhp. The bucket capacity range for the 72-61 model was 5.5 to 6 cubic yards.

to 5 cubic yards. In 1970, a 72-31S "basic" model was also introduced at the same time as the 72-21S model. In 1971, more power was available from the GM Detroit Diesel 4-71N, with increased ratings of 151 gross horsepower and 146 fhp. The 72-31 later received an upgraded two-speed Allison TT-2221 transmission in 1974. Except for a spiffy new ROPS (Rollover Protection Structures) cab, the unit looked as it did back in 1968.

In June 1975, the first prototype Terex 72-31B model was built for engineering evaluation testing, and it would eventually replace the older unit in the product line in 1977. The 72-31B had a bucket capacity range of 3 to 3.75 cubic yards, and was powered by a GM Detroit Diesel 4-71T, two-cycle, turbocharged engine rated at 170 gross horsepower and 160 fhp. This was connected to a two-speed Allison TT-2221-1 dual range transmission. The 72-31B was a new machine overall, and featured the Terex keystone rear-end design. It was superior to the older 72-31 in every way. In late 1982, the 72-31B nomenclature was changed to the Terex 60C model, and it remained in the product line until being phased out of production in 1988.

The Terex 72-41 front end loader was unchanged from its 1968 Euclid version, and did not receive any noticeable changes until 1971, when power ratings for its GM Detroit Diesel 4-71N engine were changed to 163 gross horsepower and 153 fhp. The transmission was the same Allison unit found in the last Euclid model. The rated bucket capacity for the 72-41 ranged from 3 to 5 cubic yards. In March 1970, a prototype of a 72-41 (BA) loader was built as an eventual replacement for the then-current 72-41. It shared the same new design look that all of the other new B model loaders were getting, but this unit never went into production. It was decided that the 72-41 model was too close in performance and capacity to the new 72-31B loader, causing the unit to be removed from the product line. The 72-41 model's last year of production was 1976.

The Euclid 72-51, like all of the rest of the former Euclid models, became a Terex loader with no immediate changes being made to the unit. In 1971, the 72-51 received revised power ratings for its GM Detroit Diesel 6-71N engine, with new outputs of 202 gross horsepower and 194 fhp. In 1974, the model received an upgraded, multi-speed Allison TT-4720 Hydro power shift transmission. The bucket capacity range for the Terex 72-51 was from 3.5 to 6 cubic yards. In January 1975, the first pilot model of the Terex 72-51B loader was built, and it was officially introduced as the replacement for the previous model in May 1977. The 72-51B was a new design for this class of loader for Terex, and was powered by a GM Detroit Diesel 6V-71T, two-cycle, turbocharged engine rated at 257 gross horsepower and 231 fhp. The transmission was a dual-range, two-speed Allison TRT-3420 full power shift unit. The bucket capacity range for the "B" version was from 4 to 5 cubic yards. In late 1982, the loader became known as the

Terex 70C, and it was offered in the product line until being phased out of production in 1988.

Terex introduced its newly designed 72-61 front end loader in mid-1976. The original pilot version of the new model had existed since March 1973, and had put in thousands of testing hours before going into full production. The 72-61 looked very much like the 72-51B loader, only larger. The loader was powered by a GM Detroit Diesel 8V-71T, 2-cycle, turbocharged, eight-cylinder engine rated at 343 gross horsepower and 307 fhp. This was connected to a dual-range, two-speed Allison TRT-4820 power shift transmission. The bucket capacity range for the 72-61 was 5.5 to 6 cubic yards. The 72-61 came standard with a full ROPS cab, like the unit mounted on the 72-51B loader. In late 1982, the loader's model identification was changed to the Terex 80C. The 80C wheel loader remained in the Terex product line until 1993, after which time it was phased out of production.

The Terex 72-71 front end loader, along with the 72-81, were considered the company's big guns in the loader product line. The 72-71 was a Terex-designed machine, and borrowed nothing from any previous Euclid model. The first pilot version of the loader was built in February 1970, and the production model was officially released in June 1971. The 72-71 was powered by a single GM Detroit Diesel 8V-71T, two-cycle, turbocharged, eight-cylinder engine rated at 360 gross horsepower and 336 fhp. The transmission was the three-speed Allison CRT-5631 full power shift unit. The Terex 72-71 series was designed specifically to do battle in the marketplace with the Caterpillar 988 wheel loader, the industry leader in that large-capacity class range.

In April 1977, the upgraded 72-71B model was released with a significant power increase over the previous version. A new GM Detroit Diesel 8V-92T, two-cycle, turbocharged, eight-cylinder engine now resided in the rear of the loader. It was connected to an upgraded three-speed Allison CRT-5633 transmission. The 72-71B was classified as a 7.5 to 8-cubic-yard capacity machine, with a maximum payload rating of 24,000 pounds. The 72-71B was a good overall performer, and was well-accepted in the marketplace. In 1988, the model identification of the 72-71B was changed to the Terex 85C, which remained in the product line until 1992.

In October 1979, Terex started testing the first pilot model of the 72-71C front end loader. This unit incor-

next: The Terex 72-71 was the second-largest wheel loader in the product line when the model was introduced in June 1971. The 72-71 was classified as a 7.5 to 8-cubic-yard machine, and was powered by a Detroit Diesel 8V-71T engine rated at 360 gross horsepower and 336 fhp. In April 1977, the upgraded 72-71B model was announced, with new power ratings of 430 gross horsepower and 388 fhp from its new DD 8V-92T engine. The first 72-71B loader was driven off the assembly line in September 1978. Shown working in August 1971 is one of the first production 72-71 loaders to be delivered into service.

The Diesel Division Continues On

When the Terex earth-moving product line passed from GM to IBH Holding AG on January 1, 1981, the diesel-electric drive haulers built at the Diesel Division, General Motors of Canada, Ltd.'s London, Ontario, Canada, plant, were not included in the deal. Because of the nature of the trucks and their relationship to the Canadian locomotive assembly plant, GM decided it was in its best interest to retain ownership in the hauler line. The Terex name was removed from the trucks' front ends and replaced with the new hauler product line identification of Titan. The Titan name was always well-liked by GM, but it caused some confusion at first in regards to the Terex 33-19 Titan hauler. One only has to remember that there was only one three-axle GM Terex Titan truck produced, while quite a few of the two-axle GM Diesel Division Titan haulers were built. Other products manufactured at the Diesel Division besides the Titan mining haulers were locomotives, buses, military vehicles, and large industrial and marine diesel engines.

The Diesel Division locomotive plant on Oxford Street in London, Ontario, had been building earth-moving equipment since 1965, when GM of Canada, Ltd. had assumed full sales responsibility for all Euclid products in Canada. The first products produced were some of the Euclid R-series haulers, and the L-20, L-25, and L-30 front end loaders. At this time, the division was referred to as GM Diesel, Ltd.

In 1981, two diesel-electric-drive rear dump haulers were offered by the Diesel Division: the 170-ton-capacity Titan 33-15B and the 350-ton-capacity Titan 33-19. The division tried to sell the giant three-axle truck, but just could not find any takers, so all sales can be traced to the 33-15 series of haulers, which were first produced in 1971. The last model to carry the Terex name was the 33-15B. The truck became a Titan 33-15B in 1981, with the only noticeable change being the name.

The Diesel Division produced 47 Titan 33-15B haulers before an improved version, the 33-15C, was introduced in late 1981. The powerplant was the same GM Detroit Diesel 16V-149TI, rated at 1,600 gross horsepower and 1,445 fhp, as that found in the "B" model. The 33-15C upgrades included better component accessibility, improved electrical system and hydraulic systems, repositioned air cleaners to improve the operator's line-of-sight, faster dump cycles, and 30 high-demand options now being made standard. The payload capacity remained at 170 tons.

This GM Titan 33-15C hauler, nicknamed "Spike," was the first produced by the Diesel Division in Canada. It is shown at the plant in July 1981. The 170-ton-capacity Titan 33-15C was the upgraded version of the previous 33-15B model. *GM Diesel Division Archives*

Shortly after Marathon LeTourneau purchased the 33-15C hauler line from GM in February 1985, the model designation of the trucks was changed to the Titan T-2000 series in September 1986, with the first prototype unit shipped in January 1987. The LeTourneau Titan T-2200 model shown is a 200-ton-capacity hauler available with either a Detroit Diesel 16V-149TI engine or a Cummins KTTA50-C unit, both rated at 2,000 fhp. The total gross weight of a loaded truck is 716,900 pounds, and it weighs 316,900 pounds empty. This hauler (now referred to as the LeTourneau T-2200 after the Titan name was retired in early 1994) is available with three engine choices: the Detroit Diesel; a Cummins K2000-E diesel; or an MTU Diesel 12V396TE44 unit, all rated at 2,000 fhp, except the MTU engine, which carries an 1,850 fhp power output. *LeTourneau, Inc.*

This Titan 33-15C hauler, at BC Coal's Balmer mine in British Columbia, Canada, in 1982, was part of the first fleet of 13 trucks to be put into service (besides the single prototype unit). The 33-15C was powered by a GM Detroit Diesel 16V-149TI engine rated at 1,600 gross horsepower and 1,445 fhp. *Bruce Kurschenska*

The first Titan 33-15C hauler, nicknamed "Spike," was shipped from the factory in November 1981. By January 1983, only 35 of the 33-15C haulers had been sold, due mainly to the mining industry's widespread economic recession. Business was so bad that for the rest of the year and for all of 1984, no 33-15C trucks were sold. Things were not looking good for the Titan hauler line.

GM had clearly lost interest in pursuing profits in the mining industry by building haul trucks. The company had enough to worry about concerning its automobile product lines, so a buyer was sought for the Titan mining hauler. By late 1984, Marathon LeTourneau of Longview, Texas, was talking seriously to GM about purchasing the truck line, including all machine tools necessary to build it. LeTourneau was no stranger to heavy equipment, and the 170-ton truck complemented the large diesel-electric-drive front end loaders LeTourneau had been building for years. The deal was signed between the two companies just before Christmas 1984, and involved the sale of all plans, drawings, toolings, and world manufacturing rights of the Titan line to Marathon LeTourneau. The Titan product line was officially transferred from GM to LeTourneau on February 1, 1985.

The 33-15C model carried over unchanged to LeTourneau, and was still referred to as a Titan hauler. LeTourneau shipped 11 of the Titan 33-15C haulers in 1985, and only six of an upgraded version, designated as a 33-15D model, in 1986.

In January 1987, Marathon LeTourneau shipped its first "T-2000" series of Titan haulers, featuring many improvements, including a newly designed operator's cab. The first prototype truck was a 190-ton-capacity Titan T-2190 hauler. Other models offered at the time were a 170-ton T-2170 and a 200-ton T-2200 model. Later, a 240-ton-capacity unit called the T-2240 was also offered. Even though the old 33-series designation was now history, all of these haulers were based on the original GM Titan 33-15C mining truck.

In all, a total of 348 diesel-electric-drive mining trucks were built at the Diesel Division, of which 266 carried the Terex name. This total includes the first dismantled prototype 33-15 "Fat Albert" from September 1970, and the one-and-only 350-ton-capacity Terex 33-19 Titan hauler.

LeTourneau, Inc. (formerly Marathon LeTourneau) still builds the big haul trucks based largely on the original Diesel Division design. Models offered include the T-2190 and the T-2200. The LeTourneau company officially broke the last remaining remnants linking the truck to GM when the Titan name was officially retired in early 1994 and dropped as the brand name of the hauler product line. Now they are simply referred to as LeTourneau T-2000 series trucks.

The largest front end loader built by Terex was its 72-81 series model, introduced in February 1969. The 72-81 started out as the Euclid 72-80 in January 1968. The production version was powered by a Detroit Diesel 12V-71T engine rated at 465 gross horsepower and 438 fhp, and it was classified as a 9- to 10-cubic-yard machine, with a payload rating of 27,000 pounds. The overall operating weight of the 72-81 loader was 114,890 pounds. This 72-81 works in August 1972 at a stone quarry in East St. Louis, Illinois.

porated the latest design innovations introduced on the smaller 72-51B and 72-61 wheel loaders, and was meant as a replacement for the 72-71B model. The 72-71C was powered by a GM Detroit Diesel 12V-71T, two-cycle, turbocharged engine rated at 484 gross horsepower and 452 fhp, connected to a three-speed Allison CRT-7033 transmission. The bucket capacity was from 7.7 to 8.5 cubic yards, with a maximum 22,500-pound payload limit. But as it turned out, the 72-71C did not replace the 72-71B model, and in fact was never released as a GM Terex Division model. The loader was officially introduced in mid-1982 as the IBH/Terex 90C model, and remained in production until the last orders for it were shipped from the plant in Scotland in 1994.

The largest of all of the front end loaders built by Terex was the model 72-81. This loader started life as the Euclid 72-80 in January 1968. The nomenclature was changed at the end of that year by Terex to the 72-81 to conform with the rest of the loader product line. In February 1969, Terex officially introduced the model to the industry.

The 72-81 was a large machine with a bucket capacity range of 9 to 10 cubic yards, and a total maximum payload of 27,000 pounds. The model released in 1969

was powered by a single GM Detroit Diesel 12V-71T, two-cycle, turbocharged, 12-cylinder engine rated at 465 gross horsepower and 438 fhp. This was connected to a three-speed Allison CRT-6033 Torqmatic transmission. In 1971, the engine's power ratings were revised to 465 gross horsepower and 434 fhp. In 1974, a new three-speed Allison CRT-7033 full power shift transmission replaced the older unit. On the outside, the upgraded loader looked just like the previous models. Terex started work on an improved version of the loader called the 72-81B in October 1973. This model was to feature the Terex trademark keystone design around the rear radiator housing. But due to the smaller market size for this type of machine, and other new loader developments aimed at generating larger-volume sales, the 72-81B upgrade project was put on hold. As it turned out, the B model project would never be resumed. The 72-81 loader stayed in the Terex product line until mid-1982, when it was replaced by the newly designed Terex 90C model.

The smallest wheel loader to be designed and built by Terex came from General Motors Scotland, Ltd.'s Motherwell plant in the form of the pivot-steer 72-11. The Terex 72-11 was a small, 1.5-cubic-yard capacity utility loader that was powered by a GM Bedford 330, four-cycle, six-cylinder engine rated at 94 gross horsepower and 90 fhp. This was mated to a dual-range, two-speed Allison TT-2220 transmission. The most distinctive design feature of the 72-11 was its single lift arm supporting the bucket, a departure from other Terex designs utilizing two arms.

The first 72-11 shipped from the factory in Scotland was transported in May 1971. The model was basically meant for home market use and none was ever imported into the United States for sale. In 1974, the loader received a revised rear-end treatment, but everything else remained the same. The Terex 72-11 was discontinued in 1975.

An off-shoot of the wheel loader product line was the Terex 74-51 Composter, aimed at companies whose business was the management of solid waste material. The 74-51 model was based on the tractor portion of the Terex 72-51 loader, with a Colby Composter unit attached to the front end. The main purpose of the unit was to re-distribute either municipal waste, sewage sludge, or animal waste material in composting heaps or rows that were constantly turned upside down and inside out by the hydraulically driven elevator action of the Colby unit. This would help keep the material supplied with oxygen to support air-breathing microorganisms that helped the waste decompose more quickly and naturally.

The first unit was built in April 1971, and was initially just referred to as a 72-51, with the Colby Composter as an option. This first design of the elevator unit was very complicated, and prone to numerous breakdowns. A redesigned Colby unit was put into service in December 1971, and proved to be more reliable. It was at this time that the unit became a stand-alone machine in the product line, becoming the 74-51 Composter. The Terex composter project was plagued with problems from the very start, compounded by the lukewarm reception that the waste management industry gave it. Terex decided to cut its losses and terminated the 74-51 project at the end of 1974.

Terex and the IBH Group

The early and mid-1970s were considered good years for the Terex Division, with the scraper product line being the strongest product segment by far. But nothing is forever. The late 1970s were troublesome for Terex, as they were for many other manufacturers of off-road heavy equipment because of a market downturn in the United States and a deepening recession in Europe. But other outside forces were controlling the Terex Division's future, namely the automotive market. Factors that affected GM's auto sales would soon cause trouble for all of its divisions.

The General Motors Corporation, like the rest of the U.S. producers of automobiles and light trucks, was heading into some of its darkest days. The giant auto producer was in the process of a gigantic and expensive new product line development program. The General could not risk making the same mistakes it did with the Chevy Vega and diesel engines for passenger cars derived from standard gasoline units. There were still too many large gas guzzlers in the product line, and the imports that got a

foot in the door during the energy crisis were not going to go home anytime soon.

At this point in the company's history, GM could not afford to concentrate on anything else except building cars that the buying public wanted. In other words, GM no longer had the time to fool around with developing and manufacturing the green iron. It just wasn't as profitable as it once had been.

In August 1980, negotiations were started between GM and IBH Holding AG, of Mainz, Germany, concerning the possible sale of the Terex Division. The IBH Group consisted of 10 subsidiary companies that, for the most part, were all European in origin. These included some of Europe's most-recognized brand names in the construction industry, Zettelmeyer, Hanomag, Hamm, Duomat, Lanz, WIBAU, Hymac, Pingon, Derruppe, and Maco-Meudon.

The IBH company was originally established on July 1, 1975, by Horst-Dieter Esch, with the intention of bringing together a number of weaker, medium-sized businesses in the construction equipment industry, and strengthening their competitive ability in a very difficult market.

The first of these acquisitions was Zettelmeyer, in July 1975, becoming the first building block of Esch's empire, which he ruled as president and chief executive. When GM contacted IBH about a possible interest in Terex, it did not take long for IBH to return the call. The IBH Group saw an opportunity to enter the lucrative North American market, something it could have only dreamed about in the past. After the signing of the Terex purchase agreement by then-GM Chairman Roger Smith and Horst-Dieter Esch in September 1980, the GM earth-moving division became a subsidiary of the IBH Group known as the Terex Corporation, effective January 1, 1981.

The sale of Terex by GM for $250 million included all major manufacturing facilities in the United States, Great Britain, and Brazil. Only a small gear-cutting plant in Peterhead, Scotland, and the diesel-electric haulers built by the Diesel Division in Canada were excluded from the deal.

In return for IBH acquiring the Terex operations, GM became an investor in IBH Holding AG, with holdings valued at $22 million, or about 13.6 percent of the company. By May 1982, GM's share holdings were approximately 17.9 percent of IBH. GM was needed as a financial backer to help prop up IBH while Terex was being integrated into the German group.

When things were better established, and profits were coming in, GM would sell its shares and finally get itself out of the earth-moving business. At least that was the plan. No one could foretell how bad world economic conditions would be, or how much worse the recession really was. The mild recession in the United States and the stagnant European economy gave way to a full-blown worldwide recession when many of the third-world countries started defaulting on their debts in the early 1980s. This would have a dire effect on the IBH Group, and would send Terex down a road that would change the company, and how people perceived the company, forever.

Military Applications, Experimental Prototypes, Specials, and other Good Ideas

Along with the many production machines created by Euclid and Terex during the GM years, and just prior to that period, numerous special-application and experimental prototypes were built. Many of these were for military use and were never available for regular sale. Others were prototype machines for new products that, for one reason or another, never went into production. Regular production equipment was regularly converted into more-specialized units by their owners, often with the assistance of Euclid or Terex, so it could perform a particular task. To some extent, these creations were a direct reflection on the engineering resourcefulness the companies would display to try out a new idea. For many of these creations, production was never an option, as they were built with the sole purpose of testing an engineering theory or a design concept.

Military Equipment

Euclid Road Machinery had been producing some of its equipment for military purposes long before GM entered the picture, dating back to World War II. These were mostly orders for tractor/bottom dump combinations, and quarry type rear dump haulers. All of these units were based on regular production models, except for paint and light dimmers. No other special modifications were necessary. For the most part, almost all of the Euclid haulers that went into military service through the 1950s and 1960s were unmodified production units.

Along with standard military equipment, which was based on regular production machines, Euclid built a series of military machines that had no real civilian counterparts. In August 1950, Euclid Road Machinery built its first 2FPM tow tractor, referred to as the Type A-2 (later reclassified as the Type MB-2), for the U.S. Air Force. The 2FPM was a dual-cab-controlled, four-wheel-drive and -steer tractor used to maneuver aircraft around an

airport by either towing from the front landing gear, or by means of a three-wheeled, detachable cart. The tractor was powered by a single GM Diesel 6-71 engine. The unit used four 16.00x25 tires. The most distinctive feature of the 2FPM was its left-side elevating cab, which, when lowered, allowed the tractor to pass underneath most aircraft wing sections.

In late 1955, another version of the tow tractor, the Euclid 7FPM, was produced for the Air Force. This model was still referred to as a Type A-2, but differed slightly from the original 2FPM in that both cabs were fixed and did not elevate. The engine was the same as the previous model, but the unit now was equipped with larger 21.00x25 tires. Both cabs on the 7FPM were winterized for extreme cold-weather operation.

Another jeep-like tow tractor, the 8-FPM-G, was developed for the Navy in late 1955, with the first approved unit delivered in 1958. The 8FPM-G was based on all of the components of the 7FPM. Only the outside sheet metal design was different. The unit was built for yard and dock use and was not meant for aircraft-moving applications.

In 1953, Euclid introduced the first in a series of wheel dozers for military use, the 1TPM, which was specially designed for use by the U.S. Army Corps of Engineers. The 1TPM was based on the earlier (1951) Euclid 3FPM model and the 4FPM, from 1952. All these units utilized the Cummins NHRS engine. The 1TPM was essentially a 4FPM with different axles and design modifications for special space limitations.

An improved version of these wheel dozers was released in 1954, as the 5FPM-G. This unit was delivered to the U.S. Navy for testing, and was equipped with a Cummins NHS engine. All of the wheel dozers mentioned were equipped with four-wheel drive and rear-wheel steering. These models have always been confusing to identify because they all looked alike. The success of these units was very limited.

The early wheel dozers were a bit on the crude side, engineering-wise, so Euclid went back to the drawing board and came up with the 6TPM-G wheel dozer, which was completed in December 1960. This unit was competing

This 105-ton-capacity Euclid R-X is shown in June 1967 at the GM Proving Grounds, and is unique to the model line as being the only diesel-electric-drive version of the unit to be produced. This 11LLD model R-X is also equipped with an experimental aluminum dump body.

The 7FPM tow tractor, introduced in late 1955, was the second model produced by Euclid for the U.S. Air Force following the release of the 2FPM in August 1950. The main differences is that the 7FPM had larger tires, and the left-hand-side operator's cab was fixed in place, while the original 2FPM's cab could be raised or lowered.

The ITPM was the largest of the prototype wheel dozers built by Euclid for evaluation testing by the U.S. Army, shown in June 1953. Other models produced by Euclid that looked very similar to the 1TPM were the 3FPM from 1951, the 4FPM from 1952, and the 5FPM-G from 1954. All were four-wheel drive, with rear-wheel steering.

for a military contract to supply a wheel dozer and a pulled scraper unit for the U.S. Army. The entire unit, including the Euclid SV-18 pull-scraper, was ready in September 1962. The 6TPM-G was powered by a single GM Diesel 8V-71 engine that drove all four wheels. The unit was also of an articulated steering design, with the pivot point located behind the operator's cab. The maximum towed load capacity was 100,000 pounds. But again, Euclid would lose out on the contract, this time to the Caterpillar 830M and Clark Michigan 290M articulated-wheel tractor dozers. On the bright side, Euclid was awarded the contract to supply the pull-scrapers to be

used with the chosen dozers. The 18-cubic-yard-capacity Euclid 58SH-G pull-scraper, introduced in December 1963, was an improved version of the original SV-18 prototype. A special Euclid 9DY-G two-wheeled dolly was also included with the scraper for when the unit had to be transported by road or rail flat car. The Euclid scraper units that were paired up with the Clark Michigan 290M were referred to as the M280 pull-scrapers.

GM Euclid and Terex both supplied rubber-tired wheel loaders and their forklift truck counterparts to various branches of the armed services. Models included the Euclid L-15 (2UPM-G) in 1965, and the Euclid 72-31MP2U/R in

Euclid made another attempt at securing a military contract from the U.S. Army for a wheel dozer and scraper with this articulated 6TPM-G tractor and SV-18 pull scraper, shown in September 1962. The tractor was the first of the set to be completed in December 1960. Eventually, only a redesigned version of the SV-18 pull scraper was accepted for use, and it was called the Euclid 58SH-G.

Both the Euclid Division and the Terex Division supplied the U.S. Marine Corps with the 82-30 (FAM) crawler dozer. The first Euclid shipment was in 1967, followed by the Terex orders in 1970 (of which this dozer was part) and 1972. The 82-30 (FAM) was powered by a GM Detroit Diesel 6-71N engine rated at 239 gross horsepower and 225 fhp, which was the same powerplant found in its civilian counterpart.

1967. Both of these versions were based on standard production units, employing the Drott 4-in-1 bucket system. A total of 418 of the Euclid/Terex 72-31MP2U/R loaders were delivered to the U.S. Marine Corps, with 369 of the units being rebuilt and updated to like-new condition between 1978 and 1981.

In 1967, Euclid delivered its first 72-31F forklift truck to be used in the U.S. Air Force 463L Materials Handling System. This model proved to be very popular, and additional models were also ordered from Terex in 1973. By then the name, like most things military, had gotten rather long and confusing, and the Terex unit was called the Adverse Terrain 10K Fork Lift Truck, 463L Materials Handling, Type A/S32 H-15. Basic components on this unit were based on the 72-31 wheel loader. Over 300 of the 72-31F forklift trucks were delivered to the Air Force, with most still in service today.

Both GM Euclid and Terex delivered track dozers to the Marine Corps for use as their primary heavy dozer. In 1967, Euclid shipped the first 142 units of the 82-30 (FAM) dozer, which shared the same mechanical specifications as the regular production models. In 1970, Terex started delivery of a second contract order for 64 of the 82-30 (FAM) crawler, with the same specifications as the previous Euclid version. The last order for this unit was placed in 1972 for 49 additional dozers. In all, 255 dozers of the 82-30 (FAM) variety were delivered to the Marine Corps. The last dozer model Terex delivered into military service was the D700A (82-20B) crawler, of which 13 were shipped in 1984 to the Air Force.

Special pieces of Terex equipment for military use were also built at the Motherwell plant in Scotland for the British Army. These included the Terex 72-51MWT

wheel loader, first ordered in 1975, with the first 70 units being delivered in 1977. An additional 53 loaders were placed into service in 1980, followed by 30 more in 1983. Basic mechanical specifications were the same as the regular production model 72-51, except for some extra options, such as a multipurpose bucket, front-mounted winch, and a ripper. The 72-51 loader's size and weight allowed it to be transported in a Hercules C130 cargo plane, a requirement of the British Army.

Other standard production equipment drafted into military service included the Terex TS-14B scraper, of which five units were delivered in 1976, followed by an additional five in 1978. Terex also delivered two batches of 82-30B dozers, 23 in 1979 and 23 in 1981, becoming the Royal Engineers Heavy Crawler Tractor for the British Army. There were no major changes between the civilian and military versions of the dozer.

Of all of the equipment built in Scotland for the British Army, one product stands out as being developed differently than the others. This model was the Terex TS-8, all-wheel-drive, twin-engined scraper, first introduced in 1976. Even though civilian and military versions of this scraper were marketed, it was designed to military specifications first, with a regular production version considered later. One of the absolute main design considerations for the TS-8 was that it had to be fully transportable in a Lockheed C130K Hercules aircraft. The TS-8 could be flown in or trucked in to construction tasks and combat engineering areas where access by larger machines was impossible due to weak bridges, culverts, or low classification routes.

The TS-8 was powered by two identical Bedford GM 330 series, four-cycle, six-cylinder diesel engines,

The twin-engined TS-8 scraper was a special model designed by Terex Equipment, Ltd. in Scotland to meet the requirements of the British Army for a scraper that could be transported inside a Lockheed C130K Hercules aircraft. The prototype TS-8 was first introduced in 1976, with the first unit delivered into service in November 1979. *Terex Equipment, Ltd.*

rated at 100 gross horsepower and 92 fhp each, for a combined rating of 200 gross horsepower and 184 fhp. The original transmissions were four-speed, automatic Allison MT-650 units, front and rear. These were later upgraded to five-speed Allison MT-653 transmissions. The TS-8 was classified as an eight-cubic-yard struck and 11.6-cubic-yard heaped capacity scraper, with a maximum payload rating of 24,000 pounds. An additional set of load-spreading wheels was also included with the scraper unit, to be used for air transport only.

They attached on the leading edges of the scraper bowl and helped reduce the main front and rear axle loads to an acceptable level for aircraft floor loading. They also helped the units' vertical articulation, while following the contours of the loading ramps, keeping the unit from getting damaged during loading and unloading. The first 23 units of the TS-8 ordered by the British Army were delivered in February 1980, followed by an additional 12 machines in early 1983. The TS-8 was removed from the Terex product line in 1988.

The first of two MX missile transporter tractors designed and built by Terex for use by the Air Force and the Department of Energy, at the Hudson plant in July 1979. The MX tractors utilized many component systems already found in the 33-11C hauler, on which the units were largely based. The mechanical drive tractor was powered by a GM Detroit Diesel 16V-92TA engine rated at 1,000 gross horsepower. This drove the front rear axle of the tandem setup; the back unit was not powered.

Once this Boeing Aerospace-designed trailer was finished, it was shipped with two Terex tractors to the Department of Energy's Nevada test site to start the mobile MX missile transporter vertical launch testing program. Shown in November 1979 at the Jackass Flats testing area located within the Nevada test site, is the entire unit, with the Terex tractors in place at both ends of the Boeing missile platform trailer, in a push-pull setup. The transporter measured 165 feet long, and weighed 1.4 million pounds with its load. *Department of Energy*

One of the most fascinating Terex creations for military applications was the MX (Missile Experimental) Missile Transporter program, a joint engineering project with Boeing Aerospace, for use by the U.S. Air Force. Terex's involvement with the MX Missile Program started in April 1976, in joint cooperation with Martin-Marietta, on concept studies involving various MX basing systems. Two of these studies were the shelter-based and buried trench systems. A decision was reached by the Air Force that rubber-tired transporters, in conjunction with either a vertical or horizontal launching system,

would be best suited to the task. The trench and rail basing systems were found unacceptable because of costs, and because deploying either system would cause too great a disturbance to the surrounding environment.

After these early studies, Terex became a subcontractor to Boeing Aerospace. In September 1978, Terex was issued a contract, lasting from October 1978 to February 1980, for the vertical shelter test program.

An additional contract was issued to Terex, effective from August 1979 to October 1979, for a vehicle definition study of the horizontal shelter system. In July 1979, Terex

A specially prepared Euclid Tandem TS-14 unit, with an additional scraper bowl attached, at work in Columbia, Illinois, in 1966. This gave the triple-bowled scraper a payload capacity rating of 42 cubic yards struck and 60 cubic yards heaped. Power available from all four of its GM Diesel engines was 640 gross horsepower and 577 fhp.

completed the assembly of two MX prototype tractors for the vertical system evaluation testing in Nevada. The two-tractor system was chosen over a more conventional truck/semi-tractor trailer because of its superior maneuverability, stability, and its bi-directional capability.

The major components of the Terex MX tractors were largely based on the 33-11C truck. These included the engine, transmission, drive axles, and operator's cab. Major custom-built and -designed components included the frame, load-sharing suspension, twin steering system, hitch for the Boeing trailer, and various electric controls and interfaces. Each tractor was powered by a single Detroit Diesel 16V-92TA, two-cycle, turbocharged and aftercooled 16-cylinder engine mated to a six-speed Allison DP-8961 automatic transmission. Each tractor was rated at 1,000 gross horsepower, for a combined output of 2,000 gross horsepower. Each unit had four axles, two of which provided front steering and were not powered; only one of the rear tandem-axles was driven.

The length of the MX Transporter, with both tractors in place, was 165 feet, with the complete unit's gross vehicle weight coming in at 1.4 million pounds, or 700 tons.

The MX Transporter was shipped to the Department of Energy's Nevada test site, located in Jackass Flats, for testing throughout early 1980. After numerous congressional hearings and cutbacks, it was decided to place the initial deployment of the MX, now officially named the "Peacekeeper," into modified Minuteman fixed-site silos. After the cancellation of the mobile launch studies, the Terex MX tractors were auctioned off to be parted out. Between 1990 and 1996, the tractors, along with the MX test trailer, were slowly dismantled and sold off as scrap.

Field Modified Machines

Another area of specialized Euclid and Terex equipment involves the machines that were modified, either by the dealers or the owners, for particular earth-moving applications. Some of the most ambitious of these projects involved the various scraper models, both new and old, that were converted into tandem-, triple-, and even quad-bowled configurations. Many of these scrapers were converted by contractors who were using them by combining two older machines into one. In certain working conditions, this proved to be a good cost-saving measure, as it increased the capacity and productivity of older scrapers, not to mention limiting the personnel need to only one operator.

In other instances, dealers would convert new scrapers into whatever configurations the contractor wanted, with the help of retrofit parts kits that could be ordered from the Parts Sales Department at the Hudson, Ohio, main plant.

Other modifications offered by the factory included repowering packages, in which scrapers that utilized the GM 6-71 engines could have them replaced with GM 8V-71 diesel units. If a customer wanted a more powerful, multibowled scraper, the factory was more than willing to do whatever was necessary to make sure they could get the parts to get the job done.

One of the most popular units to be "tandemized" was the TS-14 scraper. The Euclid TS-14 had actually been converted into tandem units by Ken Harris, a Euclid dealer in South Dakota, a couple of years before the company offered a production version of its own. The conversion kit offered by the factory consisted of a new scraper bowl, powertrain, drawbar, and pull yoke assembly. The used TS-14 unit would be separated at the pull yoke and scraper bowl connecting points, and the new unit would be placed between the two older halves. The scraper could quickly be returned to single-bowl operation by simply disengaging the ball and socket and hydraulic control hoses of the rear scraper unit.

In some rare cases, the Tandem TS-14 scrapers were turned into Triple TS-14 units by adding another scraper bowl, all controlled by a single operator. Tests were also

Euclid tested the concept of connecting two Tandem TS-14 scrapers together by means of an A-frame ball-and-socket hitch in 1965. This unit was referred to as the Euclid Quad TS-14. Two operators were required to control the combined 960 gross horsepower and 866 fhp that both units put out, along with their combined payload capacity of 56 cubic yards struck and 80 cubic yards heaped.

Many contractors who needed larger capacity scrapers simply modified the older machines already in their fleets. This Euclid Tandem S-18/TS-18, nicknamed "Piggy-Back," was built by G.E. Smith & Sons, of Noble, Oklahoma, by combining an older S-18 scraper with the rear bowl section of a TS-18 unit. This setup produced a scraper that had a power output of 518 gross horsepower and a payload capacity of 36 cubic yards struck and 48 cubic yards heaped. The tandem scraper is seen here working in July 1963 on a portion of the Oklahoma Turnpike.

The largest of all of the Ken Harris-designed machines utilizing used Euclid components was the huge Tandem TS-33. Usually referred to as "Big Daddy," the scraper was fashioned out of a Euclid 39LOT over-hung tractor front and two SS-33 scraper bowls, rated at 66 cubic yards struck and 86 cubic yards heaped. Big Daddy was powered by three engines: a GM Diesel 12V-71T resided in the front tractor, a GM 16V-71T powered the two center axles between the scraper bowls, and a GM 8V-71T unit brought up the rear. Total power output was in the neighborhood of 1,500 gross horsepower. Big Daddy is at work here in October 1964 on a section of Interstate I-90 near Sheridan, Wyoming. That's a Harris-built Euclid Tandem TS-24 in the background.

The largest scraper unit ever built utilizing older Euclid equipment and components was the massive Western Tri-Bowl, produced by Western Contracting Corporation in May 1966. The Tri-Bowl consisted of a 43LDT tractor and three heavily modified SS-40, model 51SH, scraper bowls. The entire unit was powered by four GM Diesel 16V-71 engines rated at 2,200 gross horsepower. The total payload capacity was 120 cubic yards struck and 156 cubic yards heaped. *Western Contracting Corp.*

performed on the feasibility of connecting two Tandem TS-14 units together by means of an A-frame ball-and-socket hitch. The Quad TS-14, as it was called, was not the same as scrapers being connected by means of a Helpmate Hitch, in which the two units could separate at will. The quad scraper was permanently hooked together in the middle, even though each tandem set had its own operator. Tests revealed that this scraper combination was a bit of a handful for the operators to control and needed a large working area to keep the unit from getting itself into trouble.

Other popular conversions of GM Euclid/Terex scrapers involved the TS-24 models. Either older units or new ones could be tandemized with the available high-arching gooseneck with the ball-and-socket hitch arrangement available from the factory. The air control system (for both the hydraulic and throttle controls), needed to operate the second bowl and rear engines, was provided by a separate vendor. Many of these Tandem TS-24 units also received the upgraded GM 8V-71 engine packages, which, when combined with a 82-80 twin-engined push dozer, made them practically unstoppable in even the hardest loading situations. The TS-24 could also be turned into a four-engined tandem setup with the use of the A-frame hitch, which hooked two standard TS-24 scrapers together by a ball-and-socket method. Both complete units were controlled by a single operator in the first cab. This setup could be converted to single-scraper operations in less than 15 minutes by disconnecting the hitch and hydraulic control lines and removing the A-frame from the rear unit. This application worked best on older type TS-24 models.

An alternative to the Tandem TS-24 was to combine an S-24 scraper and a TS-24 bowl and engine unit, producing the Tandem S/TS-24 configuration. The "tandemizing" of these two units was the simplest of all of conversions with the factory kits, consisting of a ball-and-socket hitch and modified operator controls. Except for the socket portion of the hitch being attached to the kingpin casting on the gooseneck, no other major changes were needed on the TS-24 rear unit. The advantages of this type of configuration over the Tandem TS-24 conversion were cost savings: it cost 15 percent less than the Tandem TS-24 conversion and 23 percent less than two S-24 scrapers. The Tandem S/TS-24 was also 8,000 pounds lighter, reducing the chances of the unit getting itself stuck. This setup proved to be very popular with contractors, and over 30 combination sets were produced.

Sometimes combining multiple scrapers was a bit more involved than just ordering a few parts, as in the case

Another of Ken Harris' creations was the Harris Blade, built for Johnson Brothers Contractors of South Dakota. The Blade consisted of various Euclid scraper components, including bits and pieces from TC-12 dozers. This concept would eventually form the basis for the RayGo "Giant" grader. The Harris Blade is shown working here in Brookings, South Dakota, in June 1967.

One of the most famous of all of Western Contracting's specialized pieces of equipment was the Western 80. This large hauler, often referred to as the "Eucnik," consisted of a modified 1LLD truck, and a one-of-a-kind fabricated rear dump trailer rated at a maximum 150-tons capacity. The 1LLD tractor was originally equipped with two Cummins "Turbo-Diesel" engines rated at 750 gross horsepower combined when the truck first went to work on the Oahe Dam Project near Pierre, South Dakota, in 1958. When the hauler was moved to its next working assignment at Kennecott's Bingham Canyon facilities in Utah in early 1960, the truck was retrofitted with two GM Diesel 12V-71 engines rated at 850 gross horsepower. Shown in Utah in early 1960, the Western 80 is equipped with the 12-cylinder engines, as indicated by the four exhaust stacks across the front hood. The early six-cylinder-engined version only had one exhaust stack. *Western Contracting Corp.*

The Euclid Heavy-Duty Dynamometer was a one-of-a-kind truck created by the Experimental Engineering Department at the GM Milford Proving Grounds in Michigan. The unit consisted of a vintage 1954 Euclid 1FFD hauler powered by its original two GM Diesel 6-71 engines rated at 380 gross horsepower. The main purpose of the FFD Dynamometer truck was to provide controlled resistance to vehicles such as dozers and tanks to test the tractive effort of the test units. Shown in July 1958 is the FFD Dynamometer, shortly after being completed. The FFD weighed 92,360 pounds, and had a 32,000-pounds drawbar capacity at 4 miles per hour. Top speed of the test truck was 35 miles per hour. *GM Corporation*

of the four-axle Harris/Euclid Tandem TS-33 "Big Daddy." The Tandem TS-33 was created by Ken Harris, the Euclid dealer and owner of Harris Construction Company in South Dakota. Big Daddy, the name given the Tandem TS-33, was built out of various Euclid scraper components. The front over-hung 39LOT tractor pulled two highly modified SS-33 scraper bowls, each with its own power source. The lead scraper bowl was powered by a GM Diesel 16V-71T, 16-cylinder engine that drove the two center axles. The rear unit was equipped with a GM Diesel 8V-71T, eight-cylinder engine. The lead tractor was equipped with a GM Diesel 12V-71T, 12-cylinder powerplant. All three engines were turbocharged, which helped push power levels up to an estimated 1,500 gross horsepower and 1,427 fhp. The Tandem TS-33 scraper's capacity was rated at 66 cubic yards struck and 86 cubic yards heaped. The big scraper was introduced in July 1964, and was first put to work on the I-90 project in Sheridan, Wyoming, in October of that year.

The largest Euclid parts-based scraper ever produced was the incredible Western Tri-Bowl built by Western Contracting Corporation of Sioux City, Iowa. The giant Western three-bowl scraper was introduced at

its first job assignment in Hennepin, Illinois, in May 1966. The Tri-Bowl was built out of various used Euclid scraper components, of which Western seemingly had an endless supply, from the massive fleets of machines the company had purchased over the years.

The Tri-Bowl was powered by four GM Diesel 16V-71, two-cycle, 16-cylinder engines rated at 2,200 gross horsepower. The front 43LDT tractor contained one GM 16V-71, and each of the modified SS-40, model 51SH scraper bowls had its own two-axle power module pushing unit, each with a 16V-71 engine. The Tri-Bowl used two operators, one driving the tractor, and another in an elevated cab on top of the first scraper's drive unit, controlling the unit's loading operations. Each scraper bowl was rated at 40 cubic yards struck and 52 cubic yards heaped, giving the scraper the combined rating of 120 cubic yards struck and 156 cubic yards heaped. Only R.G. LeTourneau produced machines with capacities greater than the Western Tri-Bowl.

The massive Western Tri-Bowl was not the only specially modified piece of Euclid earth-moving equipment to be produced by the company. In 1958, Western Contract-

Developing new equipment concepts was a never-ending process that led to many fine machines being conceived, along with a few that, for one reason or another, never made it past the prototype stage. Shown in the late 1970s undergoing preliminary evaluation testing at the Proving Grounds is this TS-14B, equipped with a front-mounted high-floatation track system with rack-and-pinion steering. This experimental scraper option did not make it into production.

ing created a 150-ton capacity hauler called the "Western 80," often referred to as the "Eucnik." When the Western 80 was commissioned, it was the world's largest rear dump-type of hauler. The engineering design talents of the C.W. Jones Engineering Company of Los Angeles were enlisted for this tractor/trailer rear dump hauler project.

The tractor front was one of Western's early Euclid 1LLD haulers, which required extensie engine and chassis modifications. In early 1960, the two original Cummins engines were removed and replaced with twin GM Diesel 12V-71, 12-cylinder engines that developed a total of 850 gross horsepower. The custom-built, two-axle trailer's capacity was 80 cubic yards struck and 100 cubic yards heaped, for a maximum load rating of 300,000 pounds. The weight of the combined unit was 290,000 pounds empty and 590,000 pounds fully loaded. Only one Western 80 was ever constructed, and it worked on many of Western's larger dam and construc-

tion projects before being taken out of service by 1970. Soon after that, the entire truck was scrapped.

Many Euclid haulers were modified into specialized earth-moving machines to fit various job requirements, but a few found new service lives outside of the dirt-hauling industry, becoming prime movers in the heavy haulage industry. The most famous of these machines were two 1954-vintage Euclid 4FFD haulers bought by Frank W. Hake Company of Philadelphia, Pennsylvania, in 1967. With a little help from Euclid engineering, these tandem-drive trucks were turned into four-axle, twin-steer, heavy haulage tractors.

To achieve this, the front ends of the FFDs were widened and fitted with a pair of Mack front axles and a six-coil-spring suspension system. Both units were powered by Cummins N220 NHB1 diesel engines powering the rear tandem-drive Euclid-built planetary axles. Each of these tractors weighed in at about 64,000 pounds. Both

The largest conventional, single-bowled, over-hung type of scraper designed by Terex was the TS-34 (55LOT-99SH), in 1973. By 1977, a modified version of the original unit, called the TS-34 "Plus" (shown) was undergoing engineering testing at the GM Proving Grounds. This model was powered by a Detroit Diesel 16V-71T engine in the tractor, and a DD 12V-71T unit in the rear scraper, providing a total power output of 1,100 gross horsepower and 1,038 fhp. The payload capacity was 36 cubic yards struck and 50 cubic yards heaped, with a maximum 117,000-pound load limit. Only one TS-34 "Plus" scraper was ever built.

of the Euclid prime movers operated with the Hake Company for many years, pulling loads in excess of 500 tons.

Another example of what could be done with a Euclid FFD hauler was demonstrated by the capable engineering talents at the GM Milford Proving Grounds, in Milford, Michigan. The Experimental Engineering Department at the Proving Grounds determined that a new heavy-duty towing dynamometer truck was needed for the Military and Heavy Vehicle Test Department. After a series of proposal options, a chance to obtain a used, experimental, 1954-vintage, 1FFD rear dump truck from the Euclid Division came about. Changes made to the truck included the installation of a new water gap, eddy current brakes designed by the Dynamatic Division of Eaton Manufacturing.

During dynamic load testing applications, the power absorbed by the brakes, caused from resistance being applied to a test vehicle that was "towing" the dynamometer truck, was dissipated as heat through a set

Shown in February 1947 is the tandem-drive Euclid 6TTD hauler, the forerunner of the FFD series in 1949. The 6TTD was powered by a single Cummins NVH12, 12-cylinder, diesel engine connected to a manual Fuller gearbox. Only one example of the 6TTD was produced, and it was classified as a 25–30-ton-capacity hauler.

of Young Radiator Company 75 MWC heat exchangers, one per brake unit.

The standard twin GM Diesel 6-71 engines, rated at 190 gross horsepower each and totaling 380 horsepower, were retained in the truck, but an extra auxiliary equipment power-plant, a modified 1957 Pontiac gasoline engine, was mounted behind the operator's cab, between the heat exchangers.

Other changes made to the 1FFD included a widened, full-width cab, front and rear drawbar hitches, and a cut-down dump box. The rear portion of the box, with its hydraulic hoist system, was left in place to carry loose open hearth slag ballast to increase the weight over the rear drive wheels.

When work on the truck was finished in 1958, no other towing dynamometer in the world had the capacity to absorb as much power for any extended length of time as the Proving Ground's FFD Dynamometer. This modified

As seen in June 1963, the prototype Euclid 72TD (Pilot No. 1) hauler, also referred to as the R-38, was an experimental concept design that carried a 38-ton load rating in its 150BY dump body. The truck was powered by a GM Diesel 12V-71 engine with a power output of 370 gross horsepower and 348 fhp. Only one unit was built.

This prototype of the Euclid 65TD (Pilot No. 1) hauler is shown in 1956 with an early proposed sheet metal design that was being introduced across the entire product line. Thankfully, this update program was canceled and the trucks continued to look like "Eucs." The 65TD was eventually released in late 1957 as the Euclid R-27.

The 76TD (Pilot No. 1) was another attempt at a more compact design for the Euclid R-35 series haulers. This truck, shown in April 1966, was powered by a GM Diesel 12V-71 engine rated at 434 gross horsepower and 394 fhp. The 76TD was classified as a 35-ton hauler.

The prototype 82-10 series was the smallest crawler dozer ever to be designed by Terex when it started its engineering evaluation field tests in April 1975. The pilot version of the 82-10 was powered by a GM Detroit Diesel 4-71T, turbocharged engine rated at 170 gross horsepower and 147 fhp. The 82-10 never went into production due to its high manufacturing costs; it was canceled in mid-1980.

Euclid was the Proving Grounds' primary heavy-duty dynamometer until 1983, when the torch was passed to a highly modified, 1972-vintage, Terex 33-07 truck, whose conversion had started in 1980 and was finished in 1983. The FFD truck was parked in the back lot, and in September 1983, the order was issued to scrap it. But luckily for the FFD, the order wasn't approved until 1991! At this time, Allison Division owned the truck, and no one really had the heart to cut up the FFD. A buyer was eventually found, and the truck was shipped out of the Proving Grounds on May 7, 1996. It has since been converted into a heavy-duty prime mover by a heavy haulage outfit in Fort Wayne, Indiana.

Seen here in September 1967 is the prototype Euclid 82-50 crawler dozer. The 82-50 dozer evolved from the C-8 project from April 1965, and it was based on a lengthened 82-30 (C-6) undercarriage, and was powered by a GM Diesel 8V-71T, turbocharged engine. The Euclid 82-50 was not the same as the Terex 82-50 model, which was developed along a different model line. The only thing the two crawlers had in common was the name.

Factory Experimental Prototypes

The Milford Proving Grounds played host to many of Euclid and Terex preproduction and experimental prototypes in their early testing phases. Many concept machines practically lived out their whole lives on the Proving Grounds without ever making it into any sort of production. Many experimental scraper models were part of the list of machines that were not to be.

Some of these included the Terex TS-24 Carston Dual Paddle Wheel scraper in 1969, the Euclid S-24 Hancock elevator scraper in 1966, the Terex TS-26 (44LOT-87SH) scraper in 1969, the TS-28 (40LOT-64SH) in 1963, and the big Terex TS-34 (55LOT-99SH) in 1973. The Terex TS-34 was the largest overhung, single-bowl, conventional scraper designed by the company, and was aimed squarely at the Caterpillar 657B scraper's market. The Terex unit was rated at 34 cubic yards struck and 44 cubic yards heaped, with a payload capacity of 110,000 pounds. The front engine in the 55LOT tractor was a GM Detroit Diesel 12V-71T, 2-cycle, turbocharged engine rated at 525 gross horsepower and 495 fhp. The rear engine in the 99SH scraper unit was the same engine rated at 495 gross

Terex was about to make a major design departure from its crawler dozer program in June 1980 with this 82-30C pilot model. Along with the repositioned hydraulic blade-control cylinders, the radiator was now mounted in the nose of the dozer, instead of the rear, as on other Terex models. The 82-30C was powered by a GM Detroit Diesel 8V-92T, turbocharged engine rated at 336 gross horsepower and 310 fhp.

horsepower and 472 fhp, for a total of 1,025 gross horsepower and 967 fhp. Both front and rear transmissions were Allison CLBT 5965 electric shift models. The TS-34 also featured a front suspension system like the one used on the TS/S-24B Loadrunner scrapers.

In April 1976, an upgrade program was approved for the unit, which was referred to as the TS-34 Plus. The tractor engine was changed to a DD 16V-71T, rated at 600 gross horsepower and 566 fhp, and the rear unit was a DD 12V-71T, rated at 500 gross horsepower and 472 fhp. Total output was now 1,100 gross horsepower and 1,038 fhp. The transmission in the tractor was changed to the Allison CLBT-6061, while the rear unit remained unchanged. Other changes included larger 43.5x43 wheels and tires (compared to the original 36.00x39 units), wider track, and a wider scraper bowl, which was rated at 36 cubic yards struck and 50 cubic yards heaped, with a maximum 117,000-pound load limit.

The new unit underwent field trials throughout 1977, but never went into production. By the time the TS-34 was ready to go, the market for that size of a machine was shifting to smaller scrapers. The Terex unit was also going to be too expensive to produce, further reducing the potential of luring possible customers away from the Cat 657B machine. In the end, the TS-34 was parked at the Proving Grounds, where it remained until 1983. Not long after that, the unit was sold off and parted out.

You would expect a company that specialized in haulers, as Euclid did, to have built numerous experimental pilot models, which it did. Some of the more unusual variations were the four-wheel drive 50FD in 1947; the 49FDT tandem-axle tractor truck, equipped with either the dirt 100W or coal 103W tandem-axle, bottom dump trailers in 1949; and the 6TTD tandem-drive, rear dump in 1947. The Euclid 6TTD was the forerunner of their FFD hauler line and was classified as a 25–30-ton-capacity hauler. The hauler looked a lot like a FFD model, except the 6TTD was powered by a single Cummins NVH12 diesel, connected to a manual Fuller 5A1550 transmission. The unit had side-by-side front-mounted radiators to keep the operating temperatures of

The clean design of the rear quarters of the pilot Terex 82-30C can be seen from this angle. The radiator is mounted in the front of the crawler. Also designed for this model was a new environmental ROPS cab, and re-engineered final planetary drives. But development costs were too high, and the project was canceled by 1981.

the big 12-cylinder engine under control. Early testing of the 6TTD confirmed to the Euclid engineers that a single, slow-revving and heavy diesel powerplant was not the way to go with a larger-capacity truck. At about this time, Allison released its Torqmatic transmission, making two engine installations possible, and making the 6TTD hauler project obsolete. Only one example of this tandem-drive hauler was built.

Most of the crawler dozer models designed and built were released by Euclid and Terex. But a few experimental models were built that were very intriguing, especially some of the Terex creations. These were the Euclid 82-50 in 1967, the Terex 82-10 in 1975, and the Terex 82-30C model in 1980.

The first and only Euclid 82-50 dozer was built in September 1967, and was powered by a GM Diesel 8V-71T, two-cycle, turbocharged engine. The first 82-50 project was developed from the Euclid C-8 large crawler tractor program from April 1965. The C-8 was powered by an experimental GM Diesel 12V engine, and was equipped with a front-mounted cable-controlled blade.

The 82-50 was designed around the single hydraulic cylinder control unit for controlling the bulldozer blade.

The 82-50's undercarriage was actually a modified and stretched version of the assembly used with the C-6-4 crawler tractor. The Euclid 82-50 was not the same as the Terex 82-50. When the Euclid 82-50 program was canceled, that model variation stopped there. The Terex 82-50 was a new design based on the prototype Terex Model 972 (82-40EA). The only thing the two 82-50 machines had in common was the name. The Euclid 82-50's predecessor, the C-8, was sacrificed in a ROPS testing program in the early 1970s at the Milford Proving Grounds. The only C-8 tractor ever built was pushed off sideways and rolled down a steep hillside to test the ROPS enclosure in a rollover accident.

The prototype Terex 82-10 crawler dozer was about the same size as Caterpillar's D6 model. The first 82-10 was built in April 1975, and was powered by a GM Detroit Diesel 4-71T, four-cylinder engine rated at 170 gross horsepower and 147 fhp, with a variable-speed hydrostatic transmission. After a few years of

In November 1964, Canadian Charles Doerr started development of an articulated, quad-track, twin-engined, diesel-electric-powered crawler dozer to be produced for Mannix Company Limited's Alberta Coal, Ltd. (since renamed Manalta Coal, Ltd.). The big Doerr-Tractor was powered by two Cummins NVH-12-525-BI diesel engines rated at 1,050 gross horsepower and 984 fhp, with the power delivered through four GE 766 traction motors. The tracks and complete side frame assemblies were Euclid TC-12 components, as was the front end. The Doerr-Tractor was 33 feet, 6 inches long, and the unit weighed 176,000 pounds. Doerr tried to interest a few manufacturers into building his creation, but there were no takers. Only one was ever built, and it put in some good years working for Alberta Coal. It's shown in May 1966 working in Calgary, Alberta, Canada.

engineering evaluation testing, a set of design changes was issued in November 1979 to address some of the shortcomings of the original pilot model. The engine was to be upgraded to the GM Detroit Diesel 6V-53T-N40, six-cylinder unit, rated at 179 gross horsepower and 161 fhp. Other proposed changes included a new track assembly, wider roller frame, and the installation of the new ROPS cab being designed for the 82-30C dozer. The original unit was scrapped and was to be used for parts on the next unit. But before this model could be finished, the 82-10 program was canceled due to the costs. The dozer was just too expensive to produce; in fact, it would have been the highest-priced model in an overcrowded and competitive class—a sure formula for disaster.

The dozer project that was going to change the market's view of Terex-designed crawlers was the 82-30C crawler program. The 82-30C was a radical departure, at least for Terex, from the way their crawlers were built. The 82-30C was powered by a GM Detroit Diesel 8V-

92T, two-cycle, turbocharged, eight-cylinder engine rated at 336 gross horsepower and 310 fhp. This was connected to a three-speed Allison CRT-7031, full power shifting transmission. The front end of the crawler now featured two nose-mounted hydraulic blade control cylinders, and a front-mounted radiator instead of the rear-mounted unit. After years of having the cooling system in the back and singing the virtues of having it there, Terex was now going to place it up front, just like everyone else. It wasn't because the rear-mounted system did not work well—it did—but it was more costly to place the cooling system in the back. Terex needed to make a dramatic statement in the crawler marketplace and felt that this was the best way of doing it.

But the high costs of the development program, the worsening economic conditions, and the impending sale of the company to the IBH Group in Germany all conspired against the 82-30C, causing its cancellation. All was not lost, though, since many engineering design features found their way onto the Terex D800 dozer,

The prototype Euclid 9FPM wheel dozer was developed from the rather crude-looking 6FPM, which looked much like the military 1TPM. The 9FPM was powered by a GM Diesel 6-71 engine, and was equipped with four-wheel drive. The wheel dozer was steered by its two rear wheels since it was not of an articulated design. The finished test unit is shown here in December 1955. *Pleichner Collection*

released in 1982. One feature that was not passed along, however, was the front-mounted radiator. It was left in the rear of the D800 model, as it had been on all the green dozers before it.

Of all of the model lines produced by Euclid and Terex over the years, none had more experimental prototypes that never went into production than the wheel dozer and track loader programs. Both companies built various models over the years, invested millions of dollars, and never introduced a single machine into full production.

The wheel dozer program got its start when the Euclid Road Machinery Company built a single concept machine called the 1FPM in November 1949. This model, along with the 3FPM in 1951 and the 4FPM, with hydraulic blade control, in 1952, were the starting points for future wheel loader and dozer developments by Euclid. This program evolved into the experimental military 1TPM wheel dozer from 1953, and the 5FPM unit in 1954. In June 1954, a civilian version of the 5FPM called the 6FPM was built. It was a rather crude-looking wheel dozer, with rear-wheel steering. The 6FPM was powered by a single, rear-mounted Cummins NH diesel

engine. In December 1955, the 6FPM was redesigned into the much better-looking 9FPM wheel dozer, this time powered by a GM Diesel 6-71 engine. This unit had four-wheel drive and rear steering like its predecessor, but the outside sheet metal was of the same rounded design that the crawler dozers and wheel loaders were receiving. While the other new product lines were gaining momentum, though, the wheel dozers were going nowhere fast. In December 1957, the first pilot 11UPM pivot-steer wheel dozer was built, heavily based on the looks and components of the early Euclid L-20 (3UPM) wheel loader. This was followed by the L-40 (10FPM) wheel dozer in 1959. Again, this was a pivot-steer unit with four-wheel drive, and like its predecessors, it was never released. At this point, Euclid halted development of a dedicated wheel dozer, and instead just offered an optional utility blade for use on the standard production front-end loaders.

In May 1969, another attempt was made to produce a rubber-tired wheel dozer, this time by the Terex Division. The model was called the Terex PX-81 wheel dozer, and was based on the large 72-81 front end

Euclid again tried to build a marketable wheel dozer, this time in the form of the articulated steering 11UPM, which was completed in December 1957. The 11UPM was a four-wheel-drive design, and was powered by a GM Diesel 4-71 engine. Records indicate that only one 11UPM wheel dozer was built.

The 10FPM was another articulated-steering, all-wheel-drive Euclid wheel dozer; it was built in mid-1959. This unit was the largest of all of the experimental models, and was powered by a GM Diesel 6-71 engine. Again, this model went nowhere, convincing Euclid to abandon the wheel dozer development program entirely.

The prototype Euclid 11FPM model, L-40 series articulated front end loader, shown in February 1960, was based heavily on the 10FPM wheel dozer tractor, and was also powered by a GM Diesel 6-71 engine. This model was to follow the preproduction L-30 wheel loader into limited production, but a complete redesign of the L-20 and L-30 loader concepts caused the L-40 program to be canceled.

loader. The PX-81 was primarily designed as a pusher-dozer for scraper loading applications. The PX-81 was powered by a GM Detroit Diesel 12V-71T, two-cycle, turbocharged engine rated at 500 gross horsepower. At first, the unit was equipped with an Allison CRT-6031 transmission, but it was soon replaced with a four-speed Clark 8421 model unit. After early baseline performance testing at the Proving Grounds, the PX-81 was shipped to a contractor's job site at Upton, Wyoming, in July 1971, for further field tests. Early on, one of the major problems was tire slippage on the wheel rims under full power push-loading situations. This led to cord breakage in many of the test unit's radial tires.

Mechanically, the dozer was performing well, and except for the tire problem, looked like it might have a chance of going into production.

Further tests were performed on the unit once it was returned to the Proving Grounds. PX-81 test program results were supposed to be used in the concept and development stage of the new Terex wheel dozer product line, to be called the "73-series," with the first model to be called the 73-81 (AA) pusher-dozer. But as late as 1977 the PX-81 was still undergoing testing, this time working with the TS-34 scraper. With the changes in the marketplace, and other recession-related concerns, Terex finally canceled the wheel dozer program, ending a pro-

Terex Division tried its hand at producing a wheel dozer in May 1969, with the completion of the PX-81 pusher-dozer that was based heavily on the 72-81 series wheel loader. The PX-81 was powered by a GM Detroit Diesel 12V-71T engine rated at 500 gross horsepower. The gross operating weight of the unit was 119,650 pounds. This tractor was supposed to be the pilot version for a production 73-81 (AA) series model, but the program was canceled before the first unit could be built. The PX-81 is shown in 1977, performing tests at the GM Milford Proving Grounds.

The Euclid C-3 (Pilot No. 1) was the company's first attempt at building a track loader. The first C-3 was completed in January 1956, and it spent the next several months undergoing field testing evaluations. The unconventional layout of the unit was ultimately its downfall. Track problems were soon encountered because of the drive sprockets facing forward. Only one C-3 unit of this design was ever produced.

By the end of 1956, an improved version of the experimental C-3 track loader was put to work; it was based on the C-2, a concept crawler tractor built by Euclid in mid-1956. Shown in January 1957 is the second pilot C-3 loader, now with its drive sprockets in the rear, where they should have been in the first place. Unfortunately, Euclid shifted all development funds away from the track loader program and concentrated loader efforts on the wheeled tractor versions.

gram that had dated back to 1949. Its hard to believe that after all that time, not a single GM-designed wheel dozer model was ever officially introduced for sale.

Another design effort that suffered the same fate was the crawler front-end loader projects that dated back to 1956. GM Euclid Division built its first track loader, the C-3, in January 1956. The Euclid C-3 was a bit on the unconventional side. It could best be described as a conventional crawler tractor with the operator's compartment and the bucket loading arms facing the rear, which was actually the front of the unit. In laying out the tractor this way, it put the main track drive sprockets in the front, causing the tracks to bunch up on the sprockets when the loader was digging. It didn't take long for the Euclid engineers to figure out that the C-3, in that form, wasn't up to the task it was designed for. By mid-1956, a redesigned crawler tractor was built called the C-2, which would be the basis of an improved track loader. By December 1956, the C-2 tractor became the redesigned Euclid C-3 loader. The unit was starting to look more like a track loader, with the engine and radiator up front and the drive sprockets in the rear. It even had the characteristic rounded body panels

like other Euclids of the day. But after months of testing, the project was put on hold indefinitely.

Years later, GM's Terex Division would take on the challenge of building a crawler front-end loader, and in November 1969, built the first pilot model of the 92-30 (AA) track loader. The Terex 92-30 looked like a conventional track loader except the radiator was in the rear, just like on the crawler dozer models. The 92-30 was in the same size class as the Caterpillar 977L track loader. After engineering testing at the Milford Proving Grounds of the first unit, a redesigned 92-30 pilot No. 2 version was built in November 1971, incorporating numerous design changes. The second machine had a sloping front hood that gave the loader a very modern look. In October 1973, pilot model No. 3 of the 92-30 was built, but the model designation on the loader had changed to the Terex 92-20. This model was powered by a GM Detroit Diesel 6-71T, two-cycle, turbocharged, six-cylinder engine rated at 250 gross horsepower and 225 fhp. The transmission was a three-speed Allison CRT-5434 Torqmatic, full power shift unit. Bucket capacities ranged from 3 to 3.5 cubic yards, with a 10,500-pound load limit. The unit also came

In November 1969, the Terex Division built its first pilot track loader called the 92-30 (AA) series. In November 1971, a second pilot version was completed of the 92-30 (shown) with numerous design changes. The 92-30 was powered by a GM Detroit Diesel 6-71T engine rated at 250 gross horsepower and 225 fhp.

Terex designed and built the 92-20 (AA), a smaller version of its track loader in May 1972. The second pilot version of the 92-20 (shown) was finished in June 1972. The 92-20 was powered by a GM Detroit Diesel 4-71N engine rated at 157 gross horsepower and 143 fhp. In mid-June 1972, the original model designation of 92-20 was changed to the 92-10 (AH).

In 1973, the model designation for the 92-30 (AA) track loader was changed to the new 92-20 series. The third and last pilot model of the 92-20/92-30 (shown) was finished in October 1973, and it was powered by the same GM DD 6-71T engine found in the other 92-30 pilot machines. The Terex track loaders were well-designed machines, but high production costs caused the cancellation of the entire program without a production version of any model ever being released.

equipped with a full ROPS cab. The 92-20 was a very good-looking machine and its initial tests at the Proving Grounds proved it was also a good performer.

As Terex was working on the 92-30/92-20 track loader, a smaller version was also being readied in May 1972, called the Terex 92-20 (AA). In June 1972, pilot No. 2 of the 92-20 was released, but on June 15, the model designation of the loader was changed to the 92-10 (AH). The quickest way to tell the two different-sized Terex loaders apart is by the track rollers—the larger 92-20 (old 92-30) models have seven track rollers per side, and the smaller 92-10 AH (old 92-20 AA) versions have only six.

The Terex 92-10 was powered by a GM Detroit Diesel 4-71N, two-cycle, four-cylinder engine rated at

157 gross horsepower and 143 fhp, and was classified as a 2.25 to 2.6-cubic-yard-capacity loader. The 92-10 was about the same size as Caterpillar's 955L track loader. Like its big brother, the 92-10 was a well-proportioned machine, and defiantly looked as if it could get the job done. But Terex was coming into this field very late in the game, and was going to be up against some tough competition that had been around for years. If that was the only reason, the Terex loaders might have stood a chance, but their development and manufacturing costs were too high for Terex to successfully compete in such a well-established playing field. The loaders were just too expensive to produce, so the entire track loader program was abandoned.

The Pioneer and the
Earth-King Live On

The 1980s were not kind to Terex, but to IBH Holding AG, they were positively disastrous. IBH tried to broaden the Terex product line by importing various Hanomag and Zettelmeyer models into North America to be sold as Terex units. But with the economic recession deepening in every industrial sector, buyers were few and far between.

In November 1983, the IBH empire, the third-largest construction equipment manufacturer in the world, came to a crashing halt. One of the major German banking firms that was a large source of financing for the company collapsed, taking IBH Holding with it. On November 5, 1983, IBH applied to the West German courts for protection from its creditors. This was quickly followed on November 8 by the Terex Corporation in the United States filing Chapter 11 bankruptcy papers for protection against possible German creditor action. On December 14, amid a growing German banking scandal, the German courts directed that IBH be liquidated immediately.

The selling of Terex was a complicated affair that took a few years to reach fruition. To go into all of the minute-by-minute details of the proceedings is not the purpose of this book. But a basic knowledge of the events is necessary to understand how the present-day company came about.

General Motors, which was a minority shareholder in IBH, wasn't going to stand idly by and watch its former earth-moving equipment division get cut to pieces during the legal proceedings. GM announced its intentions to repurchase Terex, Ltd.'s U.K. operations on February 19, 1984, and reform it as Terex Equipment, Ltd. Since GM was a major creditor of IBH, and still remained the freeholder of the factory itself in Scotland, GM feared the plant might be lost through liquidation proceedings. By buying it back outright, GM eliminated the possibility of losing the operations in Scotland. To continue production, GM arranged a licensing agreement with the Terex Corporation, in Hudson, Ohio, so it could keep selling and building machines. The Terex-USA operations were still being administered under the Chapter 11 bankruptcy laws and were not a part of the U.K. purchase by GM.

In March 1984, Horst-Dieter Esch, the founder and chief executive of IBH Holding, was arrested in Germany for a banking fraud scheme that funded his empire. Most of the fingers were pointing at Esch as the main culprit in the IBH mess, and the German courts were going to throw the book at him. He was quickly found guilty by the German courts in October 1984, and sentenced to 3 1/2 years in prison. In October 1986, Esch was sentenced to an additional 6 1/2 years in prison for breach of corporate ethics with a principal Saudi investor.

In January 1985, Terex's creditors' committee agreed in principle to proceed on a reorganization plan that would be developed in cooperation with the First Boston Corporation, a leading investment banking firm. Part of the plan to make Terex-USA viable again was to combine certain portions of its operations with the U.K. Terex Equipment, Ltd. operation, which was now a subsidiary of GM. During this time, Terex Corporation in the United States and Terex Equipment, Ltd. in the U.K. were to continue daily business activities as independent companies, separate from the parent company, GM. During this time, sales plummeted as customers took a wait-and-see attitude. After months of uncertainty, Terex Corporation emerged from Chapter 11 proceedings in August 1986 as a stand-alone company. All GM needed to do was find a buyer for both Terex concerns, and it would finally be clear of the earth-moving manufacturing industry.

The Terex 4066C is the largest articulated truck currently being produced at the Motherwell plant in Scotland, and it has been on the market in various model versions since 1989. The truck's 4066C model designation stands for a 40-ton capacity and all-wheel-drive from its six wheels (6x6). The hauler is powered by a Detroit Diesel Series 60 engine rated at 400 gross horsepower and 375 fhp. In October 1996, the 4066C received an updated grille, which now features the Terex keystone design. This 4066C works in April 1995. *Terex Equipment, Ltd.*

The largest hauler currently built by Terex Equipment Limited is the 100-ton-capacity 33100 mining truck, which was introduced in May 1996. The mechanical-drive 33100 is powered by a Cummins KTA38-C engine rated at 1,050 gross horsepower and 975 fhp at 2,100 rpm. This hauler is the direct descendent of the Terex 33-11 series truck that was introduced in July 1972. The biggest visual differences between this model and any of the previous 33-11 versions is the new design for the dump body and the front end, featuring the distinctive Terex keystone grille, which has been updated and simplified to match the other new trucks in the hauler product line. *Terex Equipment, Ltd.*

On December 31, 1986, Northwest Engineering of Green Bay, Wisconsin, purchased the Terex Corporation, and an option to later acquire Terex Equipment, Ltd. from GM. Not included in this deal were the Hudson factory properties, which were returned to GM. On June 30, 1987, Northwest Engineering exercised its option to purchase the Terex U.K operations, freeing GM from all Terex connections. In this transaction, all U.K. plants and properties were included in the sale. Terex Corporation and Terex Equipment, Ltd. were now part of Northwest Engineering, which was owned by Randolph W. Lenz. This was just the latest acquisition that Lenz had made concerning heavy construction equipment. Before Terex, he had successfully purchased the assets of the Construction Machinery Division of Bucyrus-Erie in 1985, and before that, Northwest Engineering itself, in 1983.

In May 1988, the parent firm's name of Northwest Engineering was dropped and was replaced with the Terex-USA company's name of Terex Corporation. The new name for the U.S. operations would be the Terex Division, while the U.K. company would continue as Terex Equipment, Ltd.

The Terex Hudson, Ohio, plant halted all manufacturing operations of earth-moving equipment in September 1988, with all remaining activities transferred to the facilities in Scotland. The Terex-West assembly plant had closed in December 1986, with the facilities returning to GM, since GM was the title holder to the property.

New equipment development was almost at a standstill during this time of reorganization for Terex, but one key area where the company did spend the necessary engineering dollars was on the development of an articulated rear dump hauler. The first of these released in early 1983 by Terex in Scotland was the 25-ton-capacity, three-axle 32-04. The 32-04 represented the future for Terex, one in which the articulated hauler would play an important part of turning the company's product line around. In 1985, the designation for the 32-04 changed to the Terex 2366, though mechanically both trucks were the same.

Today, Terex is alive and well, with a much more scaled-back product line than during the GM years. Terex is lean and mean, building what it knows how to do best: haulers and scrapers. As of 1997, six models of rear dump trucks, four models of articulated three-axle trucks, and four scraper models are being produced. All Terex models are built at the Motherwell plant in Scotland.

Terex Corporation is now divided into two distinct business divisions, Terex Trucks and Terex Cranes. The Terex Trucks' name covers all of the various parts of Terex Corporation's earth-moving, construction, and mining equipment manufacturing companies. These include Terex Equipment, Ltd., which is also the headquarters for Terex Trucks; Terex Americas in the U.S.; Unit Rig Lectra Haul trucks; and North Hauler in China.

The Terex off-highway, mechanical-drive, rear dump haulers include the following models: the 35-ton-capacity 3335; the 40-ton 3340; the 45-ton 3345; the 60-ton 3360; the 66-ton 3310E; and the largest in the model line, the 100-ton-capacity 33100.

The latest Terex articulated models include: the 25-ton-capacity 2566C; the 27.5-ton 2766C; the 30-ton 3066C; and the 40-ton-capacity 4066C. This truck model design has proved to be a very strong seller for the company, and these trucks are considered some of the best available on the market.

Current Terex scrapers include: the TS-14D, the S24C, the TS24C, and the TS46C Coal Scraper. All share their heritage with GM-designed machines produced in the 1970s. As far as scrapers go, they don't come any better than these.

Terex no longer offers front end loaders or crawler dozers. But in 1996, Halla Engineering and Heavy Industries Company, Ltd., a subsidiary of the Halla Group of Korea, purchased all rights, including designs, and all engineering information, on the old Terex 82-20B dozer. Even though it will no longer be considered a Terex machine, the distinctive crawler tractor with the radiator in the rear will now have a second chance to prove its worth, but this time it will be in the Asian earth-moving industry.

As we come to this point in our story, one might wonder whatever happened to Euclid, Inc. after it became a part of White Motor Corporation in 1968. For Euclid, the years between 1968 and 1997 had many ups and downs, similar to Terex's experiences, but not to such extremes. In August 1977, Euclid, Inc. became a wholly

Euclid officially introduced its massive diesel-electric-drive R-260 hauler at the National Mining Association's "MINEXPO '96" show, held in Las Vegas, Nevada, in September 1996. The truck is powered by a Detroit Diesel/MTU S-4000, four-cycle, turbocharged, 16-cylinder engine rated at 2,500 gross horsepower and 2,390 fhp at 1,900 rpm. With its maximum payload capacity of 262 tons, the gross weight of a fully loaded truck is 850,800 pounds. Shown here in November 1996 is the prototype R-260, starting its preliminary testing operations at a mine site in Ely, Nevada. *ECO*

owned subsidiary of Daimler-Benz AG of Stuttgart, Germany, when the company was purchased from White Motors. In January 1984, Daimler-Benz sold Euclid, Inc. to the Clark Michigan Company, the construction machine-producing subsidiary of Clark Equipment Company. Because of the continuing poor economic conditions in the marketplace at the time, Clark sought out a partner to help bolster its construction equipment division, and found one in Sweden.

In April 1985, AB Volvo and Clark Equipment Co. formed a 50/50 joint venture company, by combining the construction equipment subsidiaries of the two companies, Volvo BM and Clark Michigan. The new company, VME Group N.V., was divided into two operating halves, VME Americas, Inc., in North America, and Volvo BM Co. in Europe. In 1989, the European part of the joint venture changed its name to simply VME. In 1991, VME Americas, Inc. was divided into separate business units. VME Industries North America would handle the Euclid hauler product line and VME Sales North America would control the Michigan/Volvo wheel loader and Volvo BM articulated truck lines.

In December 1993, another joint venture was announced, this time involving VME Industries North America and Hitachi Construction Machinery Company, Ltd. of Japan. The new company, Euclid-Hitachi Heavy Equipment, Inc. was formed out of the U.S. Euclid operations, in which Hitachi now owned a 19.5-percent share.

In May 1995, the parent company of AB Volvo purchased the 50-percent holdings that Clark Equipment still held in the VME Group, making AB Volvo the sole owner

of the construction equipment group. The new company name became Volvo Construction Equipment Corporation, and the old VME name was eliminated. Product lines carried by Volvo Construction Equipment include Volvo BM wheel loaders and articulated trucks, Zettelmeyer utility loaders, Champion motor graders, and Volvo (formerly Akerman) hydraulic excavators. Euclid haulers were still in the Volvo empire, but they existed as part of the Euclid-Hitachi joint venture company. By the end of 1996, Hitachi's share of Euclid-Hitachi Heavy Equipment had increased to 40 percent of the company, with Volvo owning the other 60 percent. If all of these business transactions sound confusing, they still were not as bad as the Terex company saga. The Euclid transactions were more cut-and-dried, while the Terex story was clouded up by the Chapter 11 proceedings, which devastated the company.

During this time of being under these various companies' wings, Euclid had its share of winners and losers. On the down side, certain new model developments during the early 1970s were very costly, and for one reason or another, never found the audience for which they were built. These included the Euclid 105-ton-capacity R-105 truck from 1969; the BV-II Super Belt Loader from 1970; and the 210-ton-capacity R-210 turbine hauler from 1971.

In 1983, Euclid introduced a 35-ton-capacity articulated hauler called the A-464 Arctic. Again, no buyers were knocking on Pioneer Pete's door. All of these products had one thing in common: They all strayed from the basic idea of what a Euclid truck or product should be. But when the company had a clear idea as to where it wanted its haulers to fit into the marketplace, it often produced trucks that were considered some of the best on the market. These included the R-75 in 1971; the R-85 in 1973; the R-100 in 1978; the R-120 in 1980; the R-170 in 1974; and the 209.5-ton-capacity R-190 in 1986.

Euclid offers 12 models of off-highway, heavy-duty haul trucks, of which five are of the diesel-electric drive type. Models include the Euclid R32 rated at 35.9 tons; the R36 rated at 40 tons; the R40 rated at 41 tons; the R60 rated at 63 tons; the R65 rated at 67.6 tons; the R90 rated at 94.5 tons; the R130B rated at 145.5 tons; the R150 rated at 154.7 tons; the R170 rated at 183 tons; the R190 rated at 202 tons; the R220 rated at 217 tons; and the R260, which was introduced in 1996, rated at 262 tons. All are built at Euclid's manufacturing facilities in Guelph, Ontario, Canada, with the exception of the R32 and R36, which are assembled in Poland. A very impressive lineup of green trucks, indeed. Euclid's technical center is still located just off of St. Clair Avenue in Euclid, Ohio.

With some of the worst times behind them, both Euclid and Terex are entering the next century with outstanding product lines. Both entities share in the great legacy of the Euclid Road Machinery Company's industry pioneering achievements, as they related to the earth-moving field. The Pioneer and the Earth-King continue to build the green iron—the metal of off-road hauling history.

Appendix

Model Introductions History, 1933–1980

The Euclid and Terex equipment listed here represents some of the more significant and noteworthy model introductions made by the companies over the years. No attempt has been made to list every model that has ever been produced by either company.

Between July 1, 1968, and September 30, 1968, after GM sold its Euclid hauler product line, the division name was referred to as the Earthmoving Equipment Division of General Motors. The Terex name did not take effect until October 1968. To help reduce confusion, any models that were introduced during this period are referred to as Terex units.

Haulers

1933: Experimental prototype Euclid Model Z (ZW) bottom dump built.

1934: Euclid Model Z "Trac-Truk" rear dump hauler starts field testing.

1934: Euclid Model 1ZW bottom dump officially introduced.

1935: First Euclid Model Z bottom dump coal haulers produced (September).

1936: Euclid 1FD hauler introduced.

1942: Euclid 1LD hauler introduced (February).

1944: Euclid 1TD hauler introduced (March).

1947: Euclid 6TTD tandem-drive hauler, experimental prototype (February).

1948: Euclid 1UD hauler introduced (June).

1949: Euclid 1FFD "Twin-engine" tandem-drive hauler introduced (February).

1951: Euclid 1LLD "Twin-engine" tandem-drive hauler introduced (May).

1954: Euclid 36TD Logger truck introduced.

1957: Euclid R-40 (9FFD) tandem-drive hauler introduced (January).

1957: Euclid R-27 (65TD) hauler introduced (April).

1960: Euclid R-40 (10LD) introduced. Model designation is changed to R-45.

1962: Euclid R-30 (69TD) hauler introduced (July).

1962: Euclid R-20 (95FD/96FD) haulers introduced (November).

1963: Euclid R-12 (3UD) introduced (January).

1965: Prototype of Euclid 7LLD (R-90) starts testing (February). Model designation changes to R-X.

1965: Euclid R-35 (74TD) introduced (April).

1965: Euclid R-50 (12LD) introduced (August).

1965: The Euclid R-X (7LLD) introduced at the American Mining Show (October).

1966: Euclid R-13 (5UD) introduced (May).

1966: Euclid R-60 (14LD) prototype built (May). Forerunner of the R-65 series of haulers.

1966: Euclid R-22 (101FD) introduced (May).

1966: Euclid R-X (10LLD) goes into limited production (December).

1967: Euclid produces its 20,000th hauler, a R-35 rear dump.

1967: Euclid Electric Drive R-X (11LLD) experimental hauler starts preliminary testing (June).

1968: Euclid R-65 (16LD) introduced (January). Hauler is eventually built in Scotland, and in Canada by the Diesel Division and released as a Terex model; not available in the United States.

1970: Terex 33-27 (AA) becomes the first of the new hauler line to start prototype testing (September). Model line designation changes to 33-05.

1971: Terex 33-15 (pilot No. 2) diesel-electric-drive hauler starts operations in Canada (May).

1971: Terex model designations for R-series haulers built by GM Diesel Division in Canada changes to 33-22 (R-22), 33-35 (R-35), 33-45 (R-45), and 33-65 (R-65) (July).

1972: Terex introduces the new 33-Series hauler line, 33-05 (28 ton), 33-07 (40 ton), and 33-11 (80 ton) (July).

1974: Terex 33-09 (55 ton) introduced (April).

1974: Terex 33-19 Titan 350-ton-capacity hauler unveiled by the Diesel Division, General Motors of Canada, Ltd., London, Ontario (June). Hauler officially introduced at the American Mining Congress Show, Las Vegas, Nevada (October).

1975: Terex 33-15B hauler introduced (January).

1975: Terex 33-11B hauler introduced (November).

1976: Terex 33-05B hauler introduced (January).

1977: Terex 34-11C trailer-type coal hauler announced with a 150-ton capacity (August). First unit built in late 1978.

1977: Terex 33-03B hauler introduced (September).

1977: Terex 33-11C hauler introduced (November).

1978: Terex 33-14 hauler introduced at the American Mining Congress Show, Las Vegas, Nevada (October).

1980: Terex 33-11D hauler with oil-cooled rear brakes introduced (May).

Scrapers and Bottom Dumps

1938: Euclid introduces experimental self-propelled scraper, the 1SH with 4FDT tractor (October).

1940: Euclid produces its first prototype over-hung tractor type scraper, the 5SH.

1948: Euclid launches new design of self-propelled scraper, the 47FDT-11SH (June). Replaced by 7TDT-14SH in 1950.

1948: Euclid introduces its first "Twin-Power" concept in the form of the 50FDT-102W bottom dump (November).

1949: Euclid's first "Twin-Power" scraper produced, the 16-cubic-yard model 51FDT-13SH (February). Replaced by the 18-cubic-yard model 51FDT-15SH (March).

1954: Euclid introduces the S-7 (3UOT-26SH), S-18 (27LOT-28SH), and TS-18 (29LOT-27SH) scraper model lines. First of the production over-hung type (September).

1955: Euclid S-12 (78FOT-29SH) scraper introduced.

1956: Euclid S-7 (3UOT) with 129W rear rock dump introduced.

1956: Euclid S-18 (30LOT) with 131W rear rock dump trailer introduced (July).

1957: Euclid introduces the SS-18 (23TDT-36SH) and SS-24 (28LDT-30SH) tractor-pulled scrapers.

1957: Euclid TS-24 (31LOT-33SH) over-hung scraper introduced (January).

1957: Euclid S-12 (78FOT) with 130W bottom dump introduced.

1958: Euclid S-12 (78FOT) with Easton TS-1622 rear rock dump trailer introduced.

1958: Euclid SS-12 (77FDT-40SH) tractor-pulled scraper introduced.

1959: Euclid TS-14 (6UOT-38SH) scraper introduced (July).

1959: Euclid SS-33 (34LDT-42SH) scraper introduced (November).

1961: Euclid S-24 (39LOT-46SH) and SS-40 (34LDT-47SH) scrapers introduced.

1962: Euclid B-63 (36LDT-144W) bottom dump introduced (April).

1962: Euclid S-28 (38LOT-50SH) scraper introduced (July).

1963: Euclid TSS-40 (43LDT-54SH) scrapers produced for Western Contracting Corporation (March).

1963: Euclid SS-28 (36LDT/49LDT-53SH) introduced (June).

1963: Euclid B-100 (45LDT-146W) bottom dump introduced (July).

1963: Euclid Tandem TS-14 (6UOT-60SH-38SH) prototype scraper introduced (September). Full production model numbers were 7UOT-63SH-62SH; also known as TTS-14.

1963: Prototype Euclid TS-28 (40LOT-64SH) starts testing (October).

1964: Euclid Tandem TSS-40 (53LDT-65SH-66SH) scrapers produced for Western Contracting Corporation (August); also known as TTSS-40.

1964: First Euclid S-7 Hancock (4UOT-12E2) elevating scraper introduced.

1965: Euclid TS-32 (47LOT-80SH) introduced (December).

1966: Euclid S-32 (47LOT-79SH) introduced.

1966: Prototype Euclid S-24 Hancock elevating scraper starts preliminary field testing. Project evolves into S-32 Hancock program.

1968: Euclid S-32 elevating scraper developed (April), officially released as the S-35E (47LOT-90SH) (August).

1969: Prototype Terex TS-26 (44LOT-87SH) scraper starts early testing program (March).

1969: Terex S-11E (16UOT-94SH) elevating scraper introduced.

1969: Prototype Terex TS-17 starts testing (November). Designation changes to TS-18.

1970: First Terex TS-18 (33TOT-92SH) scraper produced (June).

1970: First Terex S-23E (33TOT-H-93SH) elevating scraper starts long-term field testing (September). Officially released in 1972.

1971: Experimental Terex TS-24+ (50LOT-95SH) scraper starts testing (September). Designation changed in 1973 to the Terex Model 979.

1971: First Terex TS-14B (17UOT-97SH) scraper introduced (November).

1973: Experimental Terex TS-34 (55LOT-99SH) scraper starts testing.

1973: Terex S-11E "Series B" (18UOT-101SH) elevating scraper introduced (July).

1977: Terex TS-24B "Loadrunner" (035-036) introduced. First production scraper with a suspension system (June). Prototype from 1975 known as 58LOT-110SH.

1977: Terex S-24B "Loadrunner" (023-024) introduced (October). Prototype in October 1972 was known as 51LOT.

1978: Terex TS-32B starts engineering preproduction testing.

1978: Terex TS-38B and TS-46B "Loadrunner" coal scrapers announced (May).

1980: Terex S-35E-B elevating scraper starts preliminary testing (March). Project canceled in early 1981.

Crawler Dozers

1954: First experimental prototype Euclid TC-12 crawler dozer with "Twin-Power" starts testing at GM Proving Grounds (July).

1955: First production prototype Euclid TC-12 rolls out of the factory (January).

1955: First Euclid C-6 crawler dozer starts preliminary field testing.

1957: Thirty Euclid C-6 prototypes put into field service for engineering evaluation.

1958: Euclid C-6-1 officially introduced.

1964: Euclid TC-12-3 dozer engineering upgrades for new model started (June); proposed design program then canceled.

1964: First Euclid C-260 dozer produced (December); model designation changed to 82-40 in 1965.

1965: Euclid C-8 prototype starts large single-engine dozer program (May). Program evolves into 82-50 series in 1967.

1966: Euclid introduces the "82-series" of crawler dozers, the 82-30EA (C-6), 82-80BA (TC-12), and the new 82-40AA (January).

1967: Prototype of Euclid 82-50 dozer starts evaluation testing (September).

1969: Terex 82-30 (FAT) Turbo and 82-40 (DAT) Turbo models introduced.

1971: Terex 82-20 dozer prototype starts testing (July).

1971: Terex Model 972 (82-40EA) dozer prototype starts field studies.

1973: Terex officially releases the 82-20 (July) and the 82-50 (August) dozers.

1973: Terex 82-30B (GA) dozer introduced (June).

1975: Prototype 82-10 dozer starts evaluation testing (April); model did not go into production.

1976: Terex 82-20B dozer introduced.

1980: Terex 82-30C dozer prototype starts production evaluation testing (June). Program canceled due to costs and the sale of the Terex Division by GM to the IBH Group.

Wheel Loaders

1956: Prototype Euclid 1QPM wheel loader built (June).

1956: Experimental Euclid 3UPM 1.5-yard front end loader starts engineering evaluations (July).

1957: Euclid 1QPM officially introduced as the L-7 (July).

1958: Prototype Euclid L-20 (3UPM) pivot-steer front end loader starts field trial testing.

1959: Prototype Euclid L-30 (5UPM) pivot-steer front end loader starts its field testing.

1960: Experimental Euclid L-40 (11FPM) pivot-steer front end loader built (February).

1961: Preproduction Euclid L-20 (7UPM) built (June).

1962: Euclid L-20 (7UPM) and L-30 (9UPM) introduced (January).

1964: Euclid L-15 (2UPM) and L-25 (8UPM) loaders introduced (February).

1965: Euclid 72-40 (17UPM) introduced (January). Replaces L-30 loader.

1965: Euclid 72-30 (16UPM) introduced (March). Replaces L-25 loader.

1965: Euclid 72-10 (2UPM) introduced (October). Replaces L-15 loader.

1966: Euclid 72-20 (15UPM) introduced (January). Replaces L-20 loader.

1966: Euclid L-X Pilot No. 1 (18UPM) wheel loader starts engineering evaluations (May).

1966: Euclid 72-21 (October), 72-31 (September), 72-41 (November), and 72-51 (November) front end loaders introduced.

1968: Euclid 72-80 (L-X) wheel loader introduced (January).

1969: Model 72-80 officially released as Terex 72-81 (February).

1970: Prototype Terex 72-71 (AA) introduced (February).

1971: Terex 72-51 with Colby Composter introduced (April). Model name changed to 74-51 for Pilot No. 2 unit (December).

1973: Prototype Terex 72-61 wheel loader built (March). Officially released in June 1976.

1975: Prototype Terex 72-51B wheel loader built (January). Officially released in May 1977.

1977: Terex 72-71B (April) and 72-31B (May) wheel loaders introduced. First 72-71B loader built in September 1978.

1979: Terex 72-21B wheel loader introduced (September).

1979: Prototype Terex 72-71C wheel loader starts field testing (October); model designation changes to the Terex 90C in mid-1982.

Track Loaders

The following machines should all be classified as experimental since none was ever commercially available.

1956: Euclid C-2 crawler built.

1956: Euclid C-3 concept track loader designed with radiator in back (January).

1956: Euclid C-3 track loader with front-mounted radiator starts testing (December).

1969: Terex 92-30 (AA) Pilot No. 1 track loader built (November).

1971: Terex 92-30 Pilot No. 2 track loader built (November).

1972: Terex 92-20 Pilot No. 1 track loader built (May).

1972: Terex 92-20 Pilot No. 2 track loader built (June). Designation for this model changes to 92-10 (AH), effective June 15.

1973: Terex 92-30 model designation changes to 92-20 for the Pilot No. 3 machine (October).

Wheel Dozers

The following machines should all be classified as experimental since none was ever commercially available.

1949: Euclid 1FPM wheel dozer built (November).

1952: Euclid 4FPM wheel dozer built with single hydraulic cylinder blade control (May).

1954: Euclid 6FPM wheel dozer built (June). Civilian version of the military 5FPM-G version.

1955: Euclid 9FPM wheel dozer built (December). Redesigned version of the 6FPM.

1957: Euclid 11UPM wheel dozer built (December).

1959: Euclid 10FPM wheel dozer built.

1969: Terex PX-81 wheel dozer starts long-term testing program (May).

Military Models

Included in this list are model lines that had military applications such as haulers, bottom dumps, and dozers. Many of these units were submitted for evaluation and did not necessarily go into limited production.

Tractor and Trailer Combinations

1943: Euclid 9FDT-G/58W-G bottom dump, U.S. Army (April); 30 built.

1943: Euclid 22FDT/77W 6,000-gallon fuel tanker, U.S. Army Air Corps (May); one built.

1944: Euclid 25FDT-G/58W-G bottom dump, U.S. Army (February); 45 built.

1951: Euclid 71FDT-G/89W-G bottom dump, U.S. Army (March).

Rear Dumps
1943: Euclid 19FD, U.S. Army (March).
1944: Euclid 27FD-G, U.S. Army (June).
1953: Euclid 82FD-G, U.S. Navy (U.S.N.). (July).
1955: Euclid 80FD-G, U.S.N. (January).
1957: Euclid 1UD-G (September).
1967: Euclid R-12 (4UD), U.S. Marine Corps (U.S.M.C.) (January).
1967: Euclid R-20 (99FD), U.S. Army (March).

Track Dozers
1967: Euclid 82-30 (FAM), U.S.M.C. (May).
1972: Terex 82-30 (FAM), U.S.M.C. (January).

Miscellaneous Wheeled Models
1950: Euclid 2FPM tow tractor (Type A-2), U.S. Air Force (U.S.A.F.) (August).
1953: Euclid 1TPM wheel dozer, U.S. Army (June).
1954: Euclid 1UPM wheel dozer (June).
1954: Euclid 5FPM-G wheel dozer, U.S.N. (July).
1956: Euclid 7FPM tow tractor (Type A-2), U.S.A.F.
1955: Euclid 8FPM-G tractor, U.S.N.; delivered 1958.
1960: Euclid 6TPM-G wheel dozer (December) with SV18 scraper unit, U.S. Army (September 1962).
1963: Euclid 58SH-G pull-scraper with 9DY dolly, U.S. Army (December).
1965: Euclid 2UPM-G (L-15) wheel loader (August).
1967: Euclid 72-31F forklift, U.S.A.F. (September).
1967: Euclid 72-31M wheel loader, U.S.N. (December).
1968: Terex 72-31M wheel loader, U.S.M.C. (August).
1973: Terex 72-31F (10K) forklift, U.S.A.F. (January).
1979: Terex MX Transporter; two units built; U.S.A.F. (July).

British Models
Following are significant model introductions and shipping dates of units built at the Motherwell plant in Scotland.

Haulers
1951: Euclid R-15 (B5FD), January.
1953: Euclid R-22 (B1TD), October.
1957: Euclid R-27 (B5TD), December.
1961: Euclid R-30 (B6TD), June.
1963: Euclid R-24 (B1TD).
1964: Euclid R-45 (B10LD), May.
1967: Euclid R-35s (B17TD), January.
1967: Euclid R-18 (B12FD), April.
1967: Euclid R-35 (B74TD), April.

1968: Euclid R-22 (B103FD), April.
1968: Euclid R-65 (B16LD), April.
1968: Terex R-17 (B15FD), August. Model originally introduced as the Euclid R-17, May.
1968: Terex R-25 (B1TD), October. Model originally introduced as the Euclid R-25, May.
1972: Terex R-50 (B19LD), April.
1972: Terex R-70 (B21LD), June.
1973: Terex R-25 (B18TD), November.
1976: Terex 33-07, March.
1976: Terex R-35B, June.
1978: Terex 33-11C, March.
1979: Terex R-50B (B24LD), February.

Wheel Loaders
1963: Euclid L-20 (B2UPM), August.
1963: Euclid L-30 (B4UPM), October.
1967: Euclid 72-31, April.
1967: Euclid 72-51, July.
1967: Euclid 72-41, September.
1970: Terex 72-21, March.
1971: Terex 72-11, May.
1975: Terex 72-71, March.
1976: Terex 72-51MWT (Military), December.
1978: Terex 72-71B, January.
1979: Terex 72-31B, 72-51B, and 72-61, April.

Scrapers and Bottom Dumps
1952: Euclid 12-yard (B6FDT-B1SH) scraper, September.
1953: Euclid 13-yard (B7FDT-B1W) bottom dump, September.
1955: Euclid S-7 (B3UOT-B3SH), July.
1956: Euclid S-18 (B3LOT-B4SH), March.
1958: Euclid S-7 (B3UOT-B2W) rock dump, March.
1958: Euclid TS-24 (B4LOT-B7SH), August.
1960: Euclid B-20 (B9FDT-B1W) bottom dump, February.
1960: Euclid TS-14 (B6UOT-B9SH), December.
1962: Euclid S-18 (B3LOT-B3W) rock dump, March.
1965: Euclid S-7 Hancock (B8UOT-12E2), October.
1966: Euclid TTS-14 (B13UOT-B19SH-B15SH), February.
1969: Terex TTS-14 (B12UOT-B16SH-B13SH), June.
1974: Terex TS-14B (B17UOT-B97SH), March.
1975: Terex TS-24 Mk V (B10LOT-B24SH), May.
1979: Terex TS-8, November. Prototype introduced in 1976.

Track Dozers
1958: Euclid C-6, October.
1967: Euclid 82-40, May.
1967: Euclid 82-30, November.
1979: Terex 82-30B, March.

Index